ESSAYS IN REGIONAL AND LOCAL HISTORY

In Honour of Eric M. Sigsworth

Edited by
Philip Swan and David Foster

HUTTON PRESS
1992

Published by the Hutton Press Ltd.
130 Canada Drive, Cherry Burton, Beverley
North Humberside HU17 7SB

Printed and bound by

Clifford Ward & Co. (Bridlington) Ltd.
55 West Street, Bridlington, East Yorkshire
YO15 3DZ

ISBN 1 872167 33 0

CONTENTS

Page

Front Cover:
The River Wharfs and St. Peter's Church Leeds in the 19th Century.

LIST OF CONTRIBUTORS

Professor **Maurice Beresford** retired in 1985 after 37 years of teaching economic history at Leeds University, latterly (since 1959) as professor. After retirement he has published *East End: West End – the Face of Leeds During Urbanisation, 1684-1842*, and (with J. G. Hurst) *Wharham Percy: Medieval Village*, reflecting his lifetime interests in urban and rural landscapes. He is the senior member of the Royal Commission on Historical Monuments and is active in prison education and welfare. He holds honorary degrees of the University of Hull and Loughborough.

Dr. **Jan Crowther** is an Open University tutor and a part-time lecturer in the Department of Adult Education of Hull University. Her main interest is in regional and local history. She has published on agriculture and enclosure.

Dr. **Ian Donnachie** is Staff Tutor and Senior Lecturer in History at the Open University in Scotland, and has taught in universities in both Victoria and New South Wales where he developed an interest in Australian history and the Scottish — Australian connection. His most recent books are *Companion to Scottish History* (with George Hewitt) and *Forward! Labour Politics in Scotland 1888-1988* (ed. with Christopher Harvie and Ian S. Wood). He is currently writing a history of New Lanark.

Dr. **David Foster** was formerly the Head of the School of Humanities, Humberside College of Higher Education, and is now Head of Academic Services, Humberside Polytechnic. His research interests are in the history of crime in the East Riding and he has published on this topic.

Dr. **Pat Hudson**, is currently located in the Department of Economic History at the University of Liverpool. She is a contributor to *Markets and Manufactures in Early Industrial Europe* edited by M. Berg, and is editor of a recent book entitled *Regions and Industries*. She is well known for her work on 'proto-industrialisation'.

Dr. **Jim Leonard**, has recently taken early retirement from his position as Reader in Local History in the Humanities Department of Teeside Polytechnic. His teaching and research supervisory roles have largely been concerned with modern local, social and urban history; his publications reflect these same interests, and they have tended more and more to specialise in urban change in the inter-war and immediate post-war period. Currently he is living in Scarborough, where his interest in these areas of historical scholarship continue to thrive.

Dr. **Hilary Marland** is a graduate of the University of Warwick, where she earned a Phd in Comparative Social and Economic History in 1984 with her thesis 'Medicine and Society in Wakefield and Huddersfield, 1780-1870', and subsequently published by Cambridge University Press in 1987. She is now employed as Research Officer at the Free University, Amsterdam and Erasmus University, Rotterdam. Her current research interests include public health and preventative medicine in the Netherlands in the nineteenth and early twentieth centuries, and the history of Dutch midwifery and of women medical practitioners.

Dr. **J. D. Marshall** is Emeritus Reader in Regional History in the University of Lancaster, and the author of numerous books and articles on regional history. His best-known regional study is *Furness and the Industrial Revolution* (1958), but he is also the editor of *A History of Lancashire County Council* (1977), and joint author of *The Lake Counties, 1830-1914* (1981). He is especially interested in the practical and philosophical aspects of regional history in Britain and abroad, and one of the founders of the Conference of Regional and Local Historians (1979).

Dr. **Margaret Noble** is Principal Lecturer in Geography at Humberside Polytechnic. Her main interest is in urban studies, and she has published a number of articles and books on the growth and development of small towns.

Liz Peretz was a research assistant to the Welcome Unit for the History of Medicine in Oxford from 1985 to 1989. She is currently a training officer with Oxfordshire Social Services, and is finishing her doctoral thesis on local maternal and child welfare services in interwar Britain. Recent publications have included 'Local Authority Maternity Care in the Interwar Period in Oxfordshire and Tottenham' in *The Politics of Maternity Care* edited by J. Garcia.

Dr **Philip Swan** is a Senior Lecturer in the School of Social and Professional Studies at Humberside Polytechnic. His main interest is in the history of medicine and publications include 'An Eighteenth Century Surgeon & Apothecary: William Elmhirst (1721-1772)', *Medical History*. No.26. 1982. He also has an interest in history and computing and information technology in general.

ESSAYS IN REGIONAL AND LOCAL HISTORY

INTRODUCTION

Eric Milton Sigsworth (1923-1992).

This collection of essays was originally intended to mark the retirement of Eric Sigsworth. For some years Eric had been suffering from a debilitating illness described as 'Total System Atrophy', and sadly he died before this volume was completed. Eric knew of the publication of this collection of essays and was very pleased and touched.

Eric Sigsworth belonged to an older school of historians — distinguished is the adjective which springs to mind — yet it is difficult to categorize him in any simple manner with regard to his published work. His research interests ranged from business history to medical history, from contemporary housing problems to biography. The unifying motif of this breadth of subject matter was often the 'region'. He was always at pains to demonstrate the necessity of considering the particular before making the general point. It was to such ends that he established at Hull College of Higher Education (now Humberside Polytechnic) a Centre for Regional and Local Studies, and a Local History Archives Unit (which has continued to research and publish local history material for use in the school classroom). In 1980 he founded *The Journal of Local Studies*, which was given the new title of *The Journal of Regional and Local Studies (JORALS)* in 1983. Eric felt that no other journal at that time published material which adequately reflected the interdisciplinary nature of regional and local studies. This period also marked the beginning of a mutually beneficial collaboration between *JORALS* and The Conference of Teachers of Regional and Local History in Tertiary Education, better known by its acronym of *CORAL*.

Eric published continually throughout his academic career but his contribution to economic and social history was also manifested through his teaching. Teaching was something at which he was extremely successful, and from which he and his students gained great satisfaction. For him teaching always seemed a pleasure, and never just a necessary but bothersome task. His commitment to his students was well known in all the academic institutions in which he worked, and for countless numbers of students of history at all levels he generated enthusiasm through his scholarly but humorous passion for his subject. A number of contributors to this present volume would count themselves amongst these students.

Much of Eric's historical work reflected his long-standing academic interest and personal connection with the West Riding of Yorkshire. He was actually born in America in a copper mining community in Michigan called Trimountain. He described his birthplace as an 'obscure village'. Eric was brought by his parents to live in Leeds in 1926 when he was three years old, and was later to attend Leeds Grammar School. During the war he served in the

Fleet Air Arm, after which he took a degree at the University of Leeds, and his first lecturing post was at that university. Maurice Beresford recalls Eric's early academic career,

'I first heard the names Eric Milton Sigsworth in April 1948, soon after my arrival in Leeds: apparently there was an especially bright undergraduate in his final year, an ex-serviceman, who was wrestling with the formidable Double Honours degree in Economics and History, and showing signs of interest in textile history. (It is possible that he was writing an undergraduate dissertation in that area but neither Professor Brown nor I can be certain: the University records are silent). At that very time a former Leeds economics graduate, the business man, W. H. Dean, was displaying interest in funding research projects relevant to the structure and history of the West Riding wool textile industry, and had made overtures to Arthur Brown, the recently appointed professor of economics and Head of my department. By the autumn of 1948 it had been arranged that Dean Research Studentships would be endowed and that Eric would combine work for his Ph.D. with the collection of business records from local wool textile firms that were then tumbling into amalgamation or extinction. The West Riding has been the backdrop for most of Eric's varied research interests throughout his career.'[1]

Beresford continues,

'My first home in Leeds was a flat on the ground floor of St. Luke's vicarage in Cemetery Road, Beeston (now demolished and rebuilt). It occupied a lofty site with a direct view across town to the new tower of the University's Parkinson Building. Cemetery Road was served directly by the number 1 tram which rattled down Beeston Hill, crossed the edge of Holbeck Moor and then headed for City Square, the University, and Lawswood. The Cemetery Road tram stop was at the spot from which J. M. W. Turner had sketched Leeds in 1816.[2] It was not long before I saw Eric frequently on this tram, since one stop after Cemetery Road was Cross Flatts Park near which Eric lived at 58 Parkfield Row. His father, Frank Sigsworth, hairdresser, appears at that address in *Kelly's Directory* for 1938 so that it was from this house that Eric must have departed for his period in the Navy. The houses from 31 to 64 were unbuilt when the previous Directory was compiled in 1936, and the Sigsworths' were then living at 23 St. Luke's Road on Beeston Hill just below Cemetery Road.

In 1948-49 my own research interests were confined to agrarian history, and I was poorly equipped to have a share in supervising researches into the nineteenth century wool textile industry, but I soon discovered that Eric and I shared an interest in walking the countryside, and there are photographs of him in a group that accompanied me when I first set foot on the deserted medieval village of East Lilling after a cross-country tramp from the bus terminus at Stensall. Reciprocally Eric introduced me to Ilkley Moor and Blubberhouses Moor and to the industrial archaeology of the abandoned mills at West End, Fewston, and Scotland Mill, Adell. He also introduced me, a Midlander, to an alien culture of terrace houses and back-to-back streets in Hunslet, Holbeck and Beeston, although I had no idea that thirty years later I should be deeply involved in researching the origins of the Leeds back-to-back.'

From 1952 to 1963 Eric lectured in economic history at Leeds University, and thereafter until 1978, he was Professor of Economic and Social History at the University of York. In 1970 he was Visiting Professor, Victorian Studies and Business History, at the University of Indiana. From 1979 he was Reader in the School of Humanities at Humberside College of Higher Education (now Humberside Polytechnic). Eric was also very involved in a range of other professional activities, and from 1972 to 1977 was a member, and subsequently Chair, of the SSRC Economic History Committee; member of the Editorial Advisory Panel of *Victorian Studies* from 1970-78; and, editor of the *Bulletin of Economic Research* 1973-78. Despite his illness Eric continued to write and publish. His most recent works include the editorship of a collection of articles under the title of *In Search of Victorian Values*, and a biography of Montague Burton. Before his death he completed a collection of reminiscences of Leeds in the 1930s.

****

The contents of this volume cover a variety of topics and periods. This was inevitable if the book was to reflect the broad diversity of themes which come under the heading of local and regional history. The readership this volume will appeal to will be those interested in the broad sweep of local and regional history, both the lay-historian and the professional. It will already be clear to such a readership that the practice of regional and local history has changed in recent years, with a move away from monographs on particular locations, towards a history based on high levels of interdisciplinarity between subject areas such as geography and sociology. John Marshall has contributed an important essay to the collection in which he discusses some of the problems, challenges and benefits of a regional approach to history. The very concept of regional history presents problems, not least of which is the need for a definition of terms together with the development of a clear methodology, both of which are essential in order to allow the regional historian to carry out his or her historical task. This article is nothing if not a call for a more rigorous approach in the methodology and the practice of regional history. Margaret Noble and Jan Crowther in their essay on 'Adult Education and the Development of Regional and Local History' testify to the growth of interest in this form of history especially in recent years, and in particular the role of adult education in stimulating interest in the subject. This has led increasingly to a crossing of the divide between 'amateur' and 'professional' practice of history,

9

although this process of change has not been without its problems.

Other contributors cover a range of specific themes not limited to any particular historical period. Pat Hudson investigates the structure of trade and production in Sowerby and Calverley, and addresses some of the major issues which also caught the imagination of Eric Sigsworth in his early years of research on the Yorkshire worsted industry. It is fitting that the essay on 'The Urban Garden in Leeds' by Maurice Beresford should provide a useful and interesting personal connection with Eric.[3] Hilary Marland and Philip Swan consider medical provision in the West Riding of Yorkshire from census data, with special reference to Wakefield, Bradford and Huddersfield. They portray the extent and type of medical provision from the middle decades of the nineteenth century and analyse some aspects of the economic and social status of medical practitioners. In his essay, David Foster looks at outbreaks of arson in East Yorkshire, and in particular considers the continuing prevalence of outbreaks of this form of rural protest in the 1860s and 1870s. He also explores rural social relationships in this period. Ian Donnachie presents a fascinating view of the transportation of Scottish convict women to the Australian colonies. Jim Leonard provides an interesting examination of the 'Max Lock' survey and plan for Middlesbrough in the inter-war period, describing planning methods, the presentation of the findings, and the short term impact of the Plan, and concludes by reflecting on the long-term significance of the survey and plan. Remaining in the inter-war period, Liz Peretz provides a considered discussion of maternal and child welfare provision. Using three case studies she explores the variation in levels of provision between the chosen areas, and offers conclusions which have a contemporary significance.

Notes.

1   Now in the Brotherton Library, University of Leeds and listed as the numerous 'B' entries in Patricia Hudson, *The West Riding Wool Textile Industry, a Catalogue.* (Erdington, 1975).
2   J. M. W. Turner, 'Leeds', a watercolour after a sketched panorama of September 1816: Yale Center for British Art, Paul Mellon Collection.
3   The editors would like to express their gratitude to Wendy Munday for her work on the illustrations in this chapter and for figure 4 in chapter five.

CHAPTER 1

Proving Ground or the Creation of Regional Identity?
The Origins and Problems of Regional History in Britain.

J. D. Marshall

Regional history is a term which in Britain is prone to mean different things to different historians. It can signify the history of a county, or the history of an arbitrarily chosen territory which may be larger or smaller than a county, or it can even mean the study of a conurbation or a city-region. It can be based on the geographical region, or it can adhere rigidly to county boundaries. Its subject-matter can, in the most literal of senses, cover every historical discipline or sub-discipline except that which has purely national connotations, and it can represent part of a most important dialogue between the decision-making centres of the nation, and the territorial divisions of which the nation is composed.

In fact, however, there are comparatively few studies of the regions or provinces of England which do more than meet the requirements of rather limited hypotheses or question-posing, or which throw intense and searching light on the evolution and development of representative areas of the country. There are numbers of very useful *descriptive* and *classificatory* works on different parts of Britain, notably those produced under the aegis of the Victoria History of the Counties of England, and these volumes represent the culmination of work carried on in a long tradition — that of the antiquary and recorder — but also, more recently, a development of it, seeking to come to terms with the elaborate and complex subject-matter of modern economic and social history.[1] However, this increasingly rich subject-matter, which can often be used only as incidental raw material in discussion, argument or the formation of hypotheses, has had to be contained and packaged within certain traditional administrative boundaries, those of the county and its sub-divisions.

Let it be said at once that the county is, and has been a valid and valuable unit for certain kinds of rough comparision, and, very often, such an area gives adequate space for research, sampling and even comparision of local statistics. Accordingly, the temptation and the pressures to use county data, and at the same time to adhere to county boundaries, are alike immense. More than this; groups of counties can be combined to form larger areas for the purpose, let us say, of demographic or economic research, and this has been done with effect by Dr. C. H. Lee in his comparative study of different regional levels of wealth in Britain.[2] This necessarily leaves aside the definition of a 'region' as more than an arbitrary choice of territory in which to experiment, and very often any arbitrariness can be defended where certain forms of disciplined economic and social investigation are concerned. The assumption here is that the aim, subject and method of the research matters more than the precise nature of the territory in which the latter is conducted. Historians are traditionally more concerned with the observation and analyses of changes in movements or policies or human interrelationships over time, than in the refined study of the spaces in which these activities take place, and, where the nation-state is itself seen as a legitimate 'region', and where its individual parts are taken for granted or discussed loosely — precise measurements can be left to geographers! —then concern with spatial relationships will seem otiose. Hence, it is possible for Professor Donald Read to write about the English Provinces[3] without any very close definition of their extent and distinctiveness, save through the generalised impact of their political and social life upon the national story. This approach is hardly surprising, because the traditional and most obviously distinctive broader regions of Britain have rarely been closely defined by historians, nor have they often been made the subjects of intensive research — a state of affairs which is the reverse of that encountered in France[4] or West Germany[5]. So, naturally enough, the researcher in the regions is quite content to make the best of his lot by using the established administrative division, the county, as a suitable area in which to work.

As we shall see, this utilisation of an old-established area has a long and honourable tradition; but it has never been *de rigueur* as far as some resourceful practitioners have been concerned. There are good reasons for this variety of approach. First of all, some counties are very large and variegated geographically and economically, and when one of the most distinguished pioneers of regional history, Dr. G. H. Tupling, produced his *The Economic History of Rossendale* in 1927, he concentrated his attention on a relatively small area in East Lancashire, the geographically distinct territory of the so-called Rossendale anticline, with the purpose of placing the earlier stages of the industrial revolution under the microscope. He performed this latter task with George Unwin's original exhortation ringing in his ears: 'examine the effect of the industrial revolution on Haslingden!'[6] Tupling found that Haslingden alone was insufficiently productive of material, and he ranged over what was probably a representative piece of upland Lancashire textile territory. To the economic historians of that time, the local and regional world lay open and largely unexplored, and a few years later, A. P. Wadsworth and Julia de Lacy Mann published their wider-ranging *The Cotton Trade and Industrial Lancashire* (1931), which paid tribute to, *inter alia*, Tawney, Daniels, Ashton, Redford, Sée and of course the Hammonds. The sheer richness and importance of the subject-matter precluded much consideration of the actual territory covered; and it is worth noticing that Yorkshire and the West Riding were hardly mentioned at all, even though Europe and the Near East, chiefly the Levant, received suitable attention. (Nor is this mere sniping; the *economic region*, which is the real subject of this fine book, offers considerable problems to the regionalist of today).

Another county study quickly followed, J. D. Chambers's elegant *Nottinghamshire in the Eighteenth Century* (1932), which was sub-titled *Life and Labour under the Squirearchy*. Chambers, like Tupling, was concerned with the

12

the evolution of an agrarian society, in his Nottinghamshire instance one overlain by developing industry, and, again, there was a reference to the Industrial Revolution. The aim of the book, in Chambers's words, was that of showing 'the movement of local history during the period preceding the Industrial Revolution on the background of national history, and local material that cannot be related to the facts of national history...has been generally excluded'.[7] This 'local material', he could have added, came strictly from within county boundaries, and there are only a dozen references to adjoining Derbyshire in the author's index, and the same number to Leicestershire. But, just as G. H. Tupling had found that Haslingden alone did not supply him with enough material, so Chambers was to revise his view of regional space very considerably, and this different view was clarified in his memorable extended essay, *The Vale of Trent, 1670-1800* (1956).[8]

In this instance, Chambers examined the social, economic and, more particularly, the demographic history of Nottingham's hinterland, which was in turn deeply influenced by the river and canal communication of its area, and that hinterland of course ignored administrative boundaries in reaching into Derbyshire, Nottinghamshire and Leicestershire. The seating and growth of industry clearly affected population. And, indeed, the study of economic history at the regional level was breaking the traditional moulds; the movement of goods, capital and people did not cease at a county boundary. It only remains to add that another distinguished pioneer, A. H. Dodd, solved this problem by combining five northern Welsh counties in his *The Industrial Revolution in North Wales* (1933),[9] which sought notably to probe into the living and social conditions of the labouring poor in its period, and which managed to produce a wealth of detail relating to the woollen and extractive industries of the region thus created. This was large enough to provide a mass of descriptive examples from contemporary and other printed sources, but, even if we set aside the implied methodological approach, there can be little doubt that Dodd's region had geographical coherence and validity, and even homogeneity in its way of life, industries and traditions. When one is choosing a region for examination, it is no small disadvantage to select an area that is half or two-thirds bounded by the sea.[10] The fact of geographical, ethnic and social distinctiveness is never to be undervalued.

However, much of inland England is not so sharply bounded and distinguished, and when W. H. B. Court came to write his *The Rise of the Midland Industries, 1600-1838* (1938), he set an example for all to follow by defining as exactly as possible his sphere of operations, which also contained a combination of counties 'including roughly Warwickshire, Shropshire, Staffordshire and Worcestershire', but which in this case rested on 'its geological uniformity and in the central importance of the Severn in its system of communications'.[11] More than this; Court pursued the study of what was really a nascent city-region with Birmingham as its centre. He pointed out that 'throughout the seventeenth and eighteenth centuries the manufacturers of Birmingham and the Black Country had close business links with the coal and iron district of East Shropshire', and that there were further business contacts between Shropshire and Staffordshire, especially on the part of iron-masters.

That some kind of community of interest, investment, movement and occupation existed cannot be doubted, although a later generation would ask for a great deal more information about its interrelationships, its operation through a variety of social levels and its expression through a number of occupational groups. (And even today, it would be very lucky to be so served.) However, the moment one mentions the possibility of the existence of 'communities' and social groups, potential trouble threatens, because their functioning presupposes the existence of a changing but genuine *human* frontier, i.e. one formed by the accident or choice of settlement, or even through the combination of varied frontiers or boundaries. Court, like the other pioneers of the subject, was obliged to assume that an administrative boundary or set of boundaries would provide a 'rough' delimitation of his region, and, working steadily inside this seemingly artificial enclosure, he was of course enabled to show the links between capitalists, changes in productive organisation, patterns of trade, growth of (county) populations and the nature and movements of labour forces. If this work was performed at a very generalised and discursive and even speculative level, then the author was labouring under the disadvantages of the early explorer, which included a severe lack of reliable information on areas at the intermediate level between nation and parish. Indeed, so marked is this absence of well organised and relevant information even today, especially in social and economic fields, that the provider of comprehensive descriptive surveys still has a most useful general contribution to make.

Having made this admission, we shall also admit that purely formal or administrative boundaries will continue to have their very real uses. The case for their use becomes even stronger if one accepts that the precise nature of historical *space* or territory can often be unimportant; it is the posing of questions, the precise nature of a project and its aims, which ultimately decide whether a collection of evidence shall be made from a highly determinate or from a rather shapeless area or group of areas. However, there is more to the matter than this, for the nature and significance of historical information can be conditioned and profoundly affected by the nature of the environment from which it comes, and a lack of interest in the territories in which they are working is not the mark of alertness.

In the case of the pioneers, their uses of county divisions were natural and proper. The major subject with which they were concerned, the Industrial Revolution, itself surely one of the most significant developments to have overtaken humankind, simply awaited exploration in an academic world which was clearly hungry for information, and this was scarcely the time to ask questions outside the necessary and indeed obvious universe of discourse — in what forms and circumstances did industry arise and grow? We shall not fail to notice that present-day European economic historians still relate this major question to the study of regions, so far-reaching is the question itself.[12] There are numerous reasons for this interest in the regional, especially when the region is related to industry, and some of these relate closely to the conditions and source material of nineteenth and twentieth century industry and society. Both Tupling and Chambers, however, were concerned with agrarian history, and we are therefore obliged to consider whether the county, or some other form of division, is a useful, appropriate or workable area in which to study themes and subjects outside those of modern industrial development.

The major problem relative to the use of administratively bounded spaces, like counties or groups of counties, may be set out very simply. Industrialisation takes no account of their official boundaries, and its associated form of development, urbanisation (and suburbanisation) is scarcely less accommodating. The great Birmingham conurbation ultimately overflowed into Warwickshire, Worcestershire, Staffordshire and Shropshire — could this fact have had anything to do with W. H. B. Court's notable choice of region? — and that of Manchester into Lancashire, Cheshire and Derbyshire. Such transformation creates sharp contrasts within counties themselves, with the result that parts of 'Tyneside' came to contrast vividly with the rural areas of Northumberland or Durham, that parts of south-east Derbyshire were startlingly different from great areas of the High and Low Peak, and that West Cumberland became a distinctive sub-region of Cumberland itself (or of what is now known as Cumbria).

But, once the reality of a separate 'industrial region' is admitted, how does one demarcate its boundaries? And, given that such a region exists in its own right, how far does one trace those boundaries not merely through space, but also over long periods of time? Clearly, social and economic boundaries change, and are identified through the historian's own researches according to given criteria; in other words, we can say for practical purposes that they are 'self-identifying' or self-revealing. But they are also conditioned, if not 'determined', by the geological factors to which W. H. B. Court drew attention, so that the Tyneside, South Yorkshire, South-East Lancashire, North Staffordshire and other coalfields came roughly to delimit areas which contained distinct industrial societies. However, it is also the case that these societies often passed through an early-industrial or preparatory phase; coal was not suddenly mined when the year 1760 was reached, nor was iron smelted only after that year, and as for Lancashire, it is noticeable that A. P. Wadsworth, in his early modern sections of the *Cotton Trade and Industrial Lancashire*, dwelt heavily on territories which were also the seats of the factory revolution in cotton textiles. The present-day discussion of 'proto-industrialisation', with its emphasis on the growth of textile and other industrial production within peasant societies, makes a sharp distinction from agrarian history virtually impossible, and, in these circumstances, the discussion of the history of agriculture within county boundaries *per se*[13] — and Chamber's pioneering work on Nottinghamshire pursued such a discussion — becomes in some instances rather pointless if one is thinking of the description of the development of an industrial-agrarian society. For this very reason, agrarian or agricultural historians often prefer to think in terms of geographical or geological areas and territories, even when they are obliged to work within the standard county divisions.[14]

It is in any case a commonplace that agriculture and industry have been closely linked in the British history of at least four centuries, and very often it is only the compulsions and inhibitions of classification (usually in textbooks and works of reference) that has made the two fields of activity seem separate. The administrative or 'political' boundaries of a country will often be seen to be irrelevant to the development of given forms of agrarian and industrial society, if only because geological formations (if not the physical features that boundaries often follow) do not correspond closely to the fortuitous divisions of territory that were made by the wielders of mediaeval power whose centres of authority helped to produce our shire territories and modern counties.

On balance, then, the existence of counties and county boundaries can be an obstacle to the work of the economic and social historian. Unfortunately, much of our English archival organisation is centred on the traditional county, and is largely and often inconveniently divided according to the latter's delimitations. J. D. Chambers's Nottinghamshire, as that distinguished historian had cause to find, comprehends only the eastern part of the Nottinghamshire-Derbyshire coalfield, and a river like the Erewash (otherwise a doubtless useful physical feature in the division of the two counties) runs through the middle of what is really a coherent local society; and, in order to study that society, the historian has to travel to archives at Matlock as well as in Nottingham itself. This may seem a small matter; but as historical research becomes more expensive and less well funded, such considerations will weigh more heavily. There is truth in the notion that archives have their own 'regions', and that organisers of research strategies have to take them into account. By utilising data from small units, like the traditional parish, historians can successfully cross the administrative boundary, but the fact remains that a variety of statistics (agricultural and economic data generally) relate to counties, or, as in the instance of birth, death and marriage registrations from 1854, to sub-districts which often correspond roughly to the older county divisions like poor law unions or even hundreds and wards.

None of this means that the study of the history of counties is useless, and that the latter do not have their significance in inter-regional comparison, especially when groups of counties are combined.[16] But, as the study of regions develops, such studies cannot be confined to these ancient administrative units.

****

During the last two decades, the phase 'county community' has crept into wide use, especially on the part of historians interested in the seventeenth century.[17] With it goes something of an emphasis on the special significance of the county as an historical entity or as a social as well as a political unit. It is only fair to add that this phrase, as used by Everitt and other scholars who have worked in the field, has political as well as social overtones. In the conditions of the seventeenth century, county gentry and magistracies recognised each other as social peers, kin, persons with equivalent responsibilities and duties, all operating within clearly marked territories in the county itself; and, this being the case, any study of the effects of a major political convulsion like the Civil War can be of absorbing interest as demonstrating the ultimately crucial strain and divisive effect of that conflict upon an apparently closely coherent 'community'. Here we have a case of the county itself conceived as a proving ground in the measurement of the extent of social conflict and political commitment within a given territory, which is in this instance a traditional administrative area.

However, there are dangers in this interesting experiment. The very nature of county administration ensured that magistrates, who were officers within the county's framework, adhered to its boundaries, and the operation of the county's functions devolved upon its landowning gentry, whose kin were occasionally in neighbouring counties and who certainly crossed the boundary from time to time. This caution aside, the general approach to seventeenth century gentry history, as exemplified in these studies, surely points to the potential usefulness of specifically county histories, the more so when the use of the word 'community' can be justified as extending to groups other than the gentry. It is at this point, unfortunately, that doubt appears. First of all, the word itself must be used clearly, consistently and with suitable definition, a point which must recommend itself to historians consequent upon the coolly ferocious essay by the sociologist Margaret Stacey (1969) on 'the myth of community studies'.[18] The very notion of community, as she has pointed out, contains so many variables and differing features that the comparison of one 'community' with another one can become, both semantically and practically, almost meaningless. To historians, the word has very largely signified 'an accumulation of detail about a group of people and their activities over time', an accumulation performed within the terms of a given set of criteria, indeed, but a process that still requires to be considerably more rigorous (or subject to rigorous criticism) than it has hitherto been. This having been accepted, there is no reason why historians should not seek to identify *social groups*, political, religious. agrarian, industrial, social and other, either within or outside county boundaries, bearing in mind that an agreement over definitions will sooner or later be necessary if the groups are to be compared across the face of the country.

This apart, does the county, as a social entity, have any historical significance? The answer to this question may appear to take a more satisfactory guise if it is acknowledged clearly and frankly that the county is an administrative mechanism with political overtones and social manifestations. Hence, if the debate over county 'communities' has been valuable — and I believe that it has — then it should be carried forward, not only into the eighteenth century and the age of petitioning county freeholders[19] and dominant gentry, but just as signally into the age of the county councils following 1889, whereby the growing and elaborate county administrations acquired a character of their own, through which county gentry and landowners found a solid medium of expression; J. M. Lee, in his book *Social Leaders and Public Persons* (1963), shows the nature of the transformations that took place in Cheshire, whereby the old gentry representatives had to give way to professional or semi-professional policitians of a different kind. Examined in these terms, county history is valuable[20] and is very noticeably neglected, just as the social history of administration generally is largely ignored. But the social groups engaged in administration may have only tenuous roots in larger social societies, and it would be very difficult to relate them convincingly to, say,

17

deep-rooted local tradition and to those varied and scattered manifestations of local and regional consciousness displayed over time in the form of county regiments (and thereby a supposed county patriotism), county clubs and societies (which are often, though not always, promoted in areas away from the county concerned), county newspapers and antiquarian societies.

Some of these awareness-manifestations are worthy of the closest examination, if only because they use language, like the newspapers, which demonstrates local and regional consciousness. But such forms of consciousness are not always specifically related to counties; far more often, indeed, they relate to towns, to localities, even to what could be described as a *pays*, like Craven with its *Craven Herald*. It is never very clear how far certain kinds of sub-regional consciousness extend, and the historical tools which serve to reveal such awarenesses are as yet limited in scope; but it can be accepted that they relate to topographical features, habitually followed routes, and common foregathering centres like market towns. In other words, beneath the generalised concept of the administrative division, there are numerous other kinds of 'region' and regional consciousness; geographical, social, economic, religious, cultural, family-group and kinship-group; it is significant, indeed, that in a restatement and development of the philosophy of the 'Leicester School' of Local History, Charles Phythian-Adams has stressed the importance of the 'societal group' as the basic unit for study, i.e. a complex group of families extending over a number of parishes and cemented by tradition and movement within a limited area.[22] It can be readily agreed that such a unit makes good sense as a basic component of regional history, and that it should be related to some larger type of unit — and here, our colleague, suggests that the traditional shire might be a candidate.[23] But, as he recognises, smaller divisions like the *pays* or the agrarian sub-region could play a part, especially that influenced by a given market town. And, when we come to the roles played by urbanisation and urban influence, we are into the vast and portentous field of progressive economic and industrial development, one which concerns most economic and social historians whether 'local' or not.

In other countries beside Britain, such historians are often concerned to find a type of space in which to study, a *raümliche Unitersuchungseinheit*,[24] and where a region is studied for highly specific purposes, then the historian will be barely concerned with the (say) social or cultural reality of the area he is investigating, and even less with its precise shape and boundaries. And, where a variety of specialist historians, content to work within a given county as a convenient unit, produce studies on topics which are presented in such a manner as to throw little light on the ultimate 'reality' of local and county society, or which do not indicate the directions that further studies should take, then the pursuit of regional history *as such* becomes rather pointless — not so much 'national history regionalised', as 'county history over-specialised'. In other words, much more discussion of the nature, shape and content of the region is called for in historical terms.

It remains true that those economic and other historians who have worked within regions, comparatively or individually, have often been concerned to throw light on national history by working, ostensibly, towards a greater illumination of the details of the national story. But, in so doing, have they illuminated the nature of the region itself?

****

The answer to this last question must be twofold; the singularities of regions, in certain important respects, are undoubtedly revealed by comparative study promoted against a national backcloth, but where those comparative surveys of regions have been necessarily superficial,[25] they have not answered ensuing and contingent questions about the deeper roots of local and regional society which could have produced those singularities. Nor are they, the contingent questions, likely to be answered if the concern is only with a broad national picture, and its filling out. It is all too apparent that the writers of national history textbooks are easily satisfied with broad explanations or with summarising the received views of 'what happened'; indeed, without such views, no textbooks could be written.

Moreover, many historians, whose research ranges over different regions, are quite content that those regions remain largely unexplored, because such areas appear to them to be sources of information — or 'quarries' — which can be drawn upon to provide 'evidence' or material in support of a thesis or case. We are continually warned against the perils of quoting part of an argument out of context, or causing the apparent distortion of an author's original meaning, yet the assembly of regional examples in the development of a thesis, when the precise historical context of the examples themselves is imperfectly understood, is a commonplace in the serious research of the present day. The local or regional background, or the predisposing or peculiar circumstances which have conditioned or influenced the nature of the examples, is frequently 'taken as read', or is subjected to what are probably improper or unsupported assumptions. Again, it may be objected that just as textbooks cannot be written without received views, so research cannot proceed without these assumptions — and the case is undoubtedly a fair one as far as it goes. It seems to the present writer, however, that the absence of real debate and question-posing in fundamental areas has combined with narrowing specialisation in many fields of historical concern, to divert attention from regional study as such. Accordingly, the study of demographic movements within the nation and internationally has been conducted from Cambridge and elsewhere without much attention to the need for basic economic and social frameworks at the regional level. Local historical demography can provide material that is fundamental to the study of localities and regions, but the data that it provides much be carefully organised in relationship to regional settings and peculiarities. Hence, Peter Laslett studied illegitimacy throughout England without having at his disposal information on specific movements within the counties whose bastardy figures he surveys, and the massive survey work by Wrigley and Schofield is unable to take regional peculiarities into account save in the most superficial and speculative of senses.[26] This is not to argue (churlishly) that our colleagues have not provided innumerable incidental pieces of information that are useful to the regionalist, and the beginning of wisdom for the latter is often to be found in the collection of region-wide population data.

We should not cavil at the thought that depth study of given regions will in effect provide a context for more specific kinds of research. Of course, there is more to the matter than this; regional history also provides a splendid arena for inter-disciplinary investigation and cross-fertilisation of ideas and methods. This important consideration, 'only connect' (following E. M. Forster), has special relevance because human activitity in regions has a variety of guides and classifications, economic, political, religious, and displays a great many forms of 'social' in organisational and other senses. It is not only a temptation but also a duty to look at men and women in all their guises, and, if in so doing, we seem to be attempting the apparently impossible in pursuing 'total' history, then so be it; this particular totality is only a part of the nation, after all, and arguments about the holistic view of the region should not divert us,[27] for a region contains a complex mass of shifting and sometimes sharply opposed groups, many of them barely conscious of each other's existence for much of the time. Nevertheless, a variety of social and economic groups, owing their origins to, let us say, farming patterns or industrial occupations and establishments, will often spread themselves more or less homogeneously, by overlap or in layers, in such a manner as to make it possible to distinguish a regional shape — and in such circumstances, the precise degree of holism (or total interaction of all the parts) within a society need not worry us. Much more importantly, the historian must work on the assumption that this society *is* a whole, and that its interactions are limitless, even though, in many respects, s/he will never be able to ascertain this to his or her satisfaction. To take the alternative attitude, that the 'region' is merely a convenience, a space for research, sampling and testing, is to narrow the historian's options. On the other hand, we must not be surprised to encounter so great and complex a variety of 'regions' that the production or recognition of a truly homogeneous-seeming specimen may, especially as one goes back in time, seem to be very difficult. The development, in density and shape, of an industrialising region may be fairly easy to trace, in the sense that it is a sharply defined island standing out in very different if much less differentiated territories.

We have mentioned 'layers', social and economic. It is not difficult to conceive at least five of these; demographic, occupational and heavy-industrial (in nineteenth century terms), economic (in a wider trade-related sense) and administrative, with a much wider and more various 'social' category, embracing religious and political groups. Where economic activity is concerned, centres of power and decision-making must also be considered, and these have political implications — and consequences for the nature of administration. It will be seen that the study of regions has to pass through a most intricate *classificatory* phase, and the precise nature of the types of classification involved has been most thoroughly rehearsed by geographers,[28] whose assumptions have not, however, been reflected or reproduced by historians, whose interest, in most regional and county historical studies produced so far has been in rudimentary classification and synthesis, but certainly not in the arbitrary assumptions of the planner and the economist.[29] The question posited by the historian is 'does it hang together economically, socially and politically?' and he or she must leave the more precise and exacting examinations of territory traditionally assigned to geographers, if only because the historian is more often concerned with the broader outlines of change and their approximate measurement. The historian cannot, of course, measure without knowing what his or her spatial boundaries are in any given piece of research, and these boundaries, which may help to form more generalised frontiers in the course of time, will relate specifically to the immediate questions that are being asked. Such research can be performed in any one of the 'layers' that have been mentioned, and comparisons between regions will have to take place within the terms of a given discipline or sub-discipline, and at the level of a given layer.

Does this then mean that the historian cannot work in cross-disciplinary and inter-disciplinary fashions? On the contrary: the region, city-region or major locality offers the best types of field for such exercises, and, as links between the economic, the social and the political are more clearly traced and understood, so will the regional environment be more fully comprehended in historical terms. But this in turn means that as the peculiarities and singularities of that environment are illuminated, so succeeding research projects at all levels, and directed to any regional purposes, will necessarily take the singularities into account. No recognisable process of this kind has taken place in the past; every region in Britain has a collection of theses and dissertations written on subjects within its territory,[30] but in very few instances do these concentrate on the development of major historical or other themes in the social sciences with a view to the systematic analysis of regional problems — if only because their original inspiration was subject-centred, not regional, and supervisors and students have chosen simply to use regional material as a convenience. Not surprisingly, little synthesis of knowledge or themes has taken place, and where common themes appear, they are 'imposed' by the workings and concerns of major disciplines like economic history, which has been internationally interested in topics like proto-industrialisation or the process of industrialisation in regions.[31] It must be said that on the whole, economic historians have tended to treat such themes rather narrowly, and that as regards modern history there is room for a synthesis of the study of economic and industrial development with the many-sided subject-matter of social history — an operation which is certainly best conducted at the regional level. Here, the foundation layer is social, in the sense that society contains within its semi-permanent traditions, memories and mentalities which may often outlast industrial development and even decline — the *longue durée* of Braudel is perhaps best expressed in these social currents. Varying levels of regional and local consciousness, too, expressed in the outward-looking manner of the inhabitant, as well as the inward-looking view of the out-migrant, are worth close examination, seen through administrators, at a number of levels, boundary commissioners, prelates and the clergy, sportsmen and landowners, newspaper editors, contributors and advertisers, and, above all, the diaries and reminiscences of humble people or their orally recorded memories. Do these items of evidence support the boundaries imposed by tradition, or those created by our own calculations?

It is almost a banality to add that boundaries are useful mainly because they distinguish *between* regions or localities, and enable us to pursue their comparison and systematic study; and it is a further commonplace that no region can or should be studied *in vacuo*. By studying the interactions of regions, we lay bare their individual identity and show their inner workings.

The historian has always been concerned with those changes which have made themselves evident within society over time. By introducing the element of change within space as well as time, it provides the chance to study a society in depth, and to measure social and economic change in a manner not otherwise achievable.

****

Change is the crucial word in this last sentence. The pursuit of regional history can never be concerned solely with static frameworks or constructs, however elaborate these may be, and its aim must be that of pursuing or tracing the most detailed processes of change over relatively short periods. Accordingly, it must be concerned with the frictions and conflicts that lie behind change, as well as with the more progressive or gradual transformations, and it must comprehend the study of movements and campaigns, and not merely the examination of states of mind or relatively static relationships.

Hence, agrarian societies, which display apparent regional homogeneities and even coherence (and inertia) in the face of change, can nevertheless be swept through by labourers' revolts, and the apparent contradiction between conflict on the one hand, and a stable class or social structure on the other, calls for explanation. On a more extensive scale, such struggles have to be interpreted against a background of known regional peculiarities affecting agrarian societies. This observation leads to another; currently renewed debate on the nature and development of regions should not concentrate largely on industrialisation, as they have recently threatened to do.[32] In point of fact, industrialising regions are relatively easy to distinguish,[33] and it is the *economic region* — a much larger category — which offers a variety of problems of definition in that it may have symbiotic relationships with other regions, including some in other countries, and in that relationships between capitalists hardly permit simple boundaries to be drawn. Because interregional relationships between groups of workers (save those connected with mass migrations) are usually far less regularly sustained, it is much easier to think of regions as resting on a foundation of social groups based on industrial and other occupations. This is certainly not a heterodox conclusion in the light of current thinking on the part of social geographers.[34] Economic measurements give indications of the nature and scope of production and consumption, and, no less relevantly, of the sources of power within society; but it is vulgarised Marxism which assumes that they, the economic measurements, have to lie at the base of all social motivation and decision-making.

The base, then, is social, whether expressed in the form of class analyses or not; the economic is closely related to it in historical analysis and measurement. With the social and the economic together goes the political; with the social

22

goes the demographic; and, where decisions are put into effect, goes the administrative. It should be the regional historian's ambition to combine these categories in order to show the processes and the movements of change within society. The long-term movements within a regional society are those which display its true identity.

Notes:

1 This 'coming to terms' was expressed in radical fashion in the *Victoria County History of Leicestershire* Vol.2, (1954) as edited by W. G. Hoskins, which introduced analytical as well as classifactory agrarian and economic history on a grand scale. Volume 3 (1955) shows the same influence. Later, similar forces were seen at work in the case of the *V.C.H. Essex*, Vol.5, (1966), edited by W. R. Powell, which makes a special point of a detailed and up to date account of 'Metropolitan Essex' seen as a whole. In fairness, it should be made clear that this revolution in approach has affected the post-Hoskins volumes in general, although the original systems of spatial classification into the traditional hundred-type divisions are still used, with the parish as basis.

2 C. H. Lee, *Regional Growth in the United Kingdom since the 1880s* (London and New York, 1971); *idem*, 'Regional Structural Change in the Long Run; Britain 1841-1971' in Pollard (ed.), *Region und Industrialisierung* (Göttingen, 1980); *Idem*. 'Regional Employment Statistics, 1841-71' (pamph., Cambridge, 1979).

3 Donald Read, *The English Provinces, c.1760-1960: a Study in Influence* (London, 1964).

4 Ralph Gibson, 'French Local and Regional History', *Journal of Regional and Local Studies*, Vol.3, No.2, Winter 1983, pp.1-6.

5 Peter Steinbach, 'Zur Diskussion Über den Begriff der "Region" — eine Grundsatzfrage der moderne Landesgeschichte', in *Hessisches Jahrbuch für Landesgeschichte*, Vol.31, 1981, pp.185-310.

6 G. H. Tupling, *The Economic History of Rossendale* (Publications of the University of Manchester Economic History Series, No.IV, 1927), v.

7 7 J. D. Chambers, *Nottinghamshire in the Eighteenth Century: a Study of Life and Labour under the Squirearchy* (London, 1932), Preface, v.

8 J. D. Chambers, *The Vale of Trent, 1670-1800*, (Economic History Review Supplement, 1956).

9 A. H. Dodd, *The Industrial Revolution in North Wales* (Cardiff, 1933). His counties were Denbigh, Merioneth, Flint, Caernarvon and Montgomery, with the addition of Anglesey.

10 The North Wales land-mass may be compared with Cumbria, as surveyed by C. M. L. Bouch and G. P. Jones, *The Lake Counties, 1500-1830* (Manchester, 1961), and J. D. Marshall and J. K. Walton, *The Lake Counties from 1830 to the mid-twentieth Century* (Manchester, 1981), or with the territory surveyed by J. D. Marshall, *Furness and the Industrial Revolution* (Barrow, 1958). There are manifest advantages in working in an area which is more than half surrounded by the sea, and which is otherwise enclosed by clearly marked physical features.

[11] W. H. B. Court, *The Rise of the Midland Industries, 1600-1838* (Oxford, 1938).

[12] The best evidence of this is not only in Steinbach's essay (cited, note 5), and in Pollard's collection (note 2), but also in R. Fremdling and Richard H. Tilly (eds.), *Industrialisierung und Raum; Studien zur regionalen Differenzierung im Deutschland des 19 Jahrhunderts* (Stuttgart, 1979), and also from the remarkable collection of essays from the Eighth International Congress on Economic History (Budapest, 1982), with its two volumes of essays on Proto-Industrialisation, at least half of which dwelt on regional or urban approaches: *VIII° Congres International d'Histoire Economique, Budapest, 16-22 août 1982; Section A2: La Proto-industrialisation: Théorie et Réalité, Rapports Tome 1 et 2* (ed. Pierre Deyon).

[13] However, we must also recognise the problems which the agrarian historian of regions faces; *vide*, for example, J. Thirsk (ed.) *The Agrarian History of England and Wales*, Vol.4, 1500-1640 (Cambridge, 1967), who writes in Chapter 1, 'The Farming Regions of England', of 'The Northern Province', combining the Lake Counties and Northumbria, (pp.16-27). These two territorial areas have greatly differing systems of agriculture, east and west, although the differences would be less marked in that period. This great *Agrarian History* performs a splendid job of *classification*, however, and that surely is its main role.

[14] The further volume of the *Agrarian History* dealing with regional farming systems, J. Thirsk (ed.), *The Agrarian History of England and Wales*, Vo.5, 1640-1750, I, *Regional Farming Systems* (Cambridge, 1984), draws expert attention to the problems involved (see *Introduction*). It is very difficult to delineate regions on the basis of farming systems alone, and in this fascinating survey, groups of counties show farming areas (based on system or type) which rarely follow the boundaries of the counties concerned, although they often follow main topographical features, and are of course affected by soil and climate.

[15] The reason for this is not however more than one of convenience. From the Census of Great Britain (1801- onward), many types of statistics have been accumulated in the county framework, to which that of the poor law unions and registration districts was afterwards added.

[16] Both the *Agrarian History* and Dr. C. H. Lee's comparative regional economic studies (mentioned in Note 2 above) use combinations of counties, the general approach here owing much to the *Census of 1851*, which divided England (for example) into districts composed of groups of counties. See esp. *Population Tables*, vol.1, 1851 lxxvii ff.

[17] Examples in this *genre* are A. M. Everitt, *The Community of Kent and the Great Rebellion* (Leicester, 1966); J. S. Morrill, *Cheshire, 1630-1660* (Oxford, 1974); A. Fletcher, *A County Community in Peace and War: Sussex, 1600-1660* (London, 1975); G. C. F. Forster, 'County Government in Yorkshire during the Interregnum', *Northern History*, XII, 1976.

[18] Margaret Stacey, 'The myth of community studies', *British Journal of Sociology*, 20, (1969), pp.134-145. It is only fair to note that this set of exacting propositions and arguments does not really take the historical dimension into account — an omission that could be regarded as fortunate.

[19] Read, *op.cit.*, pp.10-17, for county freeholders' associations. County consciousness could be an abiding matter as expressed through more long-lived institutions; Prof. Peter Clark has collected details of numerous county and large-town patriotic societies for the seventeenth and eighteenth centuries. Cf., for

a detailed study of individual examples, J. D. Marshall, 'Cumberland and Westmorland societies in London', *Trans. of the Cumberland and Westmorland Antiq. and Arch. Soc.* LXXXIV, (1984), pp.239-254.

[20] J. M. Lee, *Social Leaders and Public Persons* (London, 1963); J. M. Lee, Wood *The Scope of Local Initiative* (London, 1974); J. D. Marshall *et al*, *The History of Lancashire County Council, 1889-1974* (London, 1977), which attempts to introduce some social setting and political analyses; B. J. Barber and M. W. Beresford, the *West Riding County Council 1889-1974*; *Historical Studies* (Wakefield, 1979), represents the commencement of a major study of that county division. J. D. Marshall and J. K. Walton, *The Lake Counties from 1830*, cited, discusses the social origins of the Cumberland and Westmorland county councils, pp. 120-23.

[21] Craven is one of those areas that cries out for special study, although its social and economic relationships within manors probably mirrored those of much wider areas of the north-west, just as its social coherence was conceivably placed under some strain by the rise of small industries in the nineteenth century; cf. for the first topic, R. W. Hoyle, 'Lords, tenants and tenant right in the sixteenth century', *Northern History*, XX, 1984, pp-38-63, which is also a study of four manors in Craven, and for the second, Richard Lawton, 'The economic geography of Craven in the nineteenth century', in D. R. Mills (ed.), *English Rural Communities* (London, 1973), pp.155-81. *The Craven Herald* (1851) certainly seems to mirror a community of interest in its 'country', although one has to ask how far this is created by the newspaper itself.

[22] Charles Pythian-Adams, *Rethinking English Local History* (Leicester, 1987) pp.27-42.

[23] *Op.cit.*,p.45. It should be noted that the author does here make a serious attempt to clarify the concept of 'community', linking the latter to wider 'spatial expressions of human relations' (p.21).

[24] Steinbach, 'Zur Diskussion über den Begriff der Region', pp.196-7. The author of this essay points out that there is a disadvantage or contradiction in the notion of a 'spatial unit for the purposes of investigation', seen purely in a restricted sense, because the process of research will test or render implausible the actual boundaries.

[25] Dr. C. H. Lee (*loc. cit.*) is the only scholar to have consistently compared English 'regions' in the economic sense; other comparative studies, stimulated by the Conference of Regional and Local Historians, are now beginning to emerge. However, geographer colleagues are also taking up the challenge, sometimes working with economic historians; cf. J. Langton and R. J. Morris (eds.), *Atlas of Industrialising Britain* (London, 1986) and Derek Gregory, *Regional Transformation and Industrial Revolution*; *a Geography of the Yorkshire Woollen Industry* (London, 1982), which formulates a structuralist-Marxist interpretation of the nature of regions, and eschews completely the empiricist historian's approach. At another level of approach altogether is Gerard Turnbull's 'Canals, coal and regional growth during the industrial revolution', *Economic History Review*, 2nd Series, Vol. XL, No.4 (1987), pp.537-60.

[26] Peter Laslett, *Family Life and Illicit Love in Earlier Generations* (Cambridge, 1977); P. Laslett, K. Oosterveen and R. M. Smith (eds.), *Bastardy and its Comparative History* (London, 1980); E. A. Wrigley and R. S. Schofield, *The Population History of England* (Cambridge, Mass., 1981).

27   M. Chisholm, *Human Geography, Evolution or Revolution?* (Pelican, 1975), p.36. Cf. also David Grigg, 'Regions, Models and Classes', in Richard J. Chorley and Peter Haggett, (eds.) *Integrated Models in Geography* (London, 1967), pp.472-6; 'For many geographers, .. the issue as to whether the region is a real entity is dead' (p.472).

28   David Grigg, pp.479-83.

29   As has been made plain, planners tend to group administrative counties together, but economists (cf. the professional journal of the Regional Studies Organisation, *Regional Studies*) are quite happy to work in any suitable and data-producing administrative region.

30   For example, U. R. E. Lawler, *North-Western Theses and Dissertations, 1850-1978* (Centre for N.W. Regional Studies, University of Lancaster, 1981, with a *Supplement*, 1988). For an idea of the scope of regional work, see also Kathleen A. Whyte (ed.), *Historical Geography Research Series: Register of Research in Historical Geography* (1984).

31   See Note 12.

32   Cf. the valuable and stimulating discussion between the historical geographers Langton and Gregory, which in some of its terms mirrors the discussions between economic as well as regional historians over the last decade; Gregory's insistence on the importance of theory should not go unmarked by historians, however, and the latter have suffered from the narrow empiricism which has dominated local studies in England over the last three or four decades: for the main exchanges, J. Langton, 'The industrial revolution and the regional geography of England', *Trans. Inst. Brit. Geographers*, 9, (1984), pp.145-67; D. Gregory, 'The production of regions in England's industrial revolution'. *Jnl. Historical Geography*, 14,1 (1988), pp. 50-58; J. Langton, 'The production of regions in England's industrial revolution: a response', *Jnl. Historical Geography*, 14, 2 (1988), pp.170-73; D. Gregory, 'Reply', *loc. cit.*, pp.174-77. To be fair to all concerned, the historical geographers have led the way in matters of conceptualisation, over a number of years, especially in the English and French-speaking countries; cf. Anne Gilbert, 'The new regional geography in the English and French-speaking countries', *Progress in Human Geography*, Vo.12, No.2, (1988), pp.208-220.

33   Hubert Kiesewetter, 'Region und Nation in der Europäischen Industrialisierung, 1815-1871' (MS of essay to be published), demonstrates how one may distinguish and identify industrialising regions throughout the world by using the following criteria; agrarian reform, population density, food imports, coal production, and railway networks. Professor Kiesewetter, to whom I am greatly indebted for a chance to read this essay, has demonstrated in depth the nature of his general approach in a major work on the economic development of the Kingdom of Saxony, *Landwirtschaft und Industrialisierung* (Bohlau-Verlag, Cologne, 1988).

34   *Vide* Gilbert, *op.cit.*, esp. pp.216-17.

CHAPTER 2

Land, the Social Structure and Industry in Two Yorkshire Townships c.1660-1800.

Pat Hudson

The aim of this paper is to examine the origins of distinctive organisational forms of largely rural, pre-factory, domestic industry.[1] Why did products of particular kinds come to be manufactured commercially in distinct manners in different regions of Britain and Europe during the centuries of 'proto-industrialisation'?[2] How did such aspects as the division of labour, the relationship between production and marketing, the sources of capital, credit and enterprise come to differ between different regions and sub-regions even where very similar commodities were the end result?

This study focuses on these issues by examining the structure of production and trade in two very different townships of the West Riding textile belt: Sowerby, in the Calder Valley, south-west of Halifax, and Calverley, a smaller township, in the Aire Valley to the north and west of Leeds. It thus represents two case studies but it is hoped that the wider experience of the textile area and other proto-industrial regions may be illuminated by them.

As is well known, the West Riding of Yorkshire grew to dominate the production of coarse and medium quality woollen and worsted products for long-distance trade during the course of the eighteenth century. Yet within the region the production of different sorts of cloths came to exhibit a distinct organisational and spatial variation. Heaton's classic study stressed this phenomenon as did Sigsworth's and other later works.[3] More recently, at the level of the region my own analysis has attempted to place these organisational variables against the backcloth of the agrarian and institional environments found in different parts of the region.[4] I argued that the traditional manufacture of woollens, organised largely on an artisan basis, survived and flourished during the eighteenth century in the east and south of the textile belt. Artisan households typically bought their raw materials on credit and sold their finished or semi-finished products at the weekly markets. Usually, clothmaking was undertaken as a by-employment alongside farming or small-holding. In the woollen belt soils and climate were suitable for a mixture of arable and grazing which had increased the attraction of large estate ownership, a legacy of the earlier manors. This institutional structure affected the land market, inheritance and, hence, the social structure. The area to the north and west moved over from woollen production to worsted manufacture during the course of the eighteenth century. The putting-out system came to dominate instead of the structure of independent and semi-independent artisan households. Considerable division of labour between households occurred and spinning was put out over a wide area which extended into the Yorkshire Dales in the north and into Lancashire in the west. The worsted belt became characterised by increasingly proletarianised weavers' households dependent on their employer (and the Parish). This region, much of it lying above the 200 metre contour, was climatically and agriculturally less attractive than the lower-lying woollen belt and was hence never strongly manorialised. Here subinfeudation, an active land-market, and the process of enfranchisement resulted in the accumulation of land in the hands of a socially diverse, but limited, class who then rented out cottages to the larger army of the landless group. I argued that this type of social structure and institutional history was a favourable environment for putting out to flourish. Potential commercially-minded employers with landed assets existed side by side with a proletarianised group whose landlessness made it difficult to function independently as household manufacturers.

In order to test these notions vigorously and to enquire exactly how the institutional and agrarian environment functioned to influence the social structure via landholding, inheritance, poor relief systems and in other ways, two townships (which have good survival of archival materials) were chosen, one from each of the major sub-regions. Although, as we shall see, Sowerby and Calverley both have distinctive histories and social features peculiar to themselves, it is hoped that they will serve as representative in many respects of the sub-regions of which they form a part. The map illustrates the spatial distribution of the woollen and worsted areas by the end of the eighteenth century and pinpoints the position of the two townships within them.

This research relies heavily upon the use of the IBM 3083 mainframe computer, using IBM database software called SQL (Structured Query Language). This package enables nominal data to be united across a range of files and also enables the storage and retrieval of tabulated information by a very large number of co-ordinates. Thus, for example, taxation data can be readily linked to occupational information from Parish Registers, probate material can be linked to township administration, vital events from Parish Registers, settlement documents, pauper apprenticeship indentures, land transfer and estate papers etc. I would be pleased to answer any questions on this technical aspect of the work.[5]

****

Sowerby was a much bigger township than Calverley in terms both of population and of land area. At the 1811 Census Sowerby had a population of 5177 compared with Calverley's 2390.[6] Their difference in population size appears to have been similar a century and more earlier as indicated in the Hearth Tax returns for 1664 which listed the exempted as well as the taxpayers for much of the West Riding.[7] At that date Calverley-cum-Farsley is recorded as having only 127 'households' of which 43 (or 34%) were exempt. By contrast, Sowerby is recorded with 219 tax-paying households and around 93 (or 30%) of the total households exempted. In noting the proportion of tax-payers who were exempted by reason of poverty no significant difference appears between the two townships although the fact that Calverley had a slightly higher proportion exempt is perhaps surprising given the premise of our initial hypotheses at regional level. We must return to this point later.

28

The dependence of both Sowerby and Calverley on the manufacture of textiles is apparent from the late seventeenth century as indicated in surviving wills and probate inventories. As illustrated in Table 1 almost half of Sowerby will-makers (1690s-1760s) had textile occupations and in Calverley the proportion was 38%. In neither case does this represent the full commitment of the township to its main branch of manufacturer, however, because will-making was biased in favour of the upper income groups whereas textile crafts on a part or full-time basis were ubiquitous amongst the poorer groups. In Calverley, because of the greater proclivities of the soils, a significant proportion of the non-textile will-makers were yeoman farmers with no obvious textile involvements, although the existence of credits on bond among the assets of many is indicative of considerable lending and borrowing between the farming and textile groups.

The textile occupations of will-makers differed between the two townships reflecting the nature of production in the two places and the organisational structure of the industry. In Calverley the majority of will-makers included in the textile trades are described as clothiers, a term which in that township covered a vast range of types of concern, from those with assets valued as low as £2 to those over £500 but typically lying in the £30-£138 range (the interquartile range). Most of these clothiers, with the exception of the very poor, held land (particularly copyhold land) and carried out arable and livestock farming alongside textile production. Often their assets were fairly equally balanced between the two, although credits and stocks on the textile side of their operations seem to have run up large (textile) assets in one or two cases. In Sowerby the term clothier seems to have been applied both to dependent weavers and to more substantial independent concerns, but assets of clothiers in that township seldom exceeded £100. Putting-out employers with assets between £50 and £800 were typically termed yeomen. These Sowerby individuals were often involved in agriculture as well as trade and industry but the bulk of their assets were clearly in trade, especially in credits and stocks of wool and cloth. The term yeoman in Calverley was, by contrast, almost exclusively applied to landholding farmers only.[8]

By the early eighteenth century the occupational information provided by the Parish Registers enables more detailed understanding of the occupational structure across the whole of the social scale. Again there is indicated a heavy reliance on weaving in Sowerby. Whether one analyses the occupations of fathers of baptised children, relatives of those buried, or the occupations of the deceased, the results are very similar.[9] Around 45% of Sowerby's male population were weavers in the second quarter of the eighteenth century, a further 20-30% had textile occupations other than weaving (principally clothiers, dressers, spinners and combers). Thus around 70% of the male employed population was dependent on textiles for their main source of livelihood. Female dependence is harder to estimate because the work experience of so few women is reflected in the Parish Register data. Where a glimpse is obtained, a very high proportion of spinsters is indicated.[10] Sowerby's other occupations in the first half of the eighteenth century were principally the service trades (shoemakers, innkeepers, victuallers), and

The Location of Sowerby and Calverley within the Worsted and Woollen areas respectively of West Yorkshire c.1780-1830.

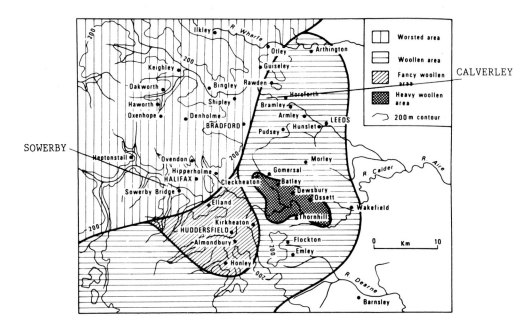

Source:- P. Hudson, *The Genesis of Industrial Capital*, Cambridge, 1986, p.28.

Table 1:
Occupations as described or listed in Probate data, Sowerby and Calverley 1690s-1760s*

Occupations	Sowerby	Median of Inv.Sowerby	Calverley	Median of Inv.Calverley
Clothiers	17	£27	38	£56
Yeomen/Putting-out merchants	16	£184	-	N/A
Weavers	14	£13	2	£8
Other textile employments	6	not calculated	2	not calculated
Non-textile employments	58	not calculated	69	not calculated
Total cases	111		111	

* Sowerby here includes Soyland and Calverley denotes Calverley Parish.
Source:- Probate Inventories and Wills, Borthwick Institute,
University of York.

building/labouring. Agricultural occupations are simply not found recorded in the Parish Registers with the exception of one or two woodcutters. Clearly the soil and its products was very much a secondary activity in the township. Many people held land (as we shall see) and worked it, but few regarded it as their main source of livelihood.

At the end of the eighteenth century the dependence on textiles remained, although the numbers concentrating on weaving had increased as had the numbers of service occupations directly associated with commercial textile production (see Table 2). The same high proportions dependent on the textile industry are found in the early nineteenth century also: 45% of the fathers of baptised children were weavers and a further 23% were involved in other aspects of textile manufacture. A large proportion of the rest were in trade and services allied to the textile industry.[11]

Interestingly, the Parish Register material provides some insights into occupational and residential mobility. Of the 855 cases of fathers of the baptised 1777-98, only 62 were recorded with more than one occupation and 48 (77%) of these were weavers (shifting to or from being soldiers, clothiers, combers and/or labourers mostly). Twelve per cent of the fathers moved one or more times, within the township, during their child-bearing years and a further 7% moved into or out of Sowerby (from or to neighbouring townships in the main). Of the total of movers, 88% were weavers showing them to be the most mobile group as well as those most likely to shift occupations or to carry on two occupations at once.

The wide use of the term clothier to cover a variety of size and type of undertaking, together with the dependence of Calverley's population on artisan cloth-making in the early eighteenth century is illustrated in Table 3 which analyses the occupational data from the Parish Register for the years 1721-26. No-one was classified as a 'weaver' or a manufacturer as in Sowerby. Apart from the overwhelming dominance of clothiers, the importance of the husbandry group, which has no direct counterpart in Sowerby, shows up. Although not yet complete, study of the Parish Register data, for Calverley, at the end of the century shows the continuing numerical dominance of the clothier group in the population, although this is reduced to nearer 50% of stated occupations.

Our earliest indications of the different social structures of the two townships during the period 1660-1820 comes from the Hearth Tax returns and are illustrated in Tables 4a and 4b which analyse the returns for 1664. The Sowerby figures are inflated by the inclusion of Soyland in the returns for the township. Soyland was to become a separate township but fell within the same Constabulary as Sowerby for Hearth Tax purposes. As Soyland appears to have been very similar in social and occupational structure to Sowerby, the Sowerby/Soyland Hearth Tax figures can be regarded as representative of the nature of Sowerby (though inflated by about 28% in terms of numbers of taxpayers).

The Calverley and Sowerby Hearth Tax returns, as illustrated in the tables, covering 1664, highlight remarkable contrasts between the two townships in social structure as reflected in hearth ownership. These, to a large extent,

Table 2:

**Fathers' occupations from Church of England Baptisms,
Sowerby St. Peters 1777-1798**

Occupations	Number	Percentage of total
Weavers	482	56
Other textiles	162	19
Service trades	77	9
Tradesmen & Merchants	30	4
Building trades	84	10
Farmers	1	0
Soldiers	19	2
Total cases	855	100

Source:-   Parish Register, Sowerby St. Peters 1777-1798

Table 3:

**Occupations as stated of fathers of children baptised at
Calverley Parish Church, 1721-26.**

Occupations	Number	% of total
Clothiers	452	70
Other textiles	5	1
Husbandmen	64	10
Innkeepers	11	2
Tailors	23	4
Masons	12	2
Blacksmiths	13	2
Shoemakers	10	1
Other services	41	6
Others	15	2
Total cases	646	100

Source:-   Calverley Parish Registers, vol.2,
West Yorkshire Archive Service, Halifax.

Table 4:
Analysis of the Hearth Tax Returns,
Sowerby and Calverley 1664.

4a) Sowerby Hearth Tax 1664 (Includes Soyland)

Hearths	Number of household heads	% of household heads
Exempt	140	30
0	3	1
1	185	39
2	72	15
3	29	6
4	27	6
5	10	2
6	2	«1
7	1	«1
8	1	«1
9	1	«1
Total	471	100

4b) Calverley Hearth Tax 1664

Hearths	Number of household heads	% of household heads
Exempt	43	34
0	0	0
1	58	45
2	18	14
3	6	5
4	1	1
5		
|		
14	1	1
Total	127	100

Source:-   Hearth Tax Returns, E179/210/393, 16 Charles II,
            Lady Day 1664, P.R.O. Chancery Lane.

accord with our initial understanding of the differences in social structure pertaining as a result of very different patterns of prior manorialism, of land-ownership, leasing, and inheritance.

In Sowerby, no tax-payer paid on more than nine hearths through the four tax points 1664-1674, but fifteen or so individuals in Sowerby paid tax on five or more hearths.[12] At the other end of the social scale (in hearth terms), 56% of the tax-paying public paid on one hearth with a further substantial group of 30% paying on between two and four hearths. Thus, although the social structure was by no means polarised at this date, there certainly appears to have been a stratum of the sort of substantial individuals who might be capable of finding the credit and capital to finance trade and putting-out on a considerable scale. These persons existed alongside a significantly large exempt class of potential employees, but the middling strata were also highly visible.

Turning to Calverley, a very different picture emerges in the distribution of hearths in the returns. Sixty-nine per cent of tax-payers (or 46% of total household heads) paid on only one hearth, in 1664, with a further 21% paying on two. Only one person paid tax on more than four hearths: Sir Walter Calverley, the largest landowner in the township by far. Thus Calverley township, as reflected in the Hearth Tax returns, had a very large group of one-hearth payers, a smaller middling stratum than Sowerby and one family, the Calverley's (succeeded by the Thornhill's during the eighteenth century) who controlled much of the land of the township. Calverley's 'one-hearth payers', as we shall see, were mainly small land-holding clothiers. It must also be borne in mind that, as in Sowerby, about one-third of householders (the landless and small-cottager group in the main) were recorded as exempt from taxation by reason of poverty.

We have thus established that Sowerby and Calverley conform to the typologies, regarding occupation and social structure, boldly stated in my earlier work although Sowerby, and possibly the other townships of the worsted area also, possessed a much more significant middle strata than was originally thought. Also, Calverley, and possibly most of the rest of the woollen area, had a class of poor and landless cottagers from the late seventeenth century which was as significant as the proletarianised element of the worsted belt. It will be necessary to discover the occupational structure of these proletarianised groups, but first we must inquire a little more into the relationship between landownership, landholding (and working), and the organisation and finance of the textile industry. For this inquiry the Land Tax assessments have proved a major source. Although the subject of much debate relating to their precise accuracy and the question of calculating acreage equivalents, these returns can provide valuable information on the structure of landholding and (from the 1780s) on land-ownership and occupation.

At this stage of the research as with the Parish Register analysis, we have much more computerised material on Sowerby than on Calverley. Thus, for Sowerby, the Land Tax analysis of owners and, where possible, occupiers has been calculated at five benchmark years — 1750, 1761, 1782, 1788, and 1794, — whilst that for Calverley has been undertaken only on the latter three. These figures have been suppplemented, where possible, with earlier miscellaneous taxation assessments, principally lay subsidies and window taxes. Additionally, for the Blackwood Quarter of Sowerby only (covering more than one-third of the land area and the population of the township) a detailed rate assessment of 1804 has been analysed against the occupational data from the Parish Registers.

Sowerby is remarkable for the survival of early Land Tax returns dating (sporadically) from 1750. The tax paid (mainly by owners rather than occupiers of land) in 1750/1 and 1761 is detailed in Table 5. Between these two dates a revision of Sowerby's assessment occurred so that individuals were made to pay an increase of some 25%. This accounts for the overall upward shift in assessments, but Table 5 is most remarkable for the stability which is shown in the distribution of taxes. In both 1750/1 and 1761, 85% and 78% respectively of tax-payers paid sums between four shillings and £2 10s. Relatively few (7% in 1750/1 and 6% in 1761) paid less than four shillings but this was matched and, in 1761, exceeded by a group of substantial tax-payers. In 1750/1 7% of tax-payers paid £2 10s and more whilst in 1761 the figure had risen to 16%, with eight people paying more than £5.

This sort of wealth distribution (in terms of land) is similarly reflected in the Poor Rate and Window Tax assessments of the mid-century. The earliest surviving Poor Rate assessment figures for 1738 are shown in Table 6 and the Window Tax figures for 1758/9 are given in Table 7. The latter are particularly clear in showing the class of substantial wealth-holders which Sowerby possessed in contrast to Calverley and other places like it. The Window Tax, like the Poor Rate but unlike the Land Tax, was assessed on the occupation of houses and is thus, perhaps, a more accurate representation of wealth-holding and social status, especially for a manufacturing township, than the Land Tax which simply reflected the ownership of landed assets.

The spread of wealth-holding in the upper-middle social range is conspicuously absent in the Calverley indicators throughout the period, although a Lay Subsidy and a War Tax of the 1690s both show a substantial social group in the lower, yet 'solid', tax-paying ranges.[13] The 1692 War Tax schedule shows clearly, for example, that Sir Walter Calverley paid three times as much as his nearest 'rival' down the social scale.[14]

The more directly comparable figures of both ownership and occupation of land in the townships highlight the same contrasts but here we can now also see the different distributions of owners, occupiers, owner-occupiers and owner-part-occupiers. If we take land-ownership first, Table 8 illustrates the percentage distribution of Land Tax payers in the two townships which reflects their differences in social structure nicely. In Calverley, Thomas Thornhill paid more than £70 in 1782 rising to £95 in 1794. By the latter year, he paid more than nineteen times that of the next person on the tax scale. In Sowerby, on the other hand, George Stansfield and Sir Watts Horton shared the top tax bracket but both paid only £25 to £35 throughout the period and several others paid more than £2 10s. Many of those in the under four shillings tax bracket in Calverley paid less than one shilling, but the lowest Sowerby payment was three shillings, indicating either the existence of a stratum of poor taxpayers in Calverley or the fact that many small-holders owned and were liable for only

Table 5:
Sowerby Land Tax Payers 1750/1 and 1761

Categories	1750/1*	1761
Less than 4 shillings	11	8
4s-«£1	79	51
£1-«£2 10s	44	46
£2 10s-«£5	7	12
£5-«£10	2	6
£10-«£20	1	1
£20 and more	-	1
Total paying tax on land	144	125

* Includes Sowerby and Westfield Quarters for 1750, Blackwood and Pallas, 1751.

Source:- Land Tax Returns, SPL 145, 146, 150, West Yorkshire Archive Service, Halifax.

Table 6:
Poor Rate Assessment, Sowerby 1738

Categories	Numbers
Listed but not taxed	10
Under 1 shilling	18
1s-«2s	33
2s-«5s	42
5s-«7s	6
7s-«£1	6
£1-«£2	1
Total rate-payers	116

Source:- SPL46, West Yorkshire Archive Service, Halifax.

Table 7:
Window Tax Analysis, Sowerby 1758/9

Windows on which Tax paid	Numbers of Tax-payers
Under 4	1
4-6	5
7-9	71
10-12	6
13-15	11
16-20	11
21 or more	8
Total tax-payers	113

Source:- SPL153 West Yorkshire Archive Service, Halifax.

part of the land which they held. Supplementary copyhold land was probably also held or small plots rented from Thornhill.

A difference is also indicated in the proportions of owner-occupiers and owner-part-occupiers. Sowerby had a much greater proportion of people directly involved in working their own land which, along with the greater dispersal of ownership, implied a much greater freedom in the land market. Most of the owner-occupiers of Sowerby were in the 4s-£1 tax category. In Calverley, owner-occupiers were predominantly found in the under four shillings group, those with bigger farms mainly consisting of tenants many of whom rented land from Thornhill who could exert considerable control over the land market.

Turning to the sizes of tenanted farm plots most common in the two townships, as detailed in Table 9, it becomes obvious that the typical farm in Calverley was one on which 4s-£1 was paid in Land Tax. There also existed a sizeable number of cottages with small patches of taxable land attached. It is my contention that these farms were the province of the dual-occupation clothier. Large units were occupied mainly by specialist yeomen farmers and graziers working to supply the Leeds market in particular. In Sowerby, the most common farm-size group was also the 4s-£1 taxed but the next category of £1-£2 10s was also very substantial and several persons occupied farms taxed at £2 10s-£5. But almost no-one classed themselves as farmers in the Parish Register entries of the period[15] and many Sowerby yeomen, as evidenced by Probate inventories were involved in textile putting-out and trade. The sizeable farms of Sowerby were thus intimately related to textile manufacture and trade, acting as a source of collateral and spreading risks just as the small farms and holdings of Calverley enabled balancing of occupations amongst the clothier group.

When research has progressed further it should be possible to match the Parish Register occupational data with the Land Tax results to get some idea of exactly which occupational groups owned and occupied the very different distributions of land in the two townships. This sort of information is currently available only for 1804 for about one-third of the township of Sowerby. Tables 10 and 11 give the results of matching the Parish Register occupational data against the Rate Valuation for that year for owners and occupiers respectively.

More than half of the landowners' occupations were identified, indicating the importance of sizeable holdings on the part of textile merchants and tradesmen and of merchant-manufacturers. Few of these individuals occupied their land however, preferring to rent it out in small farms for additional income where it could also form a valuable collateral on mortgage for credit and loans. Those weavers who owned land typically did the same. Only two, John Whitely and Jonathan Speak, worked their nine acre plots, the rest appear to have concentrated on manufacturing, supplementing their income with rent. A similar split between weaver-farmers and those, mostly landless, who concentrated just on the manufacturing becomes evident in the analysis of tenants' occupations given in Table 11. These findings considerably sophisticate our understanding of the weavers of Sowerby, previously thought to be almost entirely a proleterianised group by the end of the eighteenth century. Clearly,

Table 8:

Percentage distribution of Land Tax payers
Sowerby and Calverley 1782, 1788 and 1794

| Land Tax Assessment Category | Percentages Paying | | | | | |
| | 1782 | | 1788 | | 1794 | |
	S	C	S	C	S	C
1. «4 shillings	14	33	15	41	14	41
2. 4s-«£1	36	48	35	39	35	36
3. £1-«£2 10s	29	15	30	16	30	19
4. £2 10s-«£5	12	2	13	2	11	2
5. £5-«£10	7	-	4	-	6	-
6. £10-«£20	-	-	1	-	1	-
7. £20 and over	2	2	2	2	2	2
Total %	100	100	100	100	100	100
Total cases	122	46	111	44 (55)*	107	42
Total cases of owner occupation	32	11	30	18	32	15
Total cases of owner with part occupation	18	5	20	3	21	4
% of owners with direct involvement with their own land	41	35	45	38	50	45

Source:-   Land tax Returns for Sowerby and Calverley,
West Yorkshire Archive Service, Wakefield.

Table 9:

Percentage distribution of Occupiers of land
in Sowerby and Calverley, 1782, 1788, and 1794

| Land Tax Assessment Category | 1782 | | 1788 | | 1794 | |
	S	C	S	C	S	C
1. «4 shillings	10	15	9.5	28	10	25
2. 4s-«£1	48	65	46	57	47.5	59
3. £1-«£2 10s	36	16	38	11	34	9
4. £2 10s-«£5	6	3	6	2	8	4
5. £5-«£10	-	-	0.5	-	0.5	-
6. £10-«£20	-	1	-	2	-	3
Total %	100	100	100	100	100	100
Total cases	221	106	211	119	208	118

Source:-   Land Tax Returns for Sowerby and Calverley,
West Yorkshire Archive Service, Wakefield.

Table 10:

**Occupation of Landowners
in the Blackwood Quarter of Sowerby, 1804.**

Occupation	Name	Land owned to nearest acre	
Weavers	Wm Clay	3	
16	Henry Cockroft	40	
	David Greenwood	11	
	Wm Greenwood	0	
	John Haigh	9	
	John Hellowell	0	
	John Meller	19	
	Geo Normanton	18	average holding
	Jno Radcliffe	8	= 11
	Jas Ratcliffe	1	
	Matthew Scott	0	
	Jonathan Speak	9	
	John Sutcliffe	0	
	Richard Sutcliffe	21	
	Wm Walker	20	
	John Whiteley	9	
Widows and Spinsters			average holding
11			= 20
Textile Merchants and Tradesmen			
5	William Barker	10	
	Richard Ingham	12	
	Peter Pickles	15	average holding
	Wm Rawson	27	= 20
	Wm Sutcliffe	38	
Putting-out Merchants/ Manufacturers			
6	Richard Hincliffe	35	
	James Holroyd	33	
	Jos Priestley	148	
	Jas Riley Junr	13	average holding
	Jas Riley Senr	33	= 31
	Geo Stansfield	43	
Reverend	Nathaniel Phillips	14	
Shopkeeper	Ogden Sawood	0	

Total of owners with 'occupations' identified = 40, acreage = 799
Total number of owners = 74, acreage = 1638

Source:-   SPL 310, West Yorkshire Archive Service, Halifax.

Sowerby's population was less proletarianised than previously thought and Calverley's was more so, although the basic division of clothier/farmer structure in Calverley and landholding employer/landless employee in Sowerby does remain the most salient observation. The landless in Calverley typically found farm or service trade work or worked for clothiers as journeymen and termed themselves clothiers.

A breakdown of the 1804 Sowerby rate assessment by size of tenancy shows just how small average landholdings were in the township and how few, especially of the small plots were owner-occupied (see Table 12). This is the clearest statement we have about the extent of proletarianisation which had occurred in Sowerby by the end of the eighteenth century.

Collating results from the Land Tax data with an early household Census of 1764, the Parish Registers, business records, pauper apprentice and settlement papers and the 1804 Rate Book has yielded important case study material illustrative of various ideal-types of textile manufacturers and merchants in Sowerby. Space precludes detailed descriptions of this data here but one example will give some idea, in summary form, of the information available on several hundred individuals. Similar information will also become available for Calverley enabling detailed comparisons to be made.

James Riley was typical of the more substantial landholding putting-out manufacturers of Sowerby. He was a shalloon-maker living at Priestly Ing, Blackwood, a sizeable farm, from the 1760s to the 1800s. He employed his family and other members of his immediate household which numbered 9 in 1764. This included three of his own children, under 16, one other child under 16 (who may have been a pauper apprentice) and four inmates, probably manufacturing and domestic servants.[16] By the 1780s and 1790s Riley owned five other smallholdings and cottages and was paying a total of £4 1s 9d in Land Tax annually. He leased these out to tenants, half of whom are identifiable as weavers who may well have been in Riley's employ.[17] James Riley died shortly after the 1804 Rating Assessment in which he is recorded as owning more than 33 acres of land.[18] He had had nine children but several died in infancy.[19] His fourth son, James, succeeded him in business, bringing a further 12 acres. James Jnr. remained a putting-out manufacturer, based at Priestly Ing, until the mid 1820s.[20]

The final part of this enquiry concerns inheritance practices. So far we have considered findings from various cross sectional observations reflecting social structure and land-ownership. A study of inheritance practices, and the changing grid of custom and practice within which these operated, indicates how landholding patterns (ownership and occupation) were perpetuated or destroyed. This then had important implications for changing social structure, wealth and status distribution over time and, hence, important implications for the structure of trade and industry in the two townships.

Over 100 wills from each township area have been examined for this study. Preliminary findings suggest that in both townships considerable care was taken in will-making to see that land-holdings passed intact to a single beneficiary. In Sowerby, the wife, if she survived, usually inherited for life first and then land was passed to a male heir, usually the eldest son. Land was only

Table 11:
Occupations of Tenants identified in the Blackwood Quarter of Sowerby, 1804

Occupations	No.	No. of owner-occupiers	Average land held to nearest acre
Weavers (land-less cottagers)	30		0
Weavers with land	33	2	19
Combers (land-less cottages	8		0
Combers with land	1		3
Tradesmen	5	1	17
Surgeon	1		12
Spinner	3		1
Labourer	1		0
Manufacturers	2	1	26
Clogger/Shoemaker	2		0
Innkeeper	1		0
Wiredrawer	1		0
Farmer	1	1	27
Total tenants with identified occupations	89		
All tenants	198		
Proportion identified	45%		

Source:-   SPL310, West Yorkshire Archive service, Halifax

Table 12:
Blackwood tenancies by size 1804

Size categories	No. of tenancies	No. owner-occupied
Landless cottages and land under 1 acre	111	2
1-4 acres	124	3
5-9 acres	17	5
10-14 acres	16	2
15-19 acres	17	2
20-24 acres	10	2
25-29 acres	6	1
30-34 acres	0	
35-39 acres	2	1
40-44 acres	4	2
More than 45 acres	4	-
Total tenancies	311	20

Source:-   SPL310, Rate Assessment 1804, West Yorkshire
             Archive Service, Halifax.

sub-divided in Sowerby in two circumstances. First, where it lay some distance away, outside the township, and formed a separate estate for a second beneficiary. Secondly where there were no male heirs but more than one female to provide for.

In Calverley land was more often sub-divided among two or more male heirs, particularly where large holdings were involved which could provide more than one farm of a size suitable to run alongside manufacturing. In Calverley also, fewer wives inherited land — brothers or even male cousins being preferred particularly where they were clothiers. There also seems to have been tighter control, by testators, over future marriage of widows in Calverley than in Sowerby.

In both townships primogeniture was accompanied by the recognised need to provide portions for younger and secondary heirs, especially females. In Calverley, female (and some male) beneficiaries extended well beyond the nuclear family throughout the period, nieces, aunts, sisters and cousins commonly received sums of money or goods to a much greater extent than occurred in Sowerby where the bulk of lands and goods were left to immediate relatives of the nuclear group or, through them, to grandchildren.

One or two examples of Calverley and Sowerby will-makers might serve to highlight the aspects mentioned. William Dawson, a Calverley clothier, died in 1693 leaving an estate worth £346 12s 6d. Interestingly, about £200 of this was in credits owing and Walter Calverley owed him £100. He left lands in the neighbouring township of Yeaden to his eldest son, his two other sons and a daughter received substantial cash portions of £60 each (largely to be used for their education), and the two elder sons were also bequeathed a loom when they reached 21 years. Sarah, his wife, was given all chattels and the right of tuition of her children but only if any remarriage was approved by 'my beloved friends', Joseph Marshall of Horsforth and William Hollings of Yeaden, clothiers. These friends were themselves left 20 shillings each.[21] In 1700 Benjamin Sandall, a clothier of Calverley, died leaving an estate of £216 11s. Of this £53 was owed to him by his creditors. He obviously died without issue but expressed considerable concern for other relatives and dependents in his will. His lands and personal estate were divided equally between his two clothier brothers but first £40 was to go to his sister, 40 shillings annually to his father for life, 20 shillings each to two uncles, 20 shillings to the poor of Idle, 20 shillings plus the use of lead and tenters to a clothier cousin, five shillings each to three servants and a new suit of clothes to Robert Brewer, his apprentice.

Sowerby wills abound with interesting illustrations of the standard inheritance practices, although considerable variation occurred. Jeremiah Riley died in 1715 leaving a movable estate of £766 14s 6d. He termed himself a yeoman but, from his inventory it is obvious that he was a putting-out merchant. His considerable landed estates, which he occupied in Sowerby, were left to his eldest son, his second son receiving £150 and a smaller estate leased out to tenants. His daughter, Abigail, was left £300 at 21 'the interest of which to be used to maintain her with meat, drink, apparel, washing, lodging with all convenient education, learning and accomplishments fit and needful for such a one...'. Riley's wife received only £50, and the remainder of the estate went to the eldest son.

A part, and in Calverley a considerable part, of land bequeathed was copyhold and had first to be surrendered to the Lord of the Manor before it could be left by a testator. Tenures unsecured by a will or by a clear lineage of hereditable descent could fall back into the hands of the Lord. In a place like Calverley, the Lord was likely to enforce this, so blocking the (normal) inheritance process as there was much profit to be made in reorganising land for leasing into the size of plots suitable for the farmer-clothier. Evidence suggests that this was a very important aspect of estate improvement on the part of Sir Walter Calverley, and in the Aire Valley generally, during the eighteenth century.[24] Lords of Manors and large estate owners with reversionary leases could call back lands into their purview thus controlling and rigidifying the land-market and perpetuating a structure of small farms at lease.

The weight of portions ensured the need for Sowerby landowners to maintain an efficient and commercial attitude to their undertakings hence the prime importance of expanding commercial manufacture and trade and the ubiquity of leasing out land rather than working it direct. The relatively freer land-market in Sowerby, compared with Calverley, did mean that male heirs being left portions could easily slip into the small landowner group or could certainly lease a plot or two.

Another feature of the inheritance systems of the two townships arising out of their very different agrarian and manorial legacies was the different 'grids of inheritance': the complex web of custom and practice concerning use-rights which accompanied the passing of land from one generation to the next.[25] E. P. Thompson has argued that these grids were being extinguished in the eighteenth century long before Parliamentary enclosure. With the disappearance of gleaning and grazing and other communal use-rights younger sons and daughters had less and less chance to make do with legacies of cash or moveables. Thus, Thompson argues, impartible inheritance with portions resulted in the decline of the yeomanry as a class. However, in the case of two manufacturing townships such as Sowerby and Calverley this process was considerably modified by the possibilities of incomes earned in manufacture and the leasing of land. Furthermore, much land was held on bond or mortgage or as security for debts especially in Calverley where most clothiers' assets included a high proportion of credit extended. This holding of land as security brought with it temporary use-rights of value to clothiers.[26]

The structure and practice of inheritance tended, in both townships, to perpetuate the traditional structure of landholding and the continued importance of leasing and short-term transfers. The proliferation of copyholders in Calverley ensured some continuation of traditional use-rights particularly until the (partial) Enclosure Act of 1758. At this point the continuation of the same inheritance practices in new circumstances accelerated the process of proletarianisation of a portion of the population whilst maintaining the more substantial ex-copyholder clothier dynasties on a stable footing.

In Sowerby enclosure by Act came late — in the 1840s — but use-rights had been all but extinguished long before. Primogeniture with portions here did not result in the decline of the 'yeomanry' but meant that those who survived, flourished, and bought up the land which others were forced to sell were those involved in the lucrative spheres of trade and putting-out. This was the new yeomanry class of Sowerby. They never called themselves clothiers (though that is what, in many respects, they were) but instead termed themselves yeomen and rose during the eighteenth century to positions of power and authority in the township elite. Here they administered the poor law relief, pauper apprenticeship and settlement in a very different manner to that found in Calverley where older landholding families continued in power. In Calverley older yeoman families functioned alongside a group of stable landholding clothiers who eventually financed Co-operative Company mills on a joint stock basis. They exhibited aspects of communal organisation, affiliations and loyalties in the sphere of familial affairs and local government. Sowerby, by contrast, seems to have manifested a more 'individualistic' culture. But this aspect of the story of Calverley and Sowerby opens a different chapter to be dealt with elsewhere.

This paper set out to test some preliminary hypotheses established at sub-regional level concerning the relationship between land-holding (ownership and leasing) patterns and the organisational structure of commercial textile manufacture. To a large extent the basic hypotheses hold good for the two townships examined although the strength of the middle-income social stratum in Sowerby, its relative absence from Calverley, plus the importance of the poor and proletarianised group in Calverley from the late seventeenth century are a surprise and necessitate come restructuring of thought on the subject of social structure and textile manufacture. Of course, it may well be the case that social structure was as much a product as a precondition of the organisational forms which the industry manifested. Thus, once established, from the mid-seventeenth century, if not earlier, the multitude of artisan clothiers in Calverley both reproduced themselves (through natural increase and inheritance practices carried out within a frame-work of substantial proportions of copyhold and leasehold land), and increasingly produced a proletarianised group of portioned offspring who failed to get a foothold on the manufacturing/landholding ladder. This group was swelled by immigration — largely from neighbouring townships, migrants being attracted by the possibilities of textile employments. We know that migration in (and out of) Sowerby was also a feature of the eighteenth century, although net migration may well have been outward here, helping to control the numbers of landless poor naturally created by the structure of landholding. Inheritance practices, together with the initial structure of landownership and holding from the sixteenth century and earlier, served in Sowerby to aid the rise of a 'new yeomanry' of commercial manufacturing employers. In Calverley it seems to have ensured the relative stability of a huge group of small land-holding clothiers in the population throughout the eighteenth century.

Notes:

1   The original version of this paper was presented at a Conference on Custom and Commerce in Early Industrial Europe held at the University of Warwick in April 1987. A revised and extended version appeared with other proceedings of that conference in M. Berg ed. *Markets and Manufactures in Early Industrial Europe* Routledge, 1990.

I wish to thank the Pasold Fund, The Twenty-Seven Foundation, The Leverhulme trust, the Nuffield Foundation, the British Academy and the E.S.R.C. for financing various parts of the major project of which this study forms a part. My research Assistant during the period 1986-87, Maria Davies was responsible for much of the data inputting vital to the present paper and I am most grateful for her assistance also with the analysis and discussion. My initial interest in the West Riding and its industrial history I owe entirely to Eric Sigsworth.

2   For surveys of the literature on proto-industrialisation, the origins and use of the term see P. Kriedte, H. Medick and J. Schlumbohm, *Industrialisation before Industrialisation*, (Cambridge, 1982); M. Berg, P. Hudson and M. Sonenscher, *Manufacture in Town and Country before the Factory*, (Cambridge, 1983); *Proceedings of the Eighth International Conference of Economic History Budapest 1982: Session A2, Proto-industrialisisation* (1982), L. A. Clarkson, *Proto-industrialization: The first phase of Industrialisization?*, (London, 1985).

3   H. Heaton, *The Yorkshire Woollen and Worsted Industries from Earliest Times to the Industrial Revolution*, (Oxford, 1920; 2nd Edn. Oxford, 1965). E. M. Sigsworth, *Black Dyke Mills: A History with introductory chapters on the development of the worsted industry in the nineteenth century*, (Liverpool, 1958). M. J. Dickenson, 'The West Riding Woollen and Worsted Industries 1689-1770: An Analysis of Probate Inventories and Insurance Policies', unpublished Ph.D. 1974, University of Nottingham. D. T. Jenkinson, *The West Riding Wool Textile Industry, 1770-1835: A Study of Fixed Capital Formation*, (Edington, 1975).

4   P. Hudson, 'Proto-industrialisation: The Case of the West Riding Wool Textile Industry in the eighteenth and nineteenth centuries' *History Workshop Journal*, XII, 1981, and *The Genesis of Industrial Capital: A study of the West Riding Wool Textile Industry c1750-1850*, (Cambridge, 1986).

5   For a fuller account of the larger project on Sowerby and Calverley (of which this study forms a part) and the use of SQL: its facilities and drawbacks see Maria Davies and Pat Hudson, 'Township reconstructional study and IBM SQL' in *Computing History Today*, 1987.

6   Census Abstracts 1811.

7   E179/210/393 16 Charles II Lady Day 1664. Hearth Tax Returns, Public Record Office, (P.R.O.) Chancery Lane.

8   The preceeding paragraph is based on a study of 222 probate documents the majority of which had probate inventories. Borthwick Institute, University of York.

9   The following results were obtained from occupational analysis of the Parish Register data of Sowerby St. Peters, first half of the eighteenth century.

Occupations of fathers of baptised 1729-40		Occupations of first relatives of those buried 1730-1736	Occupations of the deceased 1730-1736
	%	%	%
Weavers	48	54	40
Other textiles	22	14	38*
Service trades	23	25	12
Building trades,		2	
labourers etc.	4	5	3
Yeomen/woodcutters	3	-	7
	100	100	100
Total cases	212	80	42

*This figure is inflated by the inclusion of several female spinners.

[10] This is apparent where occupations of deceased females and of mothers of baptised (usually illegitimate) children are specified.

[11] These figures are derived from a study of 685 cases covering the period 1812-25.

[12] The four returns analysed for this study were 1664 (E179/210/393), 1666 (E179/210/394a), 1672 (E179/210/413), and 1674 (E179/262/13). All at the P.R.O. Chancery Lane. The distributions of hearths of tax-payers did not change markedly from one return to the next and only 1664 gives the figures of households exempt by reason of poverty.

[13] Double Lay Bill, 1694, Calverley, WYAS Leeds.

[14] ibid, 1692.

[15] See Table 2.

[16] Sowerby Religious Census 1764, West Yorkshire Archive Service (WYAS), STA215/3 Halifax, Sowerby St. Peters Parish Registers, Leeds.

[17] Land Tax Returns, Sowerby 1780s, 1790s, WYAS, Wakefield and Parish Registers ibid.

[18] 1804 Rating Assessment SPL310, WYAS Halifax.

[19] Sowerby St. Peters Parish Registers, WYAS Leeds.

[20] ibid.

[21] William Dawson Probate Papers, 23.5.1693. Borthwick Institute, University of York.

[22] Benjamin Sandall Probate Papers, 3.9.1700. Borthwick Institute, University of York.

[23] Jeremiah Riley Probate Papers, 15.9.1715. Borthwick Institute, University of York.

[24] P. Hudson, *The Genesis of Industrial Capital*, p.86.

[25] E. P. Thompson, 'The Grid of Inheritance: a comment', in J. Goody, J. Thirsk and E. P. Thompson (eds.) *Family and Inheritance: Rural Society in Western Europe 1200-1800*, (Cambridge, 1976).

[26] For a more pessimistic view of the effect of portions for female heirs on the viability of estates in part of a neighbouring township of the West Riding before the mid-eighteenth century see J. Harber et al *Shore in Stansfield: a Pennine Weaving Community 1660-1750*, (Cornholme W.E.A. 1986).

CHAPTER 3

The Urban Garden in Leeds

Maurice Beresford

It is appropriate to begin this short essay at Parkfield Row where no. 58 (See Introduction) is the fourth from the end of a row made up of identical houses. They were built, as we have seen, between 1936 and 1938, and although I have not been inside no. 58 for forty years it is plain that it is one (the north) half of a back-to-back pair, with the southern half of the pair facing Parkfield Grove: separate ownership (or tenancy) is clearly indicated today by the different colours in which front- and back-dwellers currently choose to paint their houses. As a building style in Leeds since 1787 the back-to-back house had always been a triumph of economy in the use of land, achieving high densities of population. Yet, front and back, twelve-foot deep garden plots were allowed to each house in the Row by the speculative builder of 1936-38. When did the urban garden appear in the streets of Leeds? There was no such allocation of space in the first back-to-back streets.

****

There had certainly once been houses at the heart of Leeds that possessed gardens although rarely lying in front of the houses. The characteristic form of the small number of streets which made up the original core of Leeds allowed for garden ground behind the houses on the street frontages, whether of houses along the former village street of Kirkgate or of those set in the burgage plots of Briggate from 1207. This combination of a narrow house frontage to the street and a long, narrow plot of land behind is found all over western Europe, and recent studies of medieval English villages have shown that regular (and presumably, therefore, planned) layouts of this sort were not confined to towns.

In a village, as in pre-burghal Kirkgate, the rear ground was not put to an ornamental or recreational use: it was available for growing vegetables, for dung heaps, for hens and pigs, and for containing animal stock, although by the early eighteenth century it is clear that encroachments were creeping back from the frontage houses with the erection of outbuildings and workshops, and eventually the piecemeal addition of one- and two-storey dwellings, usually of one room. Those earlier uses, for crops and keeping stock, are indicated by the names commonly found in Kirkgate property deeds of that period, *garths* or *folds*, the latter term mirroring the backyard Folds which still survived in Beeston village when Beresford and Sigsworth shopped there in 1948. One of the earliest insurance policies for a Kirkgate property placed it in Kay's Fold, and an insurance policy of 1791 for another Kirkgate house placed it in a 'fold yard'.[1]

There were other uses for the garths: the historian and antiquary, Ralph Thoresby, whose family house was on the north side of Kirkgate just west of the Vicarage, found room to build his museum as 'a more convenient retirement

47

place in the garden behind the house where I live'.[2] Until 1787 the Kirkgate garths east of the Vicarage had uninterrupted views northwards, and houses on the south side looked across Kirk Ings to the river. Sufficient nectarines and peaches were growing in Alderman Cookson's garden in August 1738 to tempt a thief,[3] and ten years earlier a neighbouring house had been advertised with 'one of the gardens going down to the River Air with a Convenience in that Garden for Bathing in the River, without being exposed to Publick View'.[4]

Where successive deeds or insurance policies survive, the submission of former garden ground in Kirkgate to commercial pressures can be detected in the growing number of references to outbuildings, tenements and workshops. The Boot and Shoe Yard, notoriously crowded in 1842, had been a garden a century earlier; and the early development of a neighbour is caught in a plan of 1767. (Figure 1).

On the more highly rated properties facing into the market place of Briggate the commercial pressures to build over a garden were greater and earlier but coverage was far from complete when John Cossins drew the first large-scale plan of Leeds c.1725.[5] From this infill came another term that occurs frequently in deeds of Briggate properties, *backsydes*.

In 1698 the traveller Celia Fiennes had noticed Leeds houses with 'good gardens and steps up to their houses and walls before them'.[6] These cannot have been houses in Briggate or Kirkgate. There is no evidence that any of the houses in the central streets had gardens in front: as in all medieval towns, the Briggate house on its burgage plot, at once home, craft workshop and retail shop, needed immediate access to the public throughfare and also needed its customers and suppliers to have immediate access; and the location of inns on Briggate frontages also demanded front access.

Celia Fiennes' comment probably related to houses elsewhere in town. The different character of the non-burghal streets of Boar Lane and the transpontine Hunslet and Meadow Lanes is shown on Cossins' map: William Milner's house in Simpson's Fold just across the bridge had three bays in one wing and four in another, and it was set back from the road and surrounded with open ground. In Boar Lane the houses of Alderman Breary and his neighbour, Alderman Rooke,

Figure 1:
A Town House with Garden, 1725
Alderman Rooke's house on the north side of Boar Lane: from the margin of John Cossins' map.

48

were also spaciously set. (Figure 2a and 2b). How this ground had been obtained is not clear: the manorial demesne may have once stretched eastwards from the Manor House on Mill Hill but the long, narrow fields remaining in 1725 between the Boar Lane houses and the Headrow suggest that there was once a block of open field selions in the vicinity. Nor did the largest house in the town at that time, Alderman Atkinson's, occupy a street frontage: it, and its surrounding garden, occupied an interior block of land south of the Kirkgate garths and east of the Briggate burgages.[7] An advertisement of 1723 for a house in New Street included a garden;[8] and there would have been no shortage of space at this Town's End site in 1634 when John Harrison first laid out New Street between the Headrow and his new church of St. John.

The antecedents of spacious garden ground around a gentleman merchant's detached house can be more certainly documented in the same quarter of the town, outside the burgage plots. On either side of the main Newcastle road, later North Street, two fine Georgian houses are shown on Cossins' map, and property deeds show that for the site of each a separate field had been purchased, one of those long, narrow two-acre fields that were characteristic of rural Leeds (deriving from the late-medieval enclosure of selions, and too large to have been village garths or burgage plots). Thus there was room for these two mansions to be set back from the road, having both a front garden and garden ground behind. The back garden ground of Robert Denison's house on the east side of the road at 'Town's End' is clearly shown in 1720 in Samuel Buck's *East Prospect of the Town of Leeds.*[9] Its back garden subsequently became covered with workshops and a mill but its front garden remained until the early twentieth century, appearing in several photographs of what had then become Sheepshanks House.

Roadside mansions with surrounding gardens of this sort did not multiply in Leeds: indeed for over forty years after 1725 there was virtually no building outside the old central streets north of the river, and it was not until 1767 that any new street was added to the old core of the town on its western side and not until 1787 on the eastern and northern sides. Neither of these developments, the West End nor the East End, provided for front gardens: nor did houses in these new streets have back gardens, although the reasons for their absence were different in the east from the west.

****

The West End streets, begun in 1767, were a development on a single estate, that of the town's principal lawyers, the Wilsons, by that time owners of the manor house and its surrounds. On this ground streets were laid out for elegant terraces looking inwards to two squares and a single terrace, south facing towards the river. The style of the houses was that of contemporary Bloomsbury, Bath and Bristol, placed almost against the pavement with room only for a railed entrance leading down to a basement entrance for tradesmen and those below stairs: no front garden.

The West End houses on the Wilson park estate did not lack ground at their rear, for the plot depths in Park Row, East Parade, South Parade and Park Place ranged between 160 and 200 feet. Perhaps in a less mercantile town than Leeds

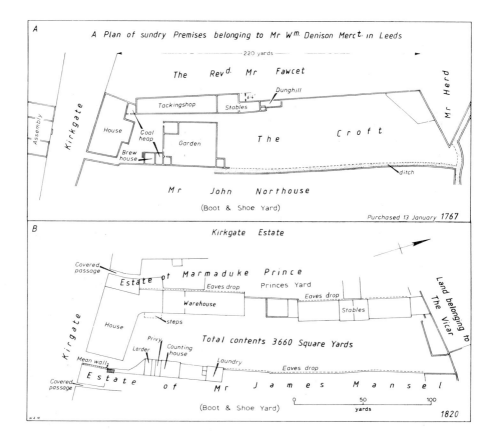

Figures 2a and 2b:

Encroachments on a Kirkgate Garth, 1767 and 1830

(a) A house between Prince's Yard (north) and the Boot and Shoe Inn (south) and opposite the first Assembly Rooms was bought by William Denison in 1767 when the former garth (croft) contained a garden, a packing shop, stables, a dunghill, two coal heaps and a brew house; there was a drainage ditch on the south side connecting with others from the north.
(Plan after University of Nottingham Library, Denison Ms. He 20)

(b) In 1820 the stables were extended and the packing shop was a warehouse; a larder, privy, counting house and laundry had also been added. For its period this garth was then remarkably open: in 1815 the Giles' map shows the Boot and Shoe Inn yard with 40 cottages.
(Plan after Denison Ms. He 21).

these back sides might have been left to horticulture but the occupants here were mainly working merchants, and from the very start both insurance policies and mortgages show that workshops, counting houses and warehouses occupied the rear ground. Thus Dunderdale's house at 19, Park Row was insured for £950 in 1784 but additional, outbuildings for another £300.[10] Thus the most elegant new town houses available in the West End were without gardens, front or back and as late as 1792 Albion Street was laid out on the same buildings or finishing shops at their rear: the exception is interesting: insured in 1792 for £1000, it was the grand eight-bay house designed by Thomas Johnson for the surgeon, William Hey, who was uninvolved with commerce or manufacture.[11] It had a walled garden large enough to give ground later for Albion Place.

The whole open ground in front of Park Row was for a while known as 'The Square' and that north of Park Place still forms Park Square: but whereas in London or Bath this ground would have been held in common by the adjoining householders and railed off for a private garden, the Wilsons retained it for development. A northern part of 'The Square' was leased to an occupant of South Parade opposite to it, and then known after him as 'Cattaneo's Garden'. From 1805 the rest of the square was put on sale for building: first for the Court House and Prison, then for the Philosophical Hall, and then from 1823 for houses and warehouses. (Figures 3a and 3b).

In 1806 there were designs to carve up the open space designated Park Square to make room for more streets had not the proprietors come together and in 1809 purchased the ground for their common enjoyment as a railed garden, the predecessor of the present public park. The major Leeds squares of the next thirty years followed this fashion:[12] Blenheim Square (1822) was intended to have 'a Pleasure Ground in the centre';[13] and the abortive 'Elmswood Square' of 1825 would have had 'Pleasure Grounds in front of each plot'.[14] When Woodhouse Square and its surrounding houses were first projected in 1825 there was to be 'a spacious open Area in Front, about to be laid out, and forever used as Pleasure Grounds by the owners and occupiers of a beautifully designed Place, to be called Woodhouse Square...'.[15] Similarly, Queen Square (begun in 1803), Hanover Square (first projected in 1791 and begun in 1825) had their private communal gardens from the first, and, like Park Square and Blenheim Square, they survive to the present day as public open spaces.

****

In the East End new streets began in 1787 but, whether the product of building clubs or of such speculative builders as Richard Paley, their density (and perhaps their back-to-back style) imitated the most closely built yards of Kirkgate in striving for the highest densities and the highest return for capital invested. Frontage houses abutted directly on to the street — as they had traditionally done in the West End — but there were neither gardens nor back access lanes behind these houses: back premises were reached through tunnels in order not to waste space on alleys, and where an irregularity in the shape of a field permitted a plot to exceed the standard rectangle other buildings were crowded in, as in Union Court behind Union Street. In a third dimension, excavations below the houses provided one-room cellar dwellings.

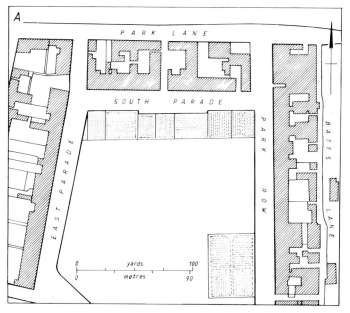

Figures 3a and 3b:

Lost Garden Ground in the West End

(a) Garden ground within 'The Square' into which the houses of Park Row, South Parade and East Parade looked: from Francis and Netlam Giles' map of 1815. Gardens behind the houses were already lost to industrial and commercial outbuildings.

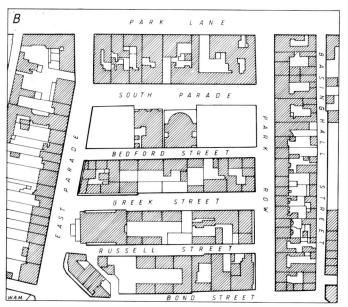

(b) The same area in 1844: from J. F. Masser, 'Plan of the Mill Hill Ward ... 1843 and 1844': Encroachments for public buildings, chapels, warehouses and private houses had begun in 1811.

There was certainly no room for front gardens here, although ironically at least two of the earliest developments were on land that had previously been market garden ground, a memory preserved in Garden Street near Crown Point bridge. Francis and Netlam Giles' plan of the town in 1815 shows a field on the east side of the Harrogate turnpike with dots and interior divisions which look suspiciously like garden ground of that type, and a conveyance indeed names it as Wilson's Garden. Other fields with this same cartographic conventional sign in 1815 were named as gardens or, nursery gardens in the 1847 O.S. plans.

Progress of building was not so rapid that other ground did not remain available near town for market gardening as late as the first edition of the Ordnance Survey (1847). It was also possible for individuals to rent small portions of fields, rather as allotments. Like Cattaneo's Garden at South Parade, ground south of Park Place had been parcelled out by the Wilsons, probably the 'New Gardens situate near the Cloth Hall' in an advertisement of 1781;[16] 'garden grounds' on the estate, probably these, had been separately rated in 1774, long before Park Place was built[17], and, as we have seen, these cannot have been gardens attached to houses. Allotments of these sort could not have been afforded by those who lived in the low-rent East End houses but the 1847 map does show an interesting agglomeration of parcels on Richmond Hill, just above the East End which may have comprised allotments and huts such as those remaining in the environs of Paris and in the Netherlands.

****

In 1816 Thomas Dunham Whitaker published his *Loidis and Elmete* to match his new edition of Thoresby's *Ducatus* of 1715. 'Could Thoresby return to survey the environs of his native town', he commented, 'no change would perhaps attract his notice than the numbers of commodious and cheerful villas which dread of smoke and desire of comfort have drawn around it...a rood of land about a country house is a little landscape'.[18] Forty two such villas have been identified, drawn around not the whole circle of the town but on the northern and western fringes.[19]

The model for this resurrection of the urban garden in Leeds was a veritable country house, Denison Hall of 1786, with thirteen acres separating it from its neighbours; the house was insured for £3100 (three times the largest houses on the Park estate),[20] rated at £82 (the largest in town), and its extensive grounds at £22 10s. As Whitaker wrote of it in 1816, 'since our Author's time the healthy and pleasant situation of this Hamlet of Little Woodhouse has occasioned the Erection of many Villas in a Style of Elegance to which he was a stranger. All these, however, indeed every Residence in the Parish, are eclipsed by [this] House...'.[21]

Whitaker's 'rood of land' may have been a poet's rood, recalling Goldsmith's rood of land that maintained its man, rather than a surveyor's quarter-acre: Beech Grove House (1799) off Woodhouse Lane had two acres, and the westernmost of the circle, Belle Vue in Little Woodhouse, had three and a half. The rate books valued Beech Grove House (Figure 4) at £12 10s and its grounds at £3 4s; Belle Vue at £12 10s and its grounds at £5; twenty other villas of this period had grounds assessed at £3 or over.[22] (Figures 5 and 6).

Although by 1847 the grounds surrounding some of these villas grounds (such as Springfield Lodge and Elmwood House) had been sold and divided for building ground, the detail on the large-scale sixty-inch-to-the-mile Ordnance Survey plan illustrates the fashion of shrubberies, lawns and

Figure 4:

The Carriage Entrance to a Villa, Beech Grove House

This villa was erected in 1799 with grounds described as 'agreeably laid out. Plantations, Gardens, Peach House and Stoves, well stocked with choice Fruit ... and about Two Acres of garden contiguous': Leeds Intelligencer, *1 April 1805. The villa and gates still stand but the grounds are occupied by the University Union, University House, and the Man-Made Fibres Building. The drawing is by John Bilbrough, 26 Dec. 1883: from sketchbook in LDA, Town Deposit*
(by courtesy of Mr. John Town).

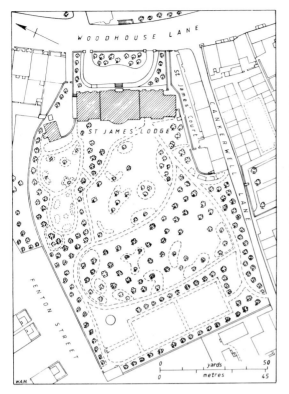

Figure 5:

**A Villa with Ornamental
Grounds, St. James Lodge, 1847**

*From the 60-inch O.S. plan. The
house was erected between 1791
and 1795 for Thomas Appleby, a
merchant, and was not
demolished until c.1960 when the
ground was taken for Leeds
Polytechnic.*

Figure 6:

The Grounds of a Villa

*Part of the gardens to the east of
Beech Grove, a villa adjoining
and similar to Beech Grove
House; erected in 1796 and
insured unfinished that May:
drawn by John Bilborough from
an attic in 1, Beech Grove
Terrace, 21 Sept. 1883 prior to
its demolition.*

55

carriage drives that occupied the roofs of land around the villas. (Figure 7).

These villas were detached and scattered, set wherever a field of sufficient size had come on the market: for villas set more closely along a road frontage one must take a knight's move, jumping over the fields of Little Woodhouse to the remoter fields of the village of Headingley where a line of villas still stands on the north side of the Leeds-Otley turnpike. These began to be erected in 1836, and many survive.[23] Like the earlier and detached villas their front gardens, many of which survive, were usually lawns and shrubberies with flower gardens behind. Eight years earlier the advertisements for plots of 'New Leeds' adjoining the Harrogate turnpike had stressed that 'the Soil is excellent and suitable for Gardens and Shrubberies.'[24]

Yet the line of detached villas at Headingley Hill did not have the form of a street: they were set wide apart, and they made up only a short row, and no similar development faced them across the road: indeed their isolation was emphasised by the width of the turnpike, greater than any street laid out as 'building ground' at that time. Where did the fashion of a line of private front gardens for a line of, non-detached houses, the style encountered at Parkfield Row, first appear?

****

Not surprisingly, front garden ground seems to appear first with the houses which were not in back-to-back streets, being modest through-houses that were erected in short Terraces (or Rows) in fields just north and north-west of town. The earliest of these was Providence Row (begun in 1797 but now demolished), near Queen Square: standing, according to *The Leeds Guide* of 1806, 'among green fields with walls and fruit trees in front of each house'[25] although it is not certain how the ornamental gardens with patterned paths shown facing the Row across the narrow Providence Place both in the 1815 Giles' map and on sheet 7 of the 1847 OS plan were related to the houses in the Row. Whereas the similar garden grounds behind the nearby Grove Place (begun between 1802 and 1806) had property boundaries that matched those of the houses in that Place, there were several mismatches in those of Providence Row. The houses of Grove Place abutted directly on to Claypit Lane having, like the neighbouring Grove Terrace and North Street, no front gardens. Nor, although not back-to-backs, had the building club houses in the nearby St. James' Street (begun in 1788).

The first dating for a front garden must therefore be sought elsewhere. On the west side of the Harrogate turnpike and just north of the Luptons' house and cloth dressing shops the 1815 map shows an empty field, known as Fountain or Tenter close; its other end abutted on to Camp Road, and there Brunswick Methodist chapel was erected in 1824-25. The eastern part of the Close was developed earlier as Brunswick Place (projected in 1813 and building from 1817 to 1821)[26] and Brunswick Street (1821-25). The two together probably made up the 'Brunswick Square' announced in 1818. (Figure 7a and 7b).

The twenty one north-facing through houses that eventually made up Brunswick Street certainly lacked front gardens, although they had garden ground at their rear. Brunswick Place, on the other hand, had the best of both worlds, for the 1847 O.S. plan shows that a substantial walled area, eight feet

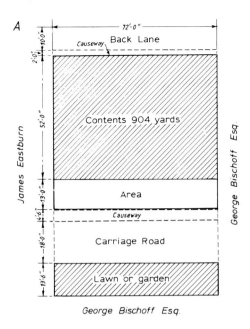

Figures 7a and 7b

The First Front Gardens in Leeds, Brunswick Place

(a) The original layout for building plots in Brunswick Place (projected in 1813) allowed for a wider carriage road than was actually built; the houses, with 52 feet depth, occupied less ground than the (private) roads and gardens which took up 67 feet: from a conveyance of 1817 (author's collection).

(b) Brunswick Place in 1847 with a drive, lawns and shrubbery separating it from the later Brunswick Street: from 60-inch O.S. plan, surveyed in 1847.

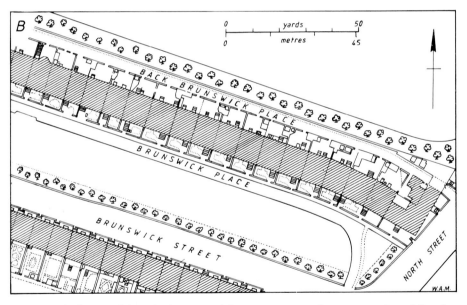

deep, lay in front of the whole row, with an ornamental gate at each end for the carriage drive:[27] it was this feature which must have given colour to the report of a projected 'Brunswick Square' in 1818.[28] Yet if the Place looked back to the private square it also looked forward in more senses than one since each of its twenty four south-facing houses was set back from the carriage drive behind a second wall, with a gate leading to the front steps and a front garden alongside. A less ambitious row was erected a little further west (1821-25) and named Brunswick Terrace, and it too had north-facing front gardens. These were small beginnings, however, for the uniform depth of the gardens both in the Terrace and in the Place was about fifteen feet.

No other building development in that part of Leeds over the subsequent decade set its houses back from the pavement although further north-west on and adjoining the present University campus there were two terrace rows which lose primacy to Brunswick Place only narrowly: and by good fortune neither has been demolished. Of the two terraces that Mrs. Julia Lyddon and her husband Captain Lyddon, initiated on their estate in 1822 the first (Lyddon Terrace) was old-fashioned enough to have only a rear garden and its front doorstep abutting on the pavement but the second (Preston Place, later Beech Grove Terrace) had both front and back gardens. Behind their wall, which still stands, the front garden of each house was forty feet deep and twenty five feet wide.[29]

Across the Woodhouse Lane from the University can be seen another runner-up, Blenheim Terrace, initiated at about the same time that Brunswick Place was completed but in quality as superior as Preston Place. It succeeded in attracting from the now-smokey West End some of the town's wealthiest spinsters and annuitants, and each pair of houses in the row shared a carriage drive through a front garden that was fifty feet wide and eighty feet deep, sufficient nowadays to corral several motor cars. (Figure 8).

It might well be objected that all these Places and Terraces of c.1825 had not yet brought the front garden to a true street; might not a purist argue that, despite its name, Brunswick Street was not a street in the way that Leeds would subsequently recognise 'street', that is, not a single row of houses but two rows of houses facing each other across the street? If this criterion is adopted we must return to the University campus and to a street now beneath it.

By this test the first Leeds street to have front gardens was Springfield Place, although it will be noticed that it thought itself too elegant to abandon 'Place' for 'Street'. It was set out on the slopes of Little Woodhouse, an area with its

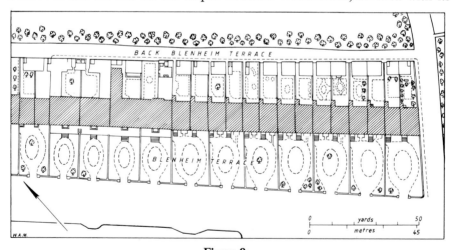

Figure 8:
Ornamental Gardens Front and Back of Blenheim Terrace
This ambitious terrace was commenced in 1825 but not completed until 1861 from 60-inch O.S. plan, surveyed in 1847.

58

ancient manor house and an array of detached villas. Next to the shrubberies of one of these, Springfield House, building ground was on offer in 1831. One 2½-acre close known as Sutton's Land was purchased by Newman Cash, stuff merchant. Two parallel back-to-back streets at least would have been packed into a field of this size elsewhere but Cash's Sale Particulars envisaged something superior.[30] (Figure 9).

Superiority was to be achieved partly by a long list of restrictive covenants binding the purchasers of the plots. 'All the houses to be erected shall be built on the lines laid down in the said plan, and fronted with dressed or good Bastard Stock bricks and covered with Blue Slate. The windows shall be in Check, the houses shall be neither more nor less than two stories high...'. The 37 houses on the east side of the road were not actually completed until 1839, when building on the west wide commenced, but already in 1833 Cash had on his part covenanted that he 'shall not build or permit to be built opposite Springfield Place (alias Woodhouse Grove) aforesaid any house or houses of an inferior description to those now standing on the east side thereof'. Each house had its back garden but there was also room for each to have its walled front garden so that by 1861 there were 74 houses facing each other as if in a mirror, their superiority assured not only by the fulfilment of the constuctional covenants but by the fact that each front window saw reflected in that mirror not only its own small, walled front garden but that of the house opposite.

****

The West End development in Leeds from 1767 had eschewed the street form in favour of terraces and squares and been indifferent to front gardens. From 1787 the East End building clubs and speculative builders had adopted the terrace form for such back-to-back streets as Union Street, Ebenezer Street and High Street but had had no room for gardens, front or rear. Then, in 1831 it rose again in Springfield Place. From Little Woodhouse the front garden spread to the better streets of the northern suburbs and occasionally to streets in Hunslet, Beeston and Holbeck, south of the river. The early-twentieth century back-to-backs in Harehills even had their front gardens.

Thus in 1948 I found the vicarage in Cemetery Road villa-like in its complete surround of garden ground, but when I moved in 1949 to a late-Victorian terrace house elsewhere in the road I discovered that I, like my neighbours, had a front garden to cultivate as did the Sigsworths in their more modest but more recent terrace in the Parkfields.

Figure 9:

The First Street with Front Gardens, Springfield Place

Occupying a complete field, Springfield Place (originally 'Woodhouse Grove') was designed in 1831 but not completed until 1856; in a neighbouring field (left) the villa, Springfield House (built in 1792 and which still stands) with its ornamental grounds: from O.S. 60-inch plan, surveyed in 1847.

Notes:

1. Kay's Fold, 1724: Guildhall Library, London, Sun Fire Insurance Registers Old Series 17/32578; 1791: Royal Exchange Registers 22/125371.

2. As sketched by Samuel Buck: *Samuel Buck's Yorkshire Sketchbook*, ed. Ivan Hall (Wakefield, 1979), p.213.

3. *Leeds Mercury*, 2 August 1738.

4. *Leeds Mercury*, 12 March 1728.

5. John Cossins, *A new and exact plan of the town of Leedes* (London, n.d. [c.1725].

6. *The Journeys of Celia Fiennes*, ed. C. Morris (London, 1949), p.20.

7. As in M. W. Beresford, *East End, West End*, Publications of the Thoresby Society, vols LX and LXI (1988), Fig. 3.3 from sketchbook 'I' of John Russell (1803-04).

8. *Leeds Mercury*, 2 April 1723.

9. As in Beresford, Fig. 3.5.

10. Sun Registers, Old Series 262/392792 and 264/ 398634.

11. Sun Registers, Country Series 22/672935.

[12] For the squares, see Beresford, pp. 280-83 and 332--47.

[13] West Yorks. Joint Archive Service, Leeds District Archives [*hereafter* LDA], LC Eng. 1/81.

[14] LDA, DB Map 411.

[15] *Leeds Intelligencer*, 18 Aug. 1825.

[16] *Leeds Mercury*, 20 Feb. 1781.

[17] West Yorkshire Joint Archive Service, Leeds District Archive Office [hereafter LDAO], LORB 32; but possibly the gardens south west of the Infirmary which certainly survived until 1815 (Giles' map).

[18] *Ducatus Leodiensis*, ed. T. D. Whitaker (London, 1816), p.87.

[19] Beresford, pp. 308 and 313.

[20] Royal Exchange Registers, 11/95834 (1786) and 26/132267 (1792).

[21] Whitaker, ed., p. 93 f.n.

[22] Data from LDA, LORB 36 (1800).

[23] C. Treen, 'The process of suburban development in north Leeds, 1870 - 1914' in F. M. W. Thompson, ed., *The Rise of Suburbia* (Liverpool, 1982), fig. 25.

[24] *Leeds Intelligencer*, 23 Oct. 1828.

[25] John Ryley (attrib.), *The Leeds Guide* (Leeds, 1806), p.82; LDA, DB204/8.

[26] Leeds Corporation Deeds, Civic Hall, no. 20952.

[27] Brunswick Place, Brunswick Street and Brunswick Terrace appear on sheet 7 of the 60-inch O.S. plan, surveyed in 1847 and published in 1850; the other streets discussed below are on sheet 6.

[28] *Leeds Intelligencer*, 18 May 1818.

[29] Illustrated in M. W. Beresford, *Walks Round Red Brick*, 1980.

[30] Leeds Corporation Deeds no. 8754; LDA, North (General), Box 89.

Acknowledgement

I am indebted to my former colleague, Gordon Dickinson, of the Department of Geography who drew my attention to the confused cartographic indication of gardens, private and market, on the contemporaneous 6-inch and 60-inch O.S. plans, and to widespread garden ground in Sheffield and Hull.

CHAPTER 4

Arson in East Yorkshire

David Foster

The historiography of the Swing Riots has focused attention on 1830/32 as the nineteenth-century highpoint of rural social protest, thereby obscuring the fact that rural incendiarism, which was only one feature of the disturbances of those years, continued to exist for much of the remainder of the century. However, recent work has drawn attention to the peaks of arson which occurred in 1843/44, 1849/52, 1862/64 and 1868/69 in different parts of the country, and which has led to the suggestion that this was 'the major form of rural protest until the late 1860s and 1870s.'[1]

During the first half of the nineteenth century, criminal and judicial statistics treated the county of York as a single entity and it was not until their revision under the terms of the County and Borough Police Act of 1856 that they began to distinguish between the three Ridings, thus facilitating studies within the ancient county. The thirty-five years subsequent to this development provide a convenient period for study since 1893 marks a further revision of the presentation of statistics.[2] During this time, 561 cases of arson are recorded in Yorkshire, an average of sixteen fires per annum. The statistics record all known and/or suspected cases of arson, including urban and rural incidents, and demonstrate the uneven spread of outbreaks across the county, with 152 (27.1%) and 126 (22.5%) in the predominantly rural East and North Ridings respectively, and 283 (50.4%) in the mixed urban and rural West Riding. These figures are in marked contrast to the northern experience in 1830/32 when, according to Hobsbawm and Rude, only thirteen disturbances occurred in the whole of Yorkshire between 1 January 1830 and 3 September 1832; of these, seven were fires, four of which were in the East Riding, seven were 'Swing' letters, and two were burglaries. This paper concentrates on the outbreaks of incendiarism in the East Riding of Yorkshire in the 1860s, with some concentration on the earlier fires of 1863/64 which generated official concern at the national level and which appear to have led to later local imitation.

The incidence of fires in the East Riding in the thirty-five year period is interesting. During the first six years from 1857/58 there were no more than twenty-three fires recorded, with none in 1861/62, whilst the twenty-two years from 1870/71 and 1891/92 had only forty-five fires with no less than four years being arson-free; in contrast the seven years from 1863/64 to 1869/70, witnessed seventy-eight fires, more than four times the annual average for the total period. In order to investigate this abnormal level of activity, this paper raises a number of detailed questions — who were the alleged perpetrators of the attacks and what were their motives?; who were the victims?; what was the reaction of the authorities, both police and courts?; what explanations were offered by contemporaries and what support is given to them by the evidence?;

and what light, if any, do these events throw on the workings of rural society in the later nineteenth century?

****

At the outset, it must be noted that the nature and context of arson render it most difficult to pursue. Premises, particularly in an area affected by parliamentary enclosure such as the East Riding, were often very isolated, offering the arsonist plenty of opportunity to learn the geography of his target and carry out his work almost with impunity. In almost all the cases with which this paper is concerned, the offence was committed at night in remote, unlit country districts and, unless detected and dealt with quickly, was likely to destroy most of the evidence in a period before the advent of forensic science facilitated the prosecution of such investigations. Thus it is no surprise to find that the sources fail to provide a complete picture of the topic and are unable to agree even of the actual number of incidents that occurred. Evidence of arsonist activity in the East Riding comes from three main sources.[3] First, the chief constable of the new county constabulary, established in 1857, made quarterly and annual reports to the Quarter Sessions in which he quantified and commented on the whole range of criminal activity. During the 1860s arson occupied considerable space in these reports and eighty-eight fires are noted, though how many of them were actually arson is not clear. The second potential source is court records, but these have proved to be extremely disappointing in the case of the East Riding. Any defendants were brought before Petty Sessions which was not a court of record and survival of any papers is purely fragmentary; at that court defendants were either discharged through lack of evidence or occasionally because they were children, or sent for trial at the Assize court held in York. Unfortunately, the complete absence of cases other than murder in the surviving files of the Northern Assize Circuit places the historian at the mercy of the third source, the local and regional press. The press were fairly assiduous in reporting actual fires and their aftermath, far less reliable in recording the activities of Petty Sessions at which defendants would first appear, but almost extravagant in their coverage of the Assizes. Perusal of the regional press suggest that there were seventy-five incidents in the period 1863-70 of which sixty-seven were known or presumed to be arson. The discrepancy between the two main sources suggests the incompleteness of press coverage of the incidents, a point confirmed by the official statistics which naturally accept authority's record of events, but a combination of these two sources enable us to form a general picture of the incidence of arson in the East Riding and use of a wider range of regional history material may point towards some explanation.

****

The fires in the East Riding between 1863 and 1870 fall into two groups, the first during the winter of 1863/64 confined to the High Wolds, and the second, possibly imitative but spread across the county throughout the subsequent six years.

The outbreak of fires at two separate farms in the village of Butterwick and another at Boythorpe, all in the north-west of the county, on the night of 18 November 1863 initiated a rash of incidents, chiefly on the High Wolds, which lasted for several months, with a total of thirteen fires occurring by 11 January 1864. The close proximity of most of the attacks fuelled rumours that the whole area of the High Wolds was under threat and the authorities reacted swiftly.

Following the example of Shropshire in 1830-32, the chief constable ordered his men to keep a particular watch on tramps and strangers and urged his superintendents to consider the use of plain-clothes officers in an attempt to trace the fire-raisers. Public reaction, particularly amongst property owners, was inevitably alarmist in the face of threats, anonymous letters and actual arson, and farmers were reported to be agitating for the establishment of bloodhound stations on the Wolds. How much fears were exaggerated by potential informers in search of reward is not clear, but the outbreak of fires was sufficiently serious to be discussed in *The Times*, and the Home Secretary, Sir George Grey, offered £50 for information leading to the discovery and conviction of the arsonists and promised to advise the grant of a pardon to accomplices willing to turn Queen's evidence; in the event both police and public contested the reward after the arrest and conviction of a man for a fire at Huggate on 23 December 1863. Whether this group of fires was orchestrated or not is unclear. Their occurrence in a limited area shortly after the end of the harvest year, their focus on the rich corn lands of the county, and the fact that suspicion fell on Wold Rangers, who travelled the district in search of work, convinced contemporaries that theirs was some kind of organised conspiracy, but no evidence has been unearthed to support such a theory.

In contrast, there is no hint of conspiracy surrounding the second group of fires which were characterised chiefly by their lack of homogeniety and are grouped together merely for the convenience of study. Since the target of the crime was normally a stack of corn, the fires occurred almost exclusively between early September and mid February, but they took place in widely scattered parts of the county. Similarly, those arrested and/or convicted for specific offences have in common nothing more than their diversity, ranging from ten-year-old boys, through farm servants and day labourers of both sexes, to tramps and unemployed persons. In so far as it is possible to speculate on motives, again it is the variety which is most noticeable, and one is driven to speculate that perhaps the Wolds outbreak of 1863/64 revived interest in arson as a means of protest which others were perhaps imitating as they sought to settle specific grievances.

****

The outbreak of arson on this scale presented a formidable challenge to the East Riding County Constabulary, newly established in 1857 under the terms of the County and Borough Police Act, initially under-funded, and therefore under-strength, largely because of the suspicion of the magistracy, and unpopular in the countryside.[4] The clandestine nature of the crime ensured that the perpetrator was difficult to trace, though some of the East Riding arsonists were careless in the extreme and contributed to their apprehension, and this may account for the high proportion of arrests which compare favourably with the number of convictions. The constabulary arrested sixty people for a total of fifty-three fires, but only sixteen were finally convicted for a total of fifteen outbreaks. Of the remainder, twenty were discharged at Petty Sessions through lack of evidence; no bill was found against three and a further thirteen were acquitted at York Assizes; and there is no record of further proceedings against eight people who were arrested and who must be presumed either to have been discharged at Petty Sessions or not even formally charged.

Information on the arsonists is difficult to discover, and it has been possible to trace from the regional press and court papers details of only thirty of those charged covering thirty-five fires; nonetheless, this represents some 44% of the fires in the period under discussion, a large enough sample to be considered representative.

Table 1.
Occupations of those arrested for arson

Labourers	17	Travelling Sweep	1
Servants	5	Destitute	1
Tramps	2	Groom	1
Wold Ranger	2	Unemployed	1

The most striking feature of the defendants is their lowly position in the social structure; whatever classification system may be used, all of these people would fall into the lowest category. Most if not all would have experienced little or no education, be accustomed to an insecure existence governed by the rhythms of agricultural life, and be fully conversant with poverty. Migrant labour played an important role in the local economy, reflected both in the annual Statute Hirings of farm servants, still a major local event in the early 1860s, and in the more casual day labourer and travelling workman personified particularly by the Wold Ranger. Nineteenth century commentators were convinced of the existence of the migratory criminal, particularly those who travelled the fairs of the land to carry out their nefarious activity, and it is interesting to note that the authorities immediately assumed that the fires on the High Wolds were likely to be the work of travelling workmen.[5]

Perhaps more difficult to establish is the status and position of the victims. Using the census enumerators' books for 1861 and 1871 it has been possible to trace thirty-two (44%) of the farmers whose property was fired.[6]

Table 2.
Arson Victims by Farm Size

2,000+ acres	1	100+ acres	17
1,000-1,999	1	Under 100	5
500-999	8		

As might be expected, the size of farms which were attacked vary widely, though the majority are amongst the larger farms in the county. It is particularly notable that the early rash of attacks, concentrated on the High Wolds where agricultural change had made the most impact, focused on larger farms; of those thirteen attacks seven Wold farmers have been traced and with one exception, they held farms in excess of 500 acres. Whilst one would not wish to push such a correlation too far, these were amongst the prosperous capitalist farms of the county where the demand for casual labour, particularly of the unskilled variety offered by Wold Rangers, was likely to be decreasing.

****

Incendiarism, had long been a traditional form of social protest in the countryside along with other attacks on property such as poaching, cattle-maiming, the theft of farm animals, machine-breaking, and the sending of anonymous and threatening letters, all of which expressed the frustrations of the rural proletariat.[7] Historians have commonly sought to explain such activity as desperate forms of opposition to low wages, high prices, and, in the 1830s and 1840s, to unpopular aspects of the reformed Poor Law; behind all of this was the generally low standard of living and all-pervading insecurity of agricultural workers which ensured that 'ill-feeling was a common commodity in rural society.' Jones's work on East Anglian incendiarism in the 1840s echoes the contemporary view of William Cobbett in *Rural Rides* and reinforces the economic explanation of such unrest as portrayed graphically by the Hammonds' work on village labourers and by Hobsbawm and Rude in their masterly study of the Labourers' Revolt of 1830.

At first sight, economic determinism fits uneasily as an explanation of the incendiarism under discussion because it occurred in the middle of the period of high farming when the lot of the agricultural labourer was improving, partly as a result of general prosperity and partly because the countryside was beginning to experience a serious labour shortage.[8] However, such confident generalisations obscure the difficulty in arriving at an accurate estimate of farm workers' incomes in any particular region of the country. In addition to the fundamental distinction between farm labourers and farm servants, the former paid by the day and living at home, the latter hired for a year and living in, highly complex piece-work payments, well-developed hierarchies of employment, and women and children's contribution complicate the task of computing workers' incomes. However, whatever the incompleteness of the statistics and notwithstanding the contemporary view that Northern agricultural wages benefited from the close proximity of alternative industrial employment, the historian of high farming has claimed that the East Riding was not a high wage county and suggested that 'the essential point is that farm labourers' living standards were appallingly low.'[9] The evidence from the attacks themselves is inconclusive. In support of the economic argument, there is some suggestion that, even in a period of general prosperity, there was sufficient economic distress locally or individually to drive people into rash action. Commenting on the High Wolds outbreak, the chief constable implied that the economic motive was the obvious explanation, but conceded that there was no local evidence of either wage reductions or class hostility. In contrast,

The Times noted that it was the comparatively wealthy farmers, the traditionally large employers, who had been fired on the High Wolds, and this selectivity was given further credence by James Sherwood who was reported to have said at his trial at York Assizes that 'he would not help put out the fire if old Burdass (the farmer) was in it.... I wish the b.... was in it.... I wish the whole bloody town was burning and the b.... burnt out of his hole.'[10]

The apparent contraction between potential poverty in a time of prosperity is not new, but light may be shed on this situation through an examination of the case of Sherwood, a notorious Wold Ranger. Though somewhat romanticised by a recent work,[11] Wold Rangers were a normal part of the East Riding scene, particulary at harvest time, but their wandering nature made them most likely to suffer from casual employment, particularly in the years following the introduction of the steam-driven harvester to the Wolds, and therefore likely to have some grievance against particular farmers. The High Wolds outbreak began with two fires at Butterwick and one at Boythorpe on 18 November 1863, and followed by another at Thwing on 21 November, and the authorities were prepared to regard them as part of the same conspiracy, if not the work of one individual. Sherwood was arrested for the Boythorpe fire, eventually tried for all the fires on the 18th, discharged through lack of evidence, and then arrested for the Thwing outbreak of which he was eventually found guilty and sentenced to fifteen years penal servitude; no one else was ever charged with the fires art Butterwick and Boythorpe. Evidence presented at his trial suggested that it was his failure to obtain employment which had prompted his attack, and the fact that the authorities also arrested and later discharged seven tramps, beggars and travellers who had been unsuccessfully looking for work suggests that this type of individual was an obvious target for suspicion. In short, no amount of statistics will reveal individual discontent felt against a farmer either for the payment of low wages or because of the refusal to offer casual employment, but the fact the Wold Rangers provided ready suspects and, in some cases, were convicted, suggests that individual grievance rather than specific income levels may well have been the source of resentment which led to incendiarism.

Vagrancy was a common problem in the lanes of rural England in the later nineteenth century and produced a ready fund of suspects for any unexplained criminal actvity; given that arson was considered second only to murder in dastardliness, it was perhaps inevitable that, in tight rural communities, strangers would be amongst the first suspects.[12] On numerous occasions, such individuals were arrested for fires in the county, often without real cause and primarily because they were either stangers or wanderers. Such unfortunates were W. & J. Marshall arrested for a fire at Rookdale (12.12.63); J. Mitchell for one at Wilberfoss (7.12.65); and an unnamed 'tramp' at Bridlington (24.12.67). The intimate connection made by the authorities between vagrancy and crime is illustrated by the case of that of George Stother, alias 'Lurcher' Slenderman. When arrested for the Thwing fire, James Sherwood sought to blame Stother and two companions who he alleged were guilty of all the fires on the High Wolds at that time; in fact Sherwood was found guilty of the Thwing blaze and one Henry Street, a travelling sweep, of another in neighbouring Huggate, whilst those at Butterwick and Boythorpe were left on the file. Stother and his companions were freed, but he was re-arrested twelve months later as a rogue and a vagabond charged with a breach of the peace, 'having threatened to set all the Wolds alight again'; hotly denying any collaboration with those found guilty of the previous year's fires, he was given two months and bound over to keep the peace. *The Beverley Guardian*, obviously convinced of his perniciousness, announced with some satisfaction that 'Lurcher' Slenderman is secured from ranging the Wolds this winter.' Similarly, the Marshall brothers were discharged because there was no evidence to connect them to the fire at Rookdale, but they were given twenty-one days for vagrancy. However, perhaps the greatest testimony to the power of the concept is seen in the rather pathetic and fatalistic case of William Branton, found guilty of arson at Withernwick in Holderness, who was reputed to have told a villager before his arrest that he assumed that he would have to be questioned on suspicion because he was the only stranger in the village and that this would not be the first time that he had been taken in on suspicion. (2.11.64).

The other major group of arsonists and attempted arsonists seem to have been prompted by personal motives other than economic, and were often committed by servants against their employers. The chief constable summarised the characteristics of this group for his Quarter Sessions audience — 'the majority of these evildoers, of course, are those who have been discharged from their employments, or punished for offences, or refused favours, or warned to be on their good behaviour, or deluded into an idea of wrong or an insult to their families.'[13] In many cases, personal animosity was the only evidence offered against those charged, but without substantial corroboration, the authorities found it difficult to obtain either a committal to the Assizes or a verdict of guilty. Thus, Elizabeth Curtis, a seventeen-year old farm servant, and John Clubley, a ten-year old boy, were both found not guilty at York Assizes of arson against their employers for fires at Bishop Burton and Walkington respectively, both close to Beverley, as was Henry Clapham for a fire at his brother's farm at Burton Pidsea in Holderness. Similarly, it proved impossible to convict James Moran of a fire at his employer's farm in Otteringham, Holderness simply because the farmer had earlier criticised Moran's ploughing, and James Wilmott of firing Mr. Jordan's farm at Eastburn, near Driffield, merely because he had been refused when begging earlier the same day. Nonetheless, some employees were convicted of arson against their employers; thus Ellen Hare received fifteen months penal servitude for arson at her employer's farm at Youlthorpe in the Vale of York and William Branton for the same offence at Withernwick, Holderness.

****

Although of some interest by themselves, the events discussed above are of value chiefly for the light they shed on wider social life in nineteenth-century rural England. Furthermore, as an element of local/regional history they offer an opportunity to test the generalisations of national scholars, thus indicating the continuity of that rich strain of provincialism which has long characterised

English society. In conclusion, this paper reflects on the relationship between the fires and the wider issues of social relations and social protest in the countryside.

One of the most striking elements of this story is the implied familiarity and localism of the northern countryside in which strangers and travellers were the natural, almost inevitable suspects of any criminal activity, and in which the authorities were prepared to make arrests purely on the grounds of suspects' transitory nature, an emphasis which was often corrected by the courts. The migratory criminal was a figure of nineteenth-century demonology; enthroned by the 1839 Chadwick Report,[14] this creature was allegedly one of the most dangerous criminal types in the land, and was blamed by authorities in almost all parts of England and Wales for their serious crime. Closely associated with and often indistinguishable from this figure in nineteenth-century demonology was the vagrant; described recently as 'the most glaring afront to the trinity of work, respectability and religion',[15] the vagrant personified all that was evil in the eyes of authority. Without respect for property or family values, the vagrant presented a serious challenge to social norms, and the principal thrust of social policy since the reform of the Poor Law in 1834 was to distinguish between the deserving and the undeserving poor into which latter category the traveller fell. Allied to this was the introduction of professional police forces in the central decades of the nineteenth century which was held by critics, with some justification, to be nothing more than a deliberate attempt to enforce the rigours of the Poor Law more effectively on the rural population; the tendency of the East Riding constabulary to arrest people merely on suspicion, and of travellers to almost expect arrest, testifies to the strength of these ideas within Victorian society. The fact that some fires, particularly those prompted by personal rather than economic motives, were started by local people, sometimes resident on the farms which they fired, seems to have escaped the authorities in their determination to fulfil their own prophecies.

The outbreak of arson also prompts speculation concerning the nature of social relations in the countryside. Clearly, those who had specific grievances, whether economic or personal, were disaffected individuals, but to what extent was this period of arson symptomatic of a wider social malaise in the countryside which, in times of greater economic difficulty, might lie closer to the surface? Evidence is at best indirect, but the chief constable's confident assertion at the height of the 1863/64 outbreaks that there was no indication of class hostility was directly challenged by the Assize judge at Sherwood's trial who noted the 'very strong evidence of that feeling of malice against farmers on the Wolds generally'.[16] Support for this view is to be found in local attitudes to two fires at Kilham on the Wolds on 13 December 1863 where agricultural labourers showed apathy and indifference when urged to assist in extinguishing the fires and were suspected of having allowed the perpetrator to escape. The regularity with which the press comments on this latter factor suggests, at least, some measure of sympathy in the villages for the fire-raisers, despite the close-knit character of rural life.

The East Riding was a county of large estates and large farms.[17] The concentration of land ownership, with twelve families with estates over 10,000 acres each controlling 30% of the county and a further 50.1% of the land held in estates over 3,000 acres, facilitated the development of high farming, both through experimentation on home farms and by the encouragement of tenants.

Consequently, by the third quarter of the nineteenth century, East Riding farms were generally above the national average with 39.4% over 100 acres and 12.4% over 300 acres compared to national figures of 29.7% and 7.6% respectively; within the county there were marked variations, with the 48.9% of the farms over 300 acres on the High Wolds, the area which suffered most from incendiarism. Thus, the county in general and the Wolds in particular, was dominated by a rural middle class, willing to invest in modernisation by the practice of family inheritance of tenancies despite the lack of long leases, and fully apprised of the virtues of capitalist economics which conflicted with the traditional paternalistic relations of the countryside. In the new society, the life of the village labourer, and moreso the travelling worker, was characterised by casual employment regulated by the rhythm of the seasons and fraught with insecurity even during the allegedly properous times of high farming, thus providing opportunities for resentment which could have found expression in indirect approval of arsonist activity, particularly where the victim was a well-known unscrupulous farmer such as Mr. Burdass of Thwing. It is also instructive that this example of incipient solidarity amongst rural workers was occurring at a time when circumstances were conspiring to heighten the profile of the travelling workman in such a way that might have been productive of hostile relations amongst the workers. Mid-century saw the beginning of a long decline in the rural population of the whole country, principally as a result of the agricultural depression from the mid-'seventies, and those areas of the East Riding which experienced arson in the 1850s were particularly badly hit.[18] However, some pressure on employment in the East Riding came from the rapid pace of mechanisation after the middle of the century. The introduction of the steam threshing machine to the county at the Bridlington Agricultural Show in 1851 led to its widespread use in the county by the 1860s, the replacement of broadcast sowing by seed-drills, and the increasing popularity of hay-making machines all contributed to a reduced demand for labour, particularly at harvest time when the casual workers of the Wolds were accustomed to finding work.[19] In such circumstances as these, the travelling stranger in search of work might have been the object of general suspicion in the countryside, but there appears to have been mutual sympathy between villagers and travellers in the face of a hard and precarious existence.

The final point worthy of note is that one of the traditional forms of exacting private vengeance by attacking property continued to exist well into the nineteenth century, despite attempts to find other and allegedly more appropriate means of dealing with workers' grievances. Dr. Charlesworth has argued that, by the 1860s agricultural labourers had learned the rules of capitalist social relations and were learning to fight effectively for their share of prosperity 'with weapons better suited for the struggle.'[20] However, a detailed search of local records, including the press, have revealed very little and unsuccessful trade union activity in the county, and that not before the early 1870's, thus leading to a prolonged life for the more ancient methods of protest.

More important still is the likelihood that even if trade unionism had made some headway in East Yorkshire, it was unlikely to have enlisted the travelling workers and youthful farm servants who seem to have committed the majority of the offences with which we are concerned. The evidence presented here suggests that workers organisations had made no impact in the East Riding by the early 1870s and that protest against the new forms of capitalist social relations, particularly amongst the more transient and younger members of the workforce, continued to take its traditional form. However, the rapid decline in the number of cases of arson from the 1870s point to the demise of the ancient forms of protest and revenge and their replacement by more temperate methods.

Notes:

[1] Jones D., 'Thomas Campbell Foster and the rural labourer; incendiarism in East Anglia in the mid nineteenth-century' in *Social History*, vol.1, no.1, January 1976. For the continuing role of incendiarism as social protest, see the debate between Wells and Charlesworth and the comment by Archer in *Journal of Peasant Studies*, vol.6, no.2 January 1979; vol.8, no.1, October 1980; vol.8, no.4, July 1981; and vol.9, no.4, July 1982.

[2] Gattrell V. A. C. & Hadden T. B., 'Criminal statistics and their interpretation' in Wrigley E. A. (ed.), *Nineteenth century society: essays on the use of quantitative methods for the study of social data* (London 1872). All figures for arson in this paper are computed from the annual judicial statistics published in *British Parliamentary Papers*.

[3] The major sources for this paper are (i) the quarterly reports of the chief constable presented to the East Riding Quarter Sessions, filed in the Humberside County Record Office, QAP 2/1; (ii) detailed reports of incidents and subsequent court proceedings in the local press — the *Beverley Guardian* held in the Humberside County Library, Beverley; the *Malton Messenger* held in the Humberside County Library, Malton; and the *York Herald* held in the North Yorkshire County Library, York; the 1863 outbreak was also commented on in *The Times*. All detailed references in this paper are from these sources unless otherwise indicated.

[4] For the origins and early history of the East Riding Constabulary see Foster D., 'The East Riding Constabulary in the nineteenth century' in *Northern History*, xxi, 1985.

[5] For migratory crime in general use see *The royal commission for inquiring as to the best means of establishing an efficient constabulary force in the counties of England and Wales,* British Parliamentary Papers. (xc), pp.19f.; in this context *Malton Messenger*, 19 December, 11863.

[6] Census enumerators' books, 1861 and 1871.

[7] For discussions of rural protest see Dunbabin J. P. D., *Rural discontent in nineteenth century Britain* (London 1974) ch.I-V, and Jones D., 'Rural crime and protest' in Mingay G. E. (ed.), *The Victorian Countryside* (London 1981).

[8] Collins J. T., 'Migrant labour in British agriculture' in *Economic History Review*, 2nd series, xxix, 1.

[9] Sheppard J. A. 'The East Yorkshire agricultural labour force in the mid nineteenth century' in *Agricultural History Review*, ix, part 1, 1961; Adams M. G., Agricultural Change in the East Riding 1850-1880; an economic and social history. Hull University Ph.D. thesis, 1977, p.396.

[10] *The Times*, 14 December 1863;l the statement was attributed to Sherwood in the report of the trial at York Assizes in the *Beverley Guardian*, 2 April 1786.

[11] Antrim A., *The Yorkshire Wold Rangers* (Beverley 1983).

[12] Jones D., 'The vagrant and crime in Victorian Britain; problems of definition and attitude', in Jones D., *Crime, protest, community and police in nineteenth-century Britain* (London 1982).

[13] Chief constable's report to Epiphany Quarter Sessions 1864; Humberside County Record Office, GAP 2/1.

[14] See note 5 above.

[15] See note 12 above.

[16] See note 13 above; comments of the judge at Sherwood's trial at York Assizes reported in *York Herald*, 2 April, 1864..

[17] Ward J. T., *East Yorkshire landed estates in the nineteenth century* (Hull 1967).

[18] Foster D., 'Population' in Dyson B. (ed.), *A guide to local studies in East Yorkshire* (Beverley 1985), pp.132-36.

[19] For agricultural change in East Yorkshire in this period see Adams thesis (note 9 above) and W. Wright, 'On the improvements in the farming of Yorkshire since the date of the last reports in this journal' in *Journal of the Royal Agricultural Society of England*, xxii, 1861.

[20] Charlesworth A., Development of English rural proletariat and social protest 1700-1850: a comment in *Journal of Peasant Studies*, vo.8, no.1, October 1980, p.106.

CHAPTER 5

Medical Practice in the West Riding of Yorkshire from Nineteenth-Century Census Data[1]

Hilary Marland and Philip Swan

A decade ago, the medical historian P. S. Brown[2] took a decisive and new step forward for historians of the medical profession, into the area of quantitative information and statistics. Through his detailed analysis of census data for one community, Bristol, in one particular census year, 1851, Brown drew together information on the number of medical men in practice in the town, the number holding hospital and dispensary appointments, their qualifications, and details of whether or not they had been born locally. Perhaps more importantly, Brown gave us some insight into an area where *still* very little is known — into the social and economic status of medical practitioners as shown in the census, by their household structures, places of residence, and their employment of apprentices, assistants and servants.

The use of census data as a source on medical practice and practitioners

From 1801 onwards, an official census of the population has been taken every ten years (apart from 1941); the census being the first body of records compiled primarily to obtain demographic or sociological information for England and Wales.[3] It is not until 1841,[4] however, with the addition of new questions on occupations and households, that the data become more interesting for historians of the medical profession. By the mid-nineteenth century, the census enumerators' books recorded details of household size and structure, and the names, ages, sex, parish of birth, and occupations of each resident, including servants. There were three distinct stages in each census. Firstly, householders' schedules were distributed, filled in by the householder, and collected. Secondly, the enumerators' books were compiled by officials appointed by local registrars of births and deaths. Thirdly, printed abstracts or reports were prepared and published in the form of parliamentary papers. Data from the last two stages have survived, in the form of the published reports and enumerators' books. Access to the enumerators' books is closed for one hundred years, so the last set available for consultation date from 1891.

Census data can be utilised in two main ways as a source on occupational groups, including medical practitioners. Firstly, published census data, taken alone or in combination with the enumerators' books, can give us information on large regions, be they counties, urban conglomerations or rural districts, or indeed, on the whole of England and Wales. A study of this type could be said to provide a global or macrocosmic survey of medical practice and practitioners. Using printed census data for the years 1841 to 1881 and the enumerators' books for 1851 and 1871, such a survey has been undertaken for the West Riding of Yorkshire.[5] This provides an overview of medical practice and practitioners within a large region over a long time span, and can be demonstrated as being of special value in distinguishing the numerical relationship between the various groups of medical personnel appearing in the census returns; physicians and surgeons, general practitioners of medicine, chemists and druggists, and 'fringe' or unqualified elements. Such data also reveal changes in the numbers in practice within each grouping, migrational patterns, and variations between the different types of town and cities represented within the West Riding.

Secondly, the census enumerators' books can be used, most beneficially in conjunction with other quantitative and qualitative information, at the micro level, to survey medical practice in individual towns. This has been carried out for several communities within the West Riding, in particular Wakefield, Huddersfield and Bradford (respectively, a market and service centre, a textile town and a large industrial city). When working at this level, and with small groups of medical practitioners, the inconsistencies in the census data become more noticeable and of increasing significance, but gaps can be filled and checks and safeguards provided by medical and trade directories, poll books, legal records, newspapers, the records of local medical charities and medical societies, and so on. Working at the level of a known community, it becomes possible to use a variety of sources of data to build up a detailed profile of medical practice and individual practitioners, using the census data as just one tool out of many, while at the macro level, working with many hundreds of individual practitioners, this is of rather doubtful practicability.

In the last few decades, the census enumerators' books in particular have attracted '...legions of historians and social scientists seeking a long-term historical perspective for their studies';[6] especially in connection with research on population, urban development and family structure.[7] Yet medical historians have largely neglected the census. Charles Rosenberg, for instance, in drawing attention to the wide range of sources available on the medical profession and medical practice, lists almost every imaginable source from hospital records to diaries, fee bills and legal records, but ignores demographic material.[8]

To date then, there has been little follow up to Brown's pioneering work on the Bristol medical profession, especially on a broader level, looking at regions rather than individual towns, and for a longer time span, instead of one particular census year. However, this neglect of the census becomes more understandable when the many serious problems associated with the collection and interpretation of census data are recognised. These problems are of particular relevance when information is being extracted for only one small occupational group, such as medical practitioners.

Perhaps the most serious problem is one of logistics; simply that, especially when working on a large region, of dealing with the massive amounts of data thrown up by the census. In spite of major improvements in facilities for data processing in recent years,[9] the large populations involved give rise to serious and time-consuming problems of data collection and collation. Almost one and

74

a half million individuals were recorded in the census enumerators' books for the West Riding in 1851; almost two million by 1871.[10]

Problems of numbers are compounded by the fact, that nineteenth-century census data are far from being wholly reliable. This is particularly so with respect to fringe or unqualified medical practitioners,[11] but also applies to qualified groups. Information given in the census enumerators' books is for the most part accurate, but not always complete or thorough.[12] To give just one example, information on the training and qualifications of medical practitioners is inconsistent and often incomplete, dependent upon the conscientiousness of both informant and enumerator. Most doctors, over 83%, indicated their place of graduation or training in the census enumerators' books for the West Riding in 1851.[13] But few stated their different places of training if there were more than one, or gave a complete list of their qualifications.[14]

Another barrier to the retrieval of accurate figures from the census, is that there are many discrepancies, often serious, between the data given in the printed reports and census enumerators' books. Both sources will be utilised here. A further difficulty is that very varied recording criteria were applied for different census years; occupational categories altered a great deal over the decades, and boundary changes were also implemented. The 1841 census report on occupations presents particular problems, one of the most serious being that students, apprentices and medical assistants were categorised together with physicians and surgeons, while in subsequent census years they were listed separately.[15]

A more serious problem if indeed it can be called a problem — perhaps it is better to describe it as something intrinsic in the use of census data — is concerned with the kind of information which the census provides. Census data it would seem can do little more than give quantitative credence to what is already 'anticipated' or 'guessed'. It can be postulated, for example, although we might be very vague about figures, that by the mid-nineteenth century most doctors would be situated in towns, that most would hold the dual qualififcation of MRCS/LSA, have been born in the locality where they set up in practice, would marry sooner or later, be heads of households, and would employ one or two servants. Census data tend to confirm what we would expect to be the case. The advantage is that such material can back our postulations up with numerical evidence where other forms of numerical evidence are lacking. Moreover, unlike much historical data, the census has the considerable advantage of being universal, covering the whole of England and Wales, throughout the second half of the nineteenth century, and of containing information '...in a standardised format capable of being treated in a uniform manner'.[16] It is also a source which lends itself particularly well to the meeting up of social and medical history; while it gives data on individual medical practitioners, the census is primarily concerned with groups.[17]

This essay will concentrate upon describing patterns of medical practice within the West Riding of Yorkshire, delineating the number of medical practitioners, physicians, surgeons and general practitioners, within the region and different communities during the mid-nineteenth century. Unqualified practitioners and chemists and druggists, though enumerated in the census returns, will be excluded from this analysis. Such a survey revealed very different patterns in the numbers of medical practitioners, with regard both to the region as a whole compared with the rest of England, and for different communities within the West Riding. The question as to why this occurred, why in fact medical practitioners chose to establish themselves in practice in particular communities or regions will also be addressed. To conclude, some idea will be given of how census data can be utilised to give an indication of the success of medical practitioners once established in practice, that is, whether their motives for setting up in particular towns were validated in economic terms. Here we will refer to just one of the economic indicators given in the census data, the employment of domestic servants.

The West Riding has been frequently utilised as a sample region on the basis of it being a county which offers a wide range of economic and social circumstances to the historian of the nineteenth century, including within its boundaries large manufacturing towns and cities, either created or much expanded by the industrial revolution, such as Leeds and Bradford, growing textile communities, of which Halifax and Huddersfield form prime examples, the steel town of Sheffield, market and service towns, exemplified by Wakefield, Ripon and Pontefract, and a vast rural hinterland. By the mid-nineteenth century the population of the Riding was distributed fairly evenly between urban and rural areas. In 1851, when the population of the West Riding was approaching one and a half million, it was distributed between town and country in a ratio of 46:54. Twenty years later, in 1871, the balance had shifted, the majority of the population of almost two million, 54%, then being resident in urban communities.

The numbers of medical practitioners in the West Riding and their ratio to the population

In terms of the crude number of medical men in practice, there was a surprising development in the West Riding between 1841 and 1881, especially in view of the massive population increase experienced within the region during this period. A large fall-off occurred in the number of medical practitioners between 1841 and 1861. After 1861, the number began to rise again, but only, by 1881, back to the 1841 level. In 1841, 861 medical practitioners were recorded in the printed census returns as being in practice in the region; by 1861 this figure had decreased to 739, and by 1881 had risen again to 864.[18] (See Table 1 and Figure 1.)[19]

Table 1.

**Percentage Changes in the Number of Medical Practitioners
and Population of the West Riding 1841-1881**

| | Numbers | | Percentage change | |
	Medical Practs.	Population	Medical Practs.	Population
1841	861	1,154,101	-12.4	16.1
1851	754	1,340,051	- 2.0	14.2
1861	739	1,530,007	-10.3	21.2
1871	815	1,854,172	6.0	18.5
1881	864	2,197,999	0.3	90.5
Percentage Change 1841-81				

Source: Printed census reports, 1841-81.

Figure 1.

**Number of Medical Practitioners at each Census
West Riding 1841-1891**

Number

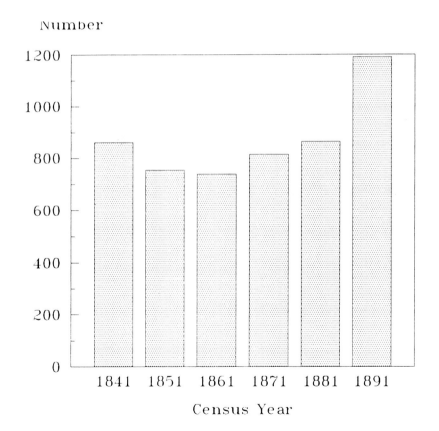

Census Year

Source: Printed census reports, 1841-91.

An examination of a selection of other English counties, both urban and rural, shows that the number of medical practitioners either remained stable or declined between the mid-nineteenth century and 1881. A decline after 1858 (1861 census) might have been anticipated, following the passing of the 1858 Medical Act which tightened up recruitment and registration. Between 1861 and 1881 the number of qualified practitioners in England and Wales increased by just 676 from 14,415 to 15,091 in 1881. This represented an increase of less than 5% compared with a 29% rise in population over the same period.[20] The 'rural' counties had a relatively low number of medical practitioners and experienced a gradual decline up to 1881, followed by a very small increase. The developments in the urbanising counties were more dramatic. Industrial Lancashire, saw an increase in medical practitioners, from 1,171 in 1851, which after an initial fall-off, rose to 1,542 in 1881, a percentage increase of 32% or one-third. In the West Riding the trend was similar, if less pronounced. In rural Norfolk the number of medical practitioners fell by 28% (from 265 in 1851 to 192 in 1881), and in Lincolnshire by 20% (from 304 to 242). (See Figure 1.) For the country as a whole, the census data also indicated a decline in the number of medical practitioners in the order of 8% between 1851 and 1881, from 15,500 to 14,500.[21]

Figure 2.
Medical Provision 1841-1891
Selected Counties

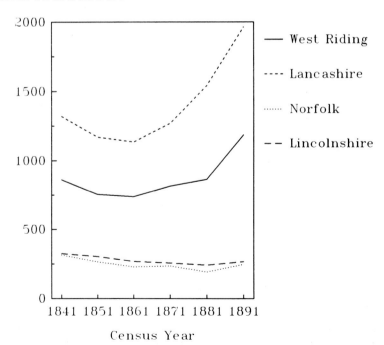

Source: Printed census reports, 1841-81.

78

Taken alone these figures signify little. In order to convey more meaning to such crude statistics, as a first step the figures for the West Riding can be related to population changes in the county. The number of medical men fell from 1841 and only re-attained the 1841 level in the 1880s. There was a decline not only in the total number of medical practitioners, but also a more dramatic decline in the ratio of medical practitioners to the population, the medical profession failing signally to keep up with the enormous population growth of the region. In 1841, according to the published census report, there was one medical practitioner to every 1,340 inhabitants of the West Riding; by 1851 the ratio had already declined to one to every 1,777, and it continued to decrease in steady stages until, by 1881, the ratio was one to every 2,544 inhabitants. (See Table 1 and Figure 2.)

Figure 3.
Ratio of Medical Practitioners to Population
West Riding, 1841-1891

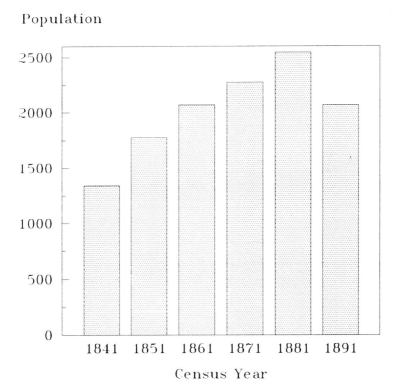

Source: Printed census reports, 1841-81.

Throughout the second half of the nineteenth century, the West Riding was badly endowed with medical practitioners compared with other regions of the country, especially southern and rural counties and London. In Yorkshire as a whole in 1861 there was one medical practitioner to every 1,400 persons; in the

79

West Riding one to every 2,070. In the South East this figure was one to every 900, and in London one to every 805 inhabitants.[22] Table 2 shows the rank order of the ratio of medical practitioners to the population of English counties for the census years 1851 to 1881. It can be seen that the West Riding was always at the lower end of the rank ordering, positioned around 40 out of the 42 counties. In general, southern and rural counties were those best served by medical practitioners; northern industrialised counties, the worst.

Table 2.

Rank Order of Ratio of Medical Practitioners to the Population in English Counties 1851-81

County	1841	1851	1861	1871	1881
London	-	1	2	2	1
Surrey EM.[a]	3	3	3	1	4
Kent EM.	4	8	9	9	6
Sussex	5	5	4	4	3
Hampshire	13	15	12	11	7
Berkshire	14	12	11	13	16
Middlesex EM.	1	2	1	3	2
Herts.	17	23	15	18	14.5
Bucks.	42	35	30	37	27
Oxfordshire	15	17	18	25	20
Northampton	26	25	33	32	34
Hunts.	33	40	40	33	32
Beds.	20	33	35	36	28
Cambridge	31	34	27	30	25
Essex	22	18	20	21	36
Suffolk	21	26	26	24	26
Norfolk	34	36	36	31	38
Wiltshire	38	28	28	20	24
Dorset	30	22	24	27	19
Devon	7	6	7	5	5
Cornwall	39	37	37	35	30
Somerset	9	7	6	7	10
Glocs.	6	4	5	6	8
Hereford	27	19	14	22	12
Shropshire	19	11	17	17	17
Staffs.	41	42	42	42	42
Worcs.	28	20	21	16	11
Warwick	16	16	23	23	33
Leicester	24	30	31	39	39
Rutland	40	31	16	14	13
Lincs.	23	21	19	19	23
Notts.	37	38	38	26	35
Derbyshire	35	32	32	29	22
Cheshire	32	29	25	28	29

Table 2. (Cont.)
Rank Order of Ratio of Medical Practitioners to the Population in
English Counties 1851-81

County	1841	1851	1861	1871	1881
Lancs.	29	39	41	40	37
West Riding	36	41	39	41	41
East "	11	9	13	10	21
North "	19	10	10	8	14.5
Durham	10	24	29	38	40
Northumberland	8	13.5	22	15	18
Cumberland	25	27	34	34	31
Westmorland	13	13.5	8	12	9
York City	2[b]	-	-	-	-
Southampton	12	-	-	-	-
Salop	18	-	-	-	-

[a]   Extra-Metropolitan

[b]   This breakdown is only available for the 1841 census. In all subsequent census they were incorporated into the relevant counties.

Source: Printed census reports, 1851-81.

Individual towns also reflected the national pattern. In the 1841 census report, for example, it was recorded that, while Oxford, Exeter and Winchester had ratios of medical practitioners to the population of 1:662, 1:530 and 1:447 respectively,[23] the figures for Leeds, Birmingham and Manchester were 1:1246, 1:1219 and 1:1075. The average figure for England was calculated as 1:1185.[24] The 1861 report on the census gave similar information, but in a rather different way, calculating the ratio between 'constantly sick' persons (according to the average annual rate of mortality) and medical practitioners for different regions of England. London had the lowest ratio, of one medical practitioner to every 24 constantly sick persons, in the South East there was one to every 37, and in Yorkshire one to every 64 constantly sick persons.[25]

When we turn more closely to the pattern of medical practice within the West Riding itself, what we find in effect is a duplication of the national pattern, with the larger, most industrialised towns and cities of the region having the least favourable ratio of medical practitioners to the population compared with smaller market towns and rural-based communities. The 1851 census enumerators' books for the West Riding recorded a total of 538 practising doctors, and 132 unqualified assistants, apprentices and pupils. The ratio of medical practitioners to the population of the region as a whole was 1:2539 (excluding apprentices, students and assistants).[26] The least favourable ratios of medical practitioners to the population were recorded in the largest communities. Bradford had the lowest ratio of one to over 3,000 inhabitants, followed by Leeds and Sheffield with one to 2,500 and 2,000 respectively. The medium-sized textile towns of Halifax and Huddersfield fell half way, with ratios of just under one to every 1,500 inhabitants. Meanwhile, the smaller, predominantly market/service towns of the West Riding had the best ratios. In Wakefield there was one practitioner to every 653 inhabitants, in Doncaster one to every 670.[27] (See Table 3.)

Table 3.

Ratio of Medical Practitioners to Population,
West Riding and Selected Towns, 1841 and 1851

	Total number of resident medical practitioners in 1841 (physicians)		Population in 1841	Ratio of medical practitioners to the population 1841	1851
West Riding	778	(56)	1,154,101	1:1483	1:2539
Sheffield Parish	87	(14)	111,091	1:1277	1:2082
Bradford Township	30	(1)	37,765	1:1259	1:3053
Leeds Borough	130	(14)	152,054	1:1170	1:2426
Huddersfield Borough	22	(3)	25,068	1:1139	1:1470
Halifax Parish[a]	67	(3)	130,743	1:1951	1:1399
Doncaster Borough	13	(1)	10,455	1:804	1:670
Wakefield Township	22	(3)	14,754	1:671	1:653

[a]   The figures for Halifax in 1841 cover the whole parish, including many outlying villages and a large rural area.

Sources: 1841 and 1851 census reports. Occupation abstracts; E. M. Sigsworth and P. Swan, 'Para-medical provision in the West Riding', *Bull. Soc. soc. Hist. Med.*, 29 (1981), 37-39.

Motives behind the selection of practice locations

Why then did medical practitioners opt to set up in practice in certain towns in large numbers, while apparently neglecting other communities? The favouring of one region or community over another has also to be seen in the context of the continuing complaints of medical men during the nineteenth century concerning the overcrowding of the profession.[28] How can we explain this when the number of medical practitioners was not keeping up with population growth in such counties as the West Riding? And why did medical practitioners appear to exacerbate what they saw as an already difficult situation by continuing to set up in practice in towns apparently well serviced by medical men?

By 1825 Dr. Simpson of Bradford was already complaining of this development in the West Riding.

The medical profession is quite overstocked... and since the Peace situations have become very difficult to meet with.... . There are in Bradford three Physicians and ten Surgeons, besides most of the villages in the vicinity have one Surgeon & some of them two. I don't

*believe that there is full employment for more than one Physician
and six Surgeons...: . We are surrounded by towns filled with
Physicians & these at no great distance. Halifax is eight miles off
where there are four Physicians, Huddersfield eleven miles & four
Physicians, Wakefield fourteen miles & five Physicians,... medical
men are ill paid here & liable to numerous bad debts.*[29]

In 1854 a Leeds general practitioner pointed to the problem faced by
'...well-taught, talented young surgeons, who are trailing along a dull round of
poverty and disappointment', cut off from the 'upper' extremes of practice by
the physician, and the 'lower' extreme *and* middle classes by the quack and
prescribing druggist.[30] Again, in 1857 a *Lancet* editorial remarked:

*There is no profession so grievously afflicted with the evil of over-
competition as that of medicine. We who are curators of the body
are infinitely more numerous than they who are curators of the soul.
Lawyers are of a rarity quite refreshing to the eye of an ambitious
physician or a pining surgeon. In short, look where we may, there is
an opening everywhere except in physic, and there are only a few
crevices which everyone is struggling to cram himself into.*[31]

The problem, it was added, was especially severe in the manufacturing
districts of Yorkshire and Lancashire, aggravated further by the presence of
enormous numbers of quacks and prescribing druggists in these regions.[32]

Judging by how individual medical practitioners summed up the situation,
the level of opposition and competition was of much importance in the
selection of a practice location.[33] However, according to information taken
from the census returns, this factor would seem to have been less influential
than might be believed, given that while some towns and regions appeared to
be distinctly over-populated by medical men, others were under-serviced. So
what reasons then can be put forward as influencing the decision? It would be
expected that the motivations would be primarily economic, that medical men
would opt for a town or locality where they believed that they, depending
upon their level of expectation, could survive or, better still, make a good
living. But other motivations played a part, not dissimilar to those which have
always influenced the migrational patterns of many different occupational
groups — the cost of setting up in a town, including the purchase of a practice,
job opportunities, family or marital ties, the physical attractiveness of a
locality, the availability and cost of housing, chances for the employment of
other family members, especially grown-up sons, and environmental and
health factors.[34]

The census data clearly indicate, in terms of patient/practitioner ratios, that
during the nineteenth century medical practitioners tended to opt for smaller
towns as locations for their practices, rather than larger manufacturing
communities. A straightforward explanation for this tendency is to be found
in the social make-up of these very different communities, and in the way
medical men perceived and interpreted the relationship between 'supply and
demand'. Market and service towns were industrially less developed than their
larger neighbours, their economies being based on trading and service

functions, and as such they were likely to have attracted a high proportion of middle-class inhabitants, the preferred and most solid and lucrative basis for a medical practice.

Wakefield, county town and market and service centre for the region, had a large middle-class population, and a high concentration of legal practitioners, bankers, agents and merchants. From the mid-eighteenth century onwards, it was said to have developed into a sought-after residential town, attracting '...persons in the higher classes, unconnected with trade;...'.[35] In 1851 7% of the population of Wakefield could be classified as 'professional', and a further 21% as 'intermediate', a broadly based middle-class group employing between one and 25 workers.[36] In 1861, the printed census summary on occupations recorded 4.2% of the male population of the Wakefield registration district as 'professionals',[37] including persons engaged in local government, defence and the learned professions. This compared with a figure of only 2.8% in Bradford.[38] Meanwhile, throughout the mid-nineteenth century, Wakefield had one of the highest practitioner/patient ratios in the West Riding.[39]

Those towns experiencing both rapid population growth and heavy industrialisation, such as Bradford and Sheffield, also attracted higher proportions of poorer inhabitants, unable to afford the services of a private medical attendant: 'It must be evident that owing to this rapid increase in the population of great towns, the proportion of the humbler classes, ...will be augmented, as the more wealthy and educated gradually withdraw themselves from these close and crowded communities'.[40] This was reflected in the low numbers of medical practitioners in relation to the population. Textile towns, such as Huddersfield and Halifax, occupied something of an intermediate position with respect to the proportion of middle-class inhabitants and doctor/patient ratios. Put simply, as the proportion of poorer inhabitants in large urban communities increased, so did the ratio of medical practitioners to the population decline.

However, it was not only a question of the numbers of rich inhabitants, or potential patients, which attracted medical practitioners to a town. Older communities, with traditional service and trading functions, and long-established economies, which experienced limited industrial expansion and a relatively steady rate of population growth proved most attractive. The 'traditional' upper and middle classes were seen as offering more lucrative and stable market conditions for medical practitioners, than the new up-and-coming commercial classes. By early in the nineteenth century, relatively large numbers of medical men were already settled in these more traditional communities. By 1821, Wakefield had 18 medical practitioners (one to every 598 inhabitants), Huddersfield 13 (1:1022) and Bradford only 9 (1:1452).[41] Results taken from the census concerning ratios of patients to practitioners do not, it should be remembered, equate directly to conscious decisions to set up in practice in certain towns; a 'time lag' has to be allowed for.

The 'social environments' of the community also played an important role. Wakefield with its large middle-, and, more particularly, large professional class, offered medical men the possiblity of achieving high levels of social integration with groups of their own class and kind, and they became much involved in elite activities; medicine, in short, was seen as a 'gentlemanly' profession.[42]

Table 4.

Selected Social Indicators for Five Yorkshire towns in 1841

Social indicators	Bradf'd	Leeds	Sheff'd	Huddsf'd	Wakef'd	County
		(percentages of the population)				
Select professions[a]	1.1	1.4	1.3	1.3	2.2	0.9
Persons of independent means	1.5	2.1	2.0	1.7	3.2	1.9
Domestic servants	2.7	3.3	3.9	4.5	6.7	3.6
Tax per. head (£)	?	0.10	0.9	?	0.15	?
Ratio of medical practitioners to the population	1:1259	1:1170	1:1277	1:1139	1:671	1:1483
Ratio of medical practitioners to select professions and persons of independent means	1:33	1:41	1:36	1:34	1:36	1:42

[a] accountants, bankers, architects, agents, surveyors, civil servants, town officials, clerks, legal profession, clergyman and ministers, medical profession, armed services, school teachers.

Sources: PP. 1841 Census. Occupation Abstract, Part 1, 1844, XXVII (587); PP. Total amount of assessed taxes for each of the years ending the 5th April, 1845, 1846 and 1847, for places sending members to parliament; also the population of each place according to the census of 1841, 1847-48, XXXIX (233-6).

On the other hand, in the larger industrialising towns and cities of the West Riding medicine was seen very much as a 'marginal' profession, and medical men as marginal to the main economic and social activities of the community.[43] From the beginning of the nineteenth century, so also 'pre-census', it was towns such as Wakefield, with a sense of continuity and tradition, and an established economic life, which, in a way similar to towns in the south of England, were capable of attracting large numbers of medical practitioners.

Bradford, meanwhile, had attracted only a small middle class, and few professionals and substantial employers, being predominantly a working-class town, rough, unsophisticated and unattractive.[44] It was also one of the least healthy towns of the region, which by the mid-nineteenth century '...exemplified in a superlative degree the deleterious effects on life and health of... rapid and intensive industrial development'.[45] Between 1801 and 1881 the population of Bradford had increased from a mere 13,000 to over 180,000. Most of this predominantly working-class population, including many Irish immigrants, resided in a congested inner basin in high density back-to-back housing, while the local gentry and middle classes, such as they were, had deserted the town centre for outer and more salubrious districts.[46] In Bradford everything combined to make the town economically and socially unattractive to the medical practitioner. The very low ratio of doctors to the population, of one to 3,000 inhabitants in 1851, also serves to emphasise the fact, that no connection appears to have existed between the state of health of communities and levels of sickness and disease, and the supply of medical practitioners.

Medical practitioners clearly saw the situation in similar terms, and to quote again from the diary of Dr. Simpson of Bradford, in 1825 he wrote of a Mr. Foster, a surgeon who had formerly lived at Whitchurch,[47] near Leeds, '...but thinking Bradford a better situation, from its great population, he removed'. However, the existence of a dense population did not ensure a successful practice, for Mr. Foster '...says he is very much disappointed in his expectations and does not know whether he shall remain or not. He perfectly agrees with me that Bradford is a bad situation for a medical man, the bulk of the population being of the lowest description of people.' Another contemporary, Dr. Sherwin, repented not having settled in Wakefield in favour of Bradford and still thought seriously of moving there. Wakefield, Simpson added, '...is a very genteel town and in my opinion for a medical man much superior to Bradford', which was not a suitable place for a 'gentleman' to practice medicine: '...people who are not gentlemen will succeed best here. The lower order of people are little removed above the brute creation, being the rudest & most vulgar people under the sun. I have been told that they are worse at Halifax and Huddersfield but I think it scarce possible'.[48]

An additional factor which emphasised the relationship between a large middle class and a high concentration of medical practitioners was the presence or otherwise of physicians in the community. Census data indicate strongly that physicians were best represented in the smaller market towns of the region. A large number of physicians was indicative of a substantial middle- and upper-class clientele, as only the wealthy could afford the services of the more specialised and expensive physician. By 1841 Bradford had only one physician for its population of almost 38,000, Leeds had fourteen physicians, or one to every 11,000 persons, and Huddersfield three, or one to every 8,500 inhabitants. Wakefield also had three resident physicians, one to every 5,000 inhabitants. Conversely, the presence of many poor and working-class elements in the community attracted a large number of chemists and druggists.

A further factor behind locational choice was the availability of jobs, ranging from sought-after hospital and dispensary posts to low-status and badly-paid Poor Law and friendly society appointments.[49] The acquisition of a post, most typically a house surgency or Union post, could be the decisive factor in attracting a medical practitioner, especially a newly-qualified one, to a town — if opportunities looked good and he made the right contacts, he might well set up in practice in the community. The post of house surgeon to a hospital or dispensary offered an especially acceptable opening, linked as it often was to a good starting salary, and board and lodgings. The house surgeon to the Wakefield Dispensary was paid £80 in the 1830s; by the 1870s, when the charity had extended into an infirmary, £125[50] (compared to a salary, during the 1850s, of only £40 per annum for the Union officer for the Wakefield Township which included payment for medicines).[51]

Posts as house surgeon, or assistant house surgeon in large institutions, provided the newly-qualified with valuable practical experience and a means of introduction to medical practice in the town; it led frequently on to successful private practice and appointment to an honorary post. When Thomas Abbey Bottomley qualified in 1851 as MRCS/LSA, for example, he immediately obtained a post as house surgeon to the Huddersfield Infirmary at a salary of £60 per annum. In 1855 he quit the position, and set up in practice in the town; ten years later he was elected honorary surgeon to the Infirmary. Some medical families established a monopoly position with regard to the acquisition of dispensary and infirmary posts, such as the Robinson family of Huddersfield. The Robinsons were connected with the institution from the establishement of the Huddersfield Dispensary in 1814, when George Robinson was elected honorary surgeon. Three generations of Robinsons served first as house surgeons to the charity, before being appointed to honorary surgical posts. The Robinson family practised in Huddersfield for well over a hundred years, building up highly successful private practices.[52]

It was not just the quality or potential of appointments that attracted medical practitioners, but also the sheer number available, and perhaps the chance of combining several paid appointments. While it would be expected that many more medical appointments would be available in the larger towns and cities of the region, this was not necessarily so. Smaller, traditional communities contained a higher proportion of wealthy individuals, and, proportionally, more charities were set up in these towns, and at an earlier date.[53] The Wakefield Dispensary, for example, was established as early as 1787, becoming the tenth dispensary to be set up in England, and first in the West Riding.[54] It was forty years later, in 1825, that a dispensary and infirmary was opened in Bradford.

A number of lucrative and prestigious posts attracted medical men to Wakefield early in the nineteenth century, which helps explain the presence of large numbers of medical practitioners in the town. In 1818 the West Riding County Lunatic Asylum was established in Wakefield, and came to provide a growing number of paid and honorary appointments. By mid-century approximately one-third of all the medical practitioners resident in Wakefield were full-time employees or part-time honorary attendants at the Asylum. Meanwhile, the prison, fever hospital, dispensary and infirmary and a number of smaller charitable enterprises offered paid or honorary appointments, together with the usual range of friendly society, Poor Law and assurance society positions. By 1851 at least 29 appointments were on offer in Wakefield, compared with only 17 in Huddersfield.[55] Little attention has been paid by medical historians to the importance of medical appointments, apart from honorary infirmary posts, emphasis being placed on private practice as the motive force behind the movements of medical practitioners. But appointments were very significant, providing income, status and a breathing space in the first critical practice-building years.

The career of Mr. Henry Dunn of Wakefield illustrates how the acquisition of posts contributed towards the successful medical practice of a not particularly well-qualified or outstanding individual. Dunn obtained the post of visiting surgeon to the Wakefield prison in 1828, largely it seems through family influence, his late father-in-law being not only his senior partner, but former prison surgeon. Dunn had qualified in 1824 as MRCS/LSA at the early age of twenty. In the same year he moved from Bradford, where he had served his apprenticeship, to Wakefield, turning down the post of apothecary to the Bradford Dispensary in favour of an equivalent appointment in Wakefield. Dunn retained the prison post at an annual salary of £250 until his death in 1858. In 1826 he was appointed honorary surgeon to the town's newly-established Fever Hospital, and this assisted in the building up of a respectable private practice, Dunn also inheriting many of his late father-in-law's patients. The prison post, meanwhile, helped fund Dunn's expensive lifestyle. The census enumerators' books for 1841 show that Dunn and his family lived in some style, employing three female domestics and a groom at their large Market Street home. Dunn achieved success at an early age — by the age of 24 he held both the prison and honorary Fever Hospital posts. He soon became a stalwart of Wakefield society, serving on the committees of many charities, as Treasurer to the Newsroom and Museum, and President of the Phil. and Lit. Society. On his death in 1858, Dunn bequeathed personal effects of just under £6,000 to his widow, a considerable sum.[56]

Dunn's success story, and its relationship not only to the acquisition of appointments, but also with an advantageous marriage, leads us on to other potential influences in 'locational decision making' — family ties, marriage, local knowledge and links established with communities or districts during training. Census data offer quantitative support to the supposed significance of what we could designate as 'local factors', giving details not only of the location of medical men at the time the census was taken, but also citing their place of birth, which provides us with a rough guide to their migrational patterns.

With regard to the West Riding, many medical practitioners either remained in or returned to the region to practise; a significant proportion of this group set up in practice in their place of birth. In 1851 nearly three-quarters of those in medical practice in the West Riding were of Yorkshire origin. Of these, 138 individuals practised in their actual place of birth.[57] Another large group had migrated from the counties bordering Yorkshire — Lancashire (4.8%), Derbyshire (2.1%), Nottinghamshire (1.5%) and Lincolnshire (1.4%). The West Riding proved unattractive to immigrants from other parts of Britain, with the exceptions of London (2.1%) and Scotland (2.6%).[58] (See Figure 4.) The local factor seems to have been of less significance for 'pure', or at least those claiming to be pure, physicians, which may well have been linked to differing patterns of training, physicians having to travel further afield to train and qualify. The published census reports for 1851 show that over 63% of surgeons and general practitioners in practice in the West Riding had been born in the region, compared with only 37% of physicians. Only 11% of physicians practised in their place of birth; for surgeons and general practitioners the figure was more than three times as high, 39%.[59]

Figure 4.

Origin of West Riding Medical Practitioners 1851[60]
(born outside West Riding)

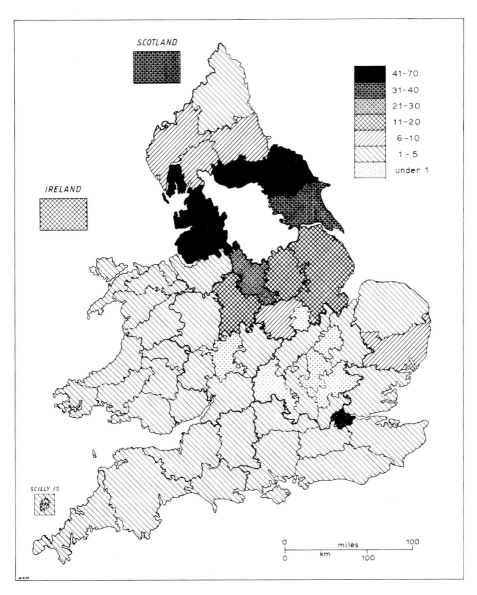

Source: Census enumerator's book 1851.

A medical practitioner who returned to his place of origin had many advantages over newcomers or 'foreigners'. Even if he had no medical connections, he could rely on family support and the possibility of building up a practice through the old-boy network (and the same would hold if he married into a well-connected family). If he came from a respected medical background, then his chances of success multiplied. Once a medical practitioner was well set up in a community, it seems that the chances of further movement were small, unless he was interested in building up a career as a consultant, given the costs of setting up in practice and problems of building up a suitable clientele.

By early in the nineteenth century, a pattern was already clearly established in Wakefield, the bulk of the town's medical profession being local men. According to the census enumerators' books for 1851, 43% of those in practise in the town had been born in Wakefield; a further 30% were Yorkshire born.[61] Both percentages were higher than the averages for the region. By the mid-nineteenth century, many of those in practice in Wakefield were the sons or relatives of established or retired local medical practitioners. Medical families had made their mark in Wakefield; for example, the Walkers, with six family members practising medicine, controlled a large part of surgical and general practice in the town and surrounding area.

Another medical career, that of William Statter of Wakefield, indicates the advantages to be gained through family links with established practitioners. In 1839, on the death of his uncle, Squire Statter, who had practised in Wakefield since early in the nineteenth century, William inherited his practice (and by implication his 'professional reputation'), property and land in Sandal Magna and Wakefield, and a pew in the Parish Church. The entry for William Statter in the census enumerators' book for 1851 confirms his level of success following the inheritance of his uncle's well-established practice. He lived in the very up-market South Parade, with his wife and family, where he was attended by four resident servants, a groom, cook, housemaid and nursemaid. His professional standing was enhanced by the acquisition of a mid-career MD in 1848, and in 1854 he became a Fellow of the Royal College of Surgeons. Statter was active in local affairs, and was appointed a JP in 1870.[62]

Economic viability of decision

When it comes to assessing the success of medical practitioners during the nineteenth-century in terms of wealth and income we are in difficult territory. Having little in the way of concrete evidence, most of what we do have is either anecdotal or relating to those at the peak of the profession. We are left very much with statements referring to the wide range of incomes which medical practice could lead to, and few hard facts and figures. The contribution of salaried appointments, as has been suggested, could range from minor, when they paid, as many Poor Law and friendly society posts did, a few pounds a year, to highly lucrative, top salaried posts paying up to several hundred pounds per annum. Fees present similar problems of precision, it being generally assumed that physicians could command fees of several guineas per consultation, while several shillings would be the norm for the general practitioner. When it comes to assessing the number of visits paid and fees actually collected by medical practitioners, we have even less to go on. The existence of such societies as the West Riding Medical Charitable Society, a charity providing for destitute medical practitioners and their widows, indicates that well into the nineteenth century poverty was not uncommon amongst medical men and their dependents. Meanwhile, other medical men within the region accumulated wealthy patients, large consulting practices, sought-after appointments, and high economic and social standing, all products of successful medical careers.

Census data enable us to evaluate the question of income from another angle, looking at what medical practitioners actually 'ended up with', in terms of household structure, place and type of residence, and the ability to employ servants and medical assistants. At the level of the known community, this evidence can be combined with other characteristics of individual practitioners, to build up a profile of their economic and social position. To conclude, we will look at one of these criteria, the employment of domestic servants. The fact that most medical men employed servants could indicate something about both their wealth and social standing, although servant employment was not necessarily indicative of high social status during this period. In 1851 almost 87% of West-Riding doctors employed resident domestics. Sixty-four per cent of servant-employing doctors had either one or two servants; a further 27% employed three. A number of grand households with grooms, coachmen and footmen, were included amongst the servant-employing group. These tended to be the households of physicians, such as that of Charles Chadwick, a 37-year-old physician, and resident of the auspicious Park Square, Leeds, who employed seven servants, including a coachman and groom, and Robert Dymond of Bolton-on-Dearne who employed nine servants.[63]

Table 5.

Numbers of Resident Domestic Servants[a] Employed by Medical Practitioners in Wakefield, Huddersfield and Bradford in 1871

	Percentage of servant-employing medical practs.	Number of servants						Mean
		0	1	2	3	4	5+	
Wakefield	100	2	4	2	5	2	1	2.3
Huddersfield	85	3	3	9	5	0	0	1.8
Bradford	79	7	11	9	5	1	0	1.4

[a]   Excluding medical assistants and apprentices.

Source: Census enumerators' books, Wakefield, Huddersfield and Bradford Townships, 1871.

Levels of servant employment have been calculated from the census enumerators' books for the Townships of Wakefield, Huddersfield and Bradford in 1871. (See Table 5.) Overall, servant employment was highest amongst Wakefield medical practitioners, in terms of both the percentage employing servants and the number of servants employed. By 1871 all Wakefield medical practitioners employed servants, the mean number employed being 2.3 servants per household (excluding medical assistants and apprentices). Meanwhile, 85% of doctors in Huddersfield had resident domestics, the mean number employed being 1.8. In Bradford servant employment was significantly lower. Although 79% of Bradford doctors employed servants,the mean number employed was only 1.4 per household; the majority had only one or two resident servants.[64]

A handful of practitioners in Wakefield ran grand households, usually, but not always, physicians or holders of honorary appointments. Dr. T. G. Wright, honorary visiting physician to the Wakefield Asylum and House of Recovery, employed five servants, and Dr. D. B. Kendell, honorary physician to the Wakefield Dispensary and Infirmary, hired four resident domestics.[65] The employment of male servants, who at £50 to £60 per annum by the 1870s, cost twice the amount of female domestics to maintain,[66] was perhaps most indicative of high social and economic status, and also of a type of 'window dressing', the hiring of servants for prestige rather than practical purposes. Both Wright and Kendell included male servants amongst their retinues. By 1851 a total of six male domestic servants were employed by Wakefield medical practitioners; in Huddersfield the figure was three.[67]

Using the calculations of contemporary observers and statisticians, we could calculate, albeit in a very tenantive way, that Wright with his five domestic servants, and Kendall with four, had incomes approaching £1,000 and £700 per annum respectively (although part of this could well have come from other sources than medical practice, most probably private incomes). During the mid-nineteenth century most servant-employing doctors had either one or two servants. Two servants fits in with the estimate of a nineteenth-century statistician, Baxter, who cited £300 as the average a doctor might have left after decucting £100 in expenses from his gross earnings in the 1860s. £300 would afford a family in an industrial town two servants and a house of about seven rooms.[68] For example, George Holdsworth, 'surgeon-apothecary' and certifying factory surgeon, resided in a small nine-roomed 'mansion' in St. John's, Wakefield, where he employed two female domestic servants and a groom on a part-time basis. Holdsworth's account books indicate that his expenditure on servants' wages in the early 1840s was somewhere in the region of £20 per annum, indicating a yearly income of approximately £300.[69] The census enumerator's books also reveal that small numbers of medical practitioners managed with one general servant or did not employ living-in servants at all, these individuals being at the lower end of the scale of earnings and social standing.

Concluding remarks

Although any conclusions relating servant employment to income must be very tentative, it could be suggested, judging by this criterium, that doctors were justified in selecting towns such as Wakefield as bases for their practices, rather than larger manufacturing communities, as represented by Bradford. Other evidence relating to the wealth and social status of medical men taken from the census and other sources not referred to here (on the social origins of medical men, their household structures, type and place of residence, investments and wills, and levels of social integration) back up this rather sweeping statement.[70] The use of data on servant employment as an indicator of income levels gives one illustration of the potential value of census data when used at a local level. In conjunction with other sources of information, it can lead to more detailed and rounded pictures of individual medical men and medical practice at the level of the known community. It can also, as this paper hopefully has shown, be used at the macro level to give more general information on levels of medical practice in large regions.

Appendix 1

References to published census reports

PP. Abstracts of the Answers and Returns made Pursuant to 'An Act for taking an Account of the Population of Great Britain' and 'An Act to amend the Acts of the last Session for taking an account of the Population'. Occupation Abstract, Part 1, 1844, XXVII (587).

PP. Census of Great Britain, 1851. Population Tables II. Ages, Civil Condition, Occupations, and Birth-Place of the People. Vol. I, 1854, LXXXVIII (1691-1).

PP. Census of England and Wales for the year 1861. Vol. III. General Report, 1863, LIII (3221).

PP. Census of England and Wales, 1871. Population Abstracts. Ages, Civil Condition, Occupations, and Birth-Places of the People. Vol. III, 1873, LXXII (c.872).

PP. Census of England and Wales, 1881. Vol. IV. General Report, 1883, LXXX (c.3797).

Notes:

[1]   An earlier version of this paper was presented by the authors at the annual conference of the Society for the Social History of Medicine, University of York, 3-5 July, 1987. 'The Economics of Health and Medicine'. It is based largely upon the Phd. thesis of Philip Swan, 'Medical Provision in the West Riding in 1851 and 1871' (Humberside College of Higher Education, 1988), and the book by Hilary Marland, *Medicine and Society in Wakefield and Huddersfield 1780-1870* (Cambridge University Press, 1987), esp. chaps. 7 and 8. For a brief summary of the paper, see Hilary Marland and Philip Swan, West Riding Medical Practice from Nineteenth-Century Census Data: A View of the Region and Selected Towns, *Bull. Soc. Soc. Hist. Med.* The authors would like to thank Margaret Pelling, Richard Smith and Eric Sigsworth for comments on earlier versions of this paper.

[2]   P. S. Brown, The Providers of medical treatment in mid-nineteenth century Bristol, *Med. Hist.*, 24 (1980), 297-314.

[3]   In Scotland civil registration of births, deaths and marriages began in 1855, under the control of a Registrar General for Scotland. A separate act of 1860 gave him responsibility for taking the first Scottish census in 1861. The organisation set up in Scotland followed similar lines to the system in England and Wales. The Scottish censuses have been excluded from this analysis.

4   The census of 1841 was the first to be carried out by officials of the recently created General Register Office. When the system of civil registration came into operation in 1837, 624 registration districts were created in England and Wales, co-extensive with the new Poor Law Unions of 1834, each having a superintendent registrar. These, in turn, were divided into 2,190 sub-districts, each with its local registrar of births, deaths and marriages. For the purpose of the census, the 2,190 registrars were directed to divide their sub-districts into enumeration districts, which numbered over 30,000 in 1841. By these means, the services of the Overseers of the Poor, who had conducted the 1801-31 censuses, were dispensed with, and it was found possible to number the people in one day, in order to obviate the chance of inaccuracy from omissions or double entry. For more details, see W. A. Armstrong, 'The Census Enumerators' Books: a Commentary', in R. Lawton (ed.), *The Census and Social Structure. An Interpretative Guide to Nineteenth Century Censuses for England and Wales* (London, Frank Cass, 1978), pp. 28-70. For a succinct account of the activities of the General Register Office, see M. Nissel, *People Count. A History of the General Register Office* (London, HMSO, 1987).

5   Swan, 'Medical Provision in the West Riding 1851 to 1871'.

6   Armstrong, 'The Census Enumerators Books', p.28.

7   Prominent amongst these studies, but no means constituting an exhaustive list, are Michael Anderson, *Family Structure in Nineteenth Century Lancashire* (Cambridge University Press, 1972); Alan Armstrong, *Stability and Change in an English County Town, a social study of York 1801-51* (Cambridge University Press 1974); Richard Dennis, *English Industrial Cities of the Nineteenth Century* (Cambridge University Press, 1984); H. J. Dyos (ed.), *The Study of Urban History* (London, Arnold, 1968); R. A. Lawton, 'The population of Liverpool in the mid-nineteenth century', *Trans. Historic Soc. Lancs. Chesh.*, 107 (1955), 89-120; R. J. Smith, 'The Social Structure of Nottingham and Adjacent Districts in the Mid-Nineteenth Century', unpublished Ph.D. thesis, Nottingham, 1968; E. A. Wrigley (ed.), *Introduction to English Historical Demography* (London, Weidenfeld and Nicolson, 1966).

8   Charles E. Rosenberg, 'The Medical Profession, Medical Practice and the History of Medicine', in Edwin Clarke (ed.), *Modern Methods in the History of Medicine.* (London, Athlone Press, 1971), pp.22-45.

9   H. J. Dyos and A. B. M. Baker, 'The Possibilities of Computerising Census Data', in H. J. Dyos, *The Study of Urban History.* pp.87-112.

10   Eric M. Sigsworth and Philip Swan, 'Para-medical Provision in the West Riding', *Bull. Soc. Soc. Hist. Med.*, 29 (1981), p.37.

11   During the nineteenth century, for example, neither the published census reports or enumerators' books throw much light on the question of how many midwives were in practise in England. The 1851 published summary of occupations recorded a total of 2,024 midwives; in 1861 there were said to be 1,913, and in 1881, 2,646. By 1901 the number of midwives in England and Wales, according to the census returns had reached 3,055. These figures were apparently hopeless underestimates. By way of comparison, a total of 24,500 midwives were recorded on the Midwives Roll of 1907. The totals recorded in the enumerators' books for the West Riding were also very unconvincing — in 1851 there were only twenty self-declared midwives in the whole region. None was recorded in the townships of Wakefield and Huddersfield.

12 P. M. Tillott, 'Sources of Inaccuracy in the 1851 and 1861 Censuses', in E. A. Wrigley (ed.), *Nineteenth Century Society. Essays in the Use of Quantitative Methods for the Study of Social Data.* (Cambridge University Press, 1972), pp.82-133.

13 Sigsworth and Swan. 'Para-medical Provision in the West Riding', p.38.

14 Yet, if we compare this level of accuracy with that of other sources of information on the qualifications of medical men, for instance, nineteenth-century medical directories, we find that the census data compare well. Irvine Loudon has pointed out that one in six entries in the 1847 *Medical Directory*, itself not a complete listing of qualified medical practitioners, consisted only of the names and addresses of medical practitioners, and did not provide any information on qualifications. Irvine Loudon, 'Two Thousand Medical Men in 1847', *Bull. Soc. Soc. Hist. Med.*, 33 (1983), p.5. For an analysis of medical practitioners recorded in 1783, in the first attempt to compile a complete medical register for Britain, see Joan Lane, 'The Medical Practitioners of Provincial England in 1783', *Med. Hist.*, 28 (1984), pp.353-71.

15 For more on problems connected with the use of census data, see, Lawton (ed.), *The Census and Social Structure*; Wrigley (ed.), *Nineteenth-Century Society*.

16 Dyos and Baker, 'The Possibilities of Computerising Census Data', p.92.

17 T. S. Ashton, *An Economic History of England; the Eighteenth Century* (London. Methuen. 1955), p.17, Cited W. A. Armstrong, 'The Use of Information About Occupation', in Wrigley, (ed.), *Nineteenth Century Society*. p.191.

18 Printed census reports, 1841, 1861 and 1881. For full references to the printed reports, see app.1.

19 Again, it should be remarked that an unknown, but presumably significant, proportion of the fall-off between 1841 and 1851 was due to the fact, that students, apprentices and assistants had been dropped from the category of physicians and surgeons by 1851, and were henceforth recorded separately.

20 Ivan Waddington, 'Competition and Monopoly in a Profession, The Campaign for Medical Registration in Britain', *Amst. Soc. Tschr.*, 2, 1979. p.314.

21 Printed census reports, 1851 and 1881.

22 Printed census reports, 1851-1881.

23 In prosperous Tunbridge Wells in Kent, there was one doctor to every 557 inhabitants by the 1850s, W. D. Foster, 'Dr. William Henry Cook: The Finances of a Victorian General Practitioner', *Proc. Roy. Soc. Med.*, 66, 1973, p.47.

24 Figures cited by Irvine Loudon, *Medical Care and the General Practitioner 1750-1850.* (Oxford. Clarendon Press. 1986). app. V. p.307.

25 PP. Census of England and Wales for the Year 1861. Vol. III. General Report, 1863, LIII (3221), app., p.248.

26 In 1975 the ratio for Yorkshire and Humberside was 1:2,500. Sigsworth and Swan, 'Para-medical Provision in the West Riding', p.37.

27 Census enumerators' books for the West Riding, 1851.

28 See Marland, *Medicine and Society in Wakefield and Huddersfield 1780-1870*, chap. 7; M. Jeanne Peterson, *The Medical Profession in Mid-Victorian London.* (Berkley, University of California Press. 1978), esp. chaps. 3 and 6, and Loudon, *Medical*

Care and the General Practitioner 1750-1850. chap. 10, for the overcrowding of the medical profession in the eighteenth and nineteenth centuries.

[29]   *The Journal of Dr. John Simpson of Bradford, 1825*, ed. E. Willmott (Bradford, City of Bradford Metropolitan Council, 1981). p.13.

[30]   G. Wilson, 'On the State of the Medical Profession in England and on Quakery in the Manufacturing Districts', *Lancet* (1854), I, p.458.

[31]   'Quakery in the Manufacturing Districts', *Lancet* (1857), II, p.326.

[32]   For the importance of prescribing chemists and druggists during the nineteenth century, see Hilary Marland, 'The Medical Activities of Mid-Nineteenth Century Chemists and Druggists, with special reference to Wakefield and Huddersfield', *Med. Hist.*, 31 (1987), 415-39; J. Austen, *Historical Notes on Old Sheffield Druggists* (Sheffield, J. W. Northend, 1961); Brown, 'The Providers of Medical Treatment in Mid-Nineteenth Century Bristol'; Irvine Loudon, 'The Vile Race of Quacks with which this Country is Infested', in W. F. Bynum and Roy Porter (eds), *Medical Fringe and Medical Orthodoxy, 1750-1850* (London, Croom Helm, 1986), pp.106-28; Stanley Chapman, *Jesse Boot of Boots the Chemists. A Study in Business History* (London, Hodder and Stoughton, 1974); M. C. Hamilton, 'The Development of Medicine in the Sheffield Region up to 1815', University of Sheffield, 1957, esp. pp.53-54; A. E. Bailey, 'Early Nineteenth Century Pharmacy', *Pharm. J.*, 185 (1960), 208-12. Nineteenth century parliamentary papers also contain much information on the prescribing activities of chemists and druggists; not only those reporting on the state of pharmacy, but also reports on the medical profession and medical provision.

[33]   The situation in the late eighteenth century was recorded by Samuel Foart Simmons, compiler of the first medical register for Britain. Simmons noted that eighteen provincial surgeon-apothecaries changed their places of practice in 1783, their reasons for change often being influenced by levels of professional opposition. R. B. Batty, for example, transferred from Huddersfield, where two other surgeon-apothecaries practised, to Dewsbury, where he had no competition. Thomas Jones left Leeds, where there were fourteen surgeon-apothecaries, for Bingley, where only one other man practised. Joseph Cartledge, MD of Edinburgh, one of three physicians in Halifax in 1783, who also practised surgery and pharmacy for a livelihood, moved to nearby Elland, where his only rival was a surgeon-apothecary. Lane, 'The Medical Practitioners of Provincial England in 1783', pp.361-62, 363.

[34]   The health factor seems to have been of greater importance than we might expect, doctors expressing much concern about the role the environment played in preserving their own health, if not always that of their patients.

[35]   William White, *History, Gazeteer, and Directory, of the West Riding of Yorkshire*, vol.1 (Sheffield, 1837), p.323.

[36]   K. A. Cowland, 'The Indentification of Social (Class) areas and their place in Nineteenth Century Urban Development', *Trans. Inst. Brit. Geogs.*, new series, 4 (1979), 239-57.

[37]   The figures would presumably be higher for the township or borough of Wakefield.

[38]   PP. Census of England and Wales for the year 1861. Vol.III. General Report, 1863, LIII (3221), app., p.130.

[39]   Other data supplying indications of wealth tend to complement the evidence taken from the census reports, on the numbers of professionals in various communities.

For example, tax returns revealed generally low levels of taxable wealth (per. head of the population) in areas of developing industry and rapid population growth, including the West Riding. During the 1840s, Leeds, Bradford and Sheffield were especially deficient, while communities such as Wakefield and Pontefract had a positive tax residual. Philips and Walton concluded that 'Towns which formerly had been important as centres of industry possessed higher levels of individual tax than those which were in the process of developing their industrial activities' (p.45); individual wealth was concentrated in smaller towns with more tradition economies. A. D. M. Phillips and J. R. Walton, 'The Distribution of Personal Wealth in English Towns in the Mid-Nineteenth Century', *Trans. Inst. Brit. Georgs.*, new series, 4 (1979)., 35-48.

[40] PP. Select Committee Report on the Health of Large Towns and Populous Districts, 1840, XI (384), p.iv.

[41] Edward Baines, *History, Directory and Gazetteer of the County of York*, vol.1, *West Riding* (Leeds, 1822; reprinted Wakefield, S. R. Pubs., 1969).

[42] Marland, *Medicine and Society in Wakefield and Huddersfield 1780-1870*, esp. pp.327-66.

[43] Ian Inkster, 'Marginal Men: Aspects of the Social Role of the Medical Community in Sheffield 1790-1850', in John Woodward and David Richards (eds), *Health Care and Popular Medicine in Nineteenth Century England. Essays in the Social History of Medicine* (London, Croom Helm, 1977), pp.128-63.

[44] D. G. Wright and J. A. Jowitt (eds), *Victorian Bradford* (Bradford, City of Bradford Metropolitan Council, 1981), p.103.

[45] Dr. J. Buchan, *Annual Report of the Medical Officer of Health, 1919* (Bradford, 1920), in Nineteenth Century Bradford', in Robert Woods and John Woodward (eds), *Urban Disease and Mortality in Nineteenth Century England* (London and New York, Batsford/St. Martin's Press, 1984), p.120.

[46] *ibid.* pp.120-121.

[47] Now known as Whitkirk.

[48] *Journal of Dr. John Simpson of Bradford.* pp.30-31, 11.

[49] Margaret Lamb, for example, has shown how, for the Glasgow case, the introduction of a number of public appointments from the mid-nineteenth century onwards provided both more stable forms of income and contributed to the career structures of medical practitioners, also enabling a small group to accumulate a large number of posts. Margaret Lamb, 'The Medical Profession', in Olive Checkland and Margaret Lamb (eds), *Health Care as Social History. The Glasgow Case* (Aberdeen University Press, 1982), pp.16-43.

[50] Annual Reports of the Wakefield Dispensary and Infirmary.

[51] PP. A Return of the Medical Officers under the Poor Law Acts,... (Wakefield Union), 1856, XLIX (434).

[52] *Huddersfield Weekly Examiner*, 2 Nov., 1912.

[53] See Charles Webster, 'The Crisis of the Hospitals during the Industrial Revolution', in E. G. Forbes (ed.), *Human Implications of Scientific Advance* (Edinburgh University Press, 1978), pp.214-33.

[54] Irvine Loudon, 'The Origins and Growth of the Dispensary Movement in England' *Bull. Hist. Med.*, 55 (1981), p.325.

55 Marland, *Medicine and Society in Wakefield and Huddersfield 1780-1870*. pp.274-80.

56 'The Late Mr. Henry Dunn, of Wakefield', *Med. Times Gaz.*, 1858 (II), pp.254-55; *Wakefield and Halifax Journal*, 21 Oct., 1831; J. Horsfall Turner, *Wakefield House of Correction* (Bingley, privately published, 1904), p.172; *Provincial Medical Directories*, 1847-1859; Census enumerators' books, Wakefield Township, 1841; Calendar of the Grants of Probate and Letters of Administration. Wakefield District Registry, 2 Sept., 1858.

57 Census enumerators' books for the West Riding, 1851.

58 *ibid.*

59 *ibid.*

60 Swan, 'Medical Provision in the West Riding in 1851 and 1871', p.263.

61 Census enumerators' books, Wakefield Township, 1851.

62 Wakefield Registry of Deeds. Memorial RB 474 733, dated 9 Sept., 1839; *Provincial Medical Directories*, 1847-1870; Census enumerators' books, Wakefield Township, 1841 and 1851.

63 Sigsworth and Swan, 'Para-medical Provision in the West Riding. p.39.

64 Census enumerators' books, Wakefield, Huddersfield and Bradford Townships, 1871.

65 See also Brown, 'The Providers of Medical Treatment in Mid-Nineteenth Century Bristol', p.307.

66 J. H. Walsh, *A Manual of Domestic Economy*, 2nd ed. (London, 1873), p.224. Cited in J. A. Banks, *Prosperity and Parenthood* (London, Routledge and Kegan Paul, 1954), p.73.

67 Census enumerators' books, Wakefield and Huddersfield, 1851.

68 R. D. Baxter, *The Taxation of the UK* (London, 1869), pp.105-106. Cited in Geoffrey Best, *Mid Victorian Britain* (London, Weidenfeld and Nicolson, 1971), p.110.

69 *'First Factory Doctors' Personal Accounts. George Holdsworth, of St. John's Square Household accts, May 1839 to Dec., 1844'*, Ms. Wakefield District Archives, John Goodchild Collection.

70 See Marland, *Medicine and Society in Wakefield and Huddersfield 1780-1870*, pp.280-301 for the situation in Wakefield and Huddersfield.

CHAPTER 6

'Utterly irreclaimable': Scottish Convict Women and Australia 1787-1852[1]

Ian Donnachie

Like many others undergoing rapid change through industrialisation and urbanisation Scottish society experienced an upturn in crime during the late eighteenth and early nineteenth centuries. As elsewhere the attitude of alarmed authorities was to clamp down on crime — with severe punishment meted out even to petty offenders regardless of sex or condition. Scotland itself had a long tradition of 'banishment' for criminal activities but after the mid-1780s resort was increasingly made to transportation on principles adopted earlier in England. Thanks to the highly centralised nature of the Scottish administrative state — and notably its legal apparatus — the record of crime in this critical period is both relatively accessible and detailed, especially proceedings of the Lord Advocates Department and the high Courts. Fortuitously the value for the social historian of the surviving Scottish evidence of criminal prosecutions and trail proceedings is matched on the other side of the world by a very different record — that of the convict settlers in New South Wales and Van Diemen's Land, where the majority of offenders ended up. While an earlier survey indicated the history and extent of transportation from Scotland during the years 1786-1852, and a subsequent case-study examined an all-male cohort transported in 1830, this article looks in a little more detail at the origins, crimes and ultimate fate (where it can be determined) of some Scottish convict women.[2] It is based on the experiences of 200 women, roughly ten percent of the total transported from Scotland, and although this can hardly claim to be a systemmatic or random sample the data obtained are nevertheless immensely valuable.

Looking first at the actual dates of transportation we find the data here broadly substantiates the findings of the earlier overall survey, for the bulk of women convicts among the 200 — over four-fifths — were transported in the 1830s and 1840s (Table 1). In fact, transportation of women from Scotland before the 1820s was unusual, despite the evidence that the earliest cohorts in the later 1780s and earlier 1790s included some women sentenced soon after the introduction of the system. Only two here were sent in the period before 1800 — with none apparently in the subsequent decade. Ten went in the decade 1810-19 and twice as many 1820-29 — both periods that saw increasing rates of crime coupled with popular protest and greater vigilance on the part of the authorities in town and countryside.[3]

Although the whole age-curve is represented (Table 2) the majority of convict women were in their 'twenties and 'thirties, one in seven was still in her 'teens, and three that we know of were actually under 15 years of age. One of the youngest, Margaret Neil, though only 14, had been in prison four times before, being sentenced to seven years transportation at the Glasgow court for theft of wearing apparel; while at the other end of the age range was Elizabeth Gordon or Young, a 54 year old widow from Banffshire, with no previous convictions, who also found herself transported from Aberdeen for both the same crime and duration. Christian Scott or Chilchrist, at 65, was the oldest. A widow with one child from Dundee, she had stolen some wine and was sentenced to seven years transportation at Perth court, subsequently sailing to New South Wales on the *Buffalo* in 1833. The earlier survey found two-thirds were in their 'twenties and 'thirties, with nearly 17 per cent in their 'teens and only 6 per cent over 50 years of age. So it seems the 200 were actually slightly older on average with a notably higher percentage over 40 years old.[4] As regards statements about marital status (Table 3) it comes as no surprise that nearly two-thirds were registered as single, either unmarried or widowed. But many, including quite likely those for whom no information is recorded, deliberately lied about their status — abandoning husbands at home knowing that this would enhance their marriage prospects in the colony. Some women — married and single — clearly abandoned children, though others had them on board with them. While some women intentionally abandoned husbands, a few actually sought to join those already transported. Others were even joined by husbands after their arrival in the colony. These men invariably came themselves as convicts, though in the odd instance we are able to document soldiers, sailors and free settlers. A few may even have jumped ship in Sydney or Hobart to join long-lost wives and sweethearts.[5]

While we have no information whatever about the religious affiliations of over 40 per cent of women, the remainder (see in Table 4) were overwhelmingly Protestant. The professed Catholics were either Irish or probably Irish descent. Contrary to expectations none of the Highland women we know of were Catholic.

The Australian convict records also provide one of the earliest statistical measures of working class literacy. They indicate that Scots men and women convicts were on the whole better educated than their English or Irish counterparts, but that women were generally less literate than men. Although we have no information about a quarter of the sample, two-thirds of the rest could read (Table 5), a quarter could both read and write, while only one in ten was illiterate. For the cohort sent out in the *Tasmania* during 1844 we have more information to go on: of 37 Scots women aboard nine could read and write, seven could only read, while 17 were described as 'imperfect'. Again one in ten seems to have been illiterate. The illiterates were most likely to be peasant girls from the Scottish Highlands or Ireland — several from the Highlands were apparently Gaelic speakers knowing next to no English and probably unable to read or write in either language.

Where did the women come from? While we lack enough information to be certain about the origins of over a quarter of the cohort we know that of the remainder (Table 6) two-thirds had native places in the industrialised districts including the counties of Lanark, Renfrew, Our, Dumbarton, Midlothian, Sterling, Fife, Perth and Angus. A third, in fact, came from Glasgow itself, while a fifth were natives of Edinburgh and its port of Leith.

Table 1.		
Date of transportation		
YEAR	TOTAL	%
1790-1799	2	1
1800-1809	-	-
1810-1819	10	5
1820-1829	20	10
1830-1839	93	46
1840-1849	75	37
	200	99

Table 2.		
Age		
AGE GROUP	No.	%
Up to 15	3 ⎱	14.5
15-19	26 ⎰	
20-24	34 ⎱	35.5
25-29	37 ⎰	
30-34	27 ⎱	24.0
35-39	21 ⎰	
40 plus	16 ⎱	12.0
50 plus	8 ⎰	
No Data	28	14.0
	200	100.0

Table 3.		
Marital Status		
STATUS	No.	%
Single	95	47.5
Married	45	22.5
Widowed	30	15.0
No Data	30	15.0
	200	100.0

Table 4.	
Religion	
Protestant	99
Catholic	14
No Data	87
	200

Table 5.	
Literacy	
Reads and Writes	38
Reads	96
Illiterate	16
No Data	50
	200

Table 6.			Table 7.		
Native Place			**Place of Conviction**		
DISTRICT/COUNTRY	No.		PLACE	No.	%
Lanark/Renfrew/Ayr/ Dumb.	47		Edinburgh	77	38
Midlothian	29		Glasgow	60	30
Perth/Angus	12		Perth	25	
North-East	10		Aberdeen	15	
Highlands	10		Stirling	4	
Stirling/Fife	4		Ayr	2	25
Dumfries/Galloway	3		Dumfries	2	
Borders	2		Jedburgh	2	
Ireland	14		Inveraray	1	
England	6		London	4	
Wales	1		Lancaster	4	5
Overseas	2		Liverpool	1	
No Data	60		Cumberland	1	
	200		No Data	2	
				200	100

One in ten was Irish and one in twenty from the Highlands and Islands. The former numbered 14, seven Catholics and seven Protestants. Their average age was 34, eight being widows, four married and two single. Most were from Ulster, though two were from Dublin, and farthest-travelled was Mary Kelly from Tipperary, who was sentenced at Perth for stealing a print in 1830.[7] Ten women were Highlanders, the majority like the Irish, migrants to the Lowlands. In one instance — a Gaelic speaker — no further information is provided but three of the others were from Caithness and two each from Argyll, Skye and Ross-shire. Half were married, the rest being either spinsters or widows, with an average age of 31. The majority were Protestant or so professed. Other rural areas, such as the Borders, Dumfries and Galloway, and the North-East, together accounted for around ten per cent, while English and Welsh migrants had only token representation.

Another interesting measure of contemporary mobility — essentially migration from rural, peasant districts to urban, industrial towns or movement from one town to another, is shown by the distance of native place from place of conviction (Table 7). Women, regardless of marital status, were apparently as mobile as men. Nearly two-thirds of women were tried locally in the busiest courts at Edinburgh, Glasgow, Aberdeen and Perth — the offences being committed in or near their home town. One in three was a migrant from a distance, the majority actually resident over 200 km. from their native place elsewhere in Scotland or in Ireland. Those travelling farthest had migrated south of the Border, Aberdeenshire to London and Caithness to Lancashire being typical. We can assume the coastal shipping connection was significant in most cases presented by the sample.

Turning now to occupations (Table 8), as one might expect a large proportion of women — over two-thirds — were domestic servants of one kind or another. Of the rest one in ten had factory or 'industrial' jobs, with the same proportion in 'country' occupations. The majority of factory workers were to be found in the textile trade — described variously as mill spinners, thread winders, weavers or bleachers; while country women included dairy maids, cheese and butter makers. Invariably one finds in the records the catch-all description 'All Work' or perhaps little bits of extra information like 'Needlewomen', 'Seamstress', or 'Dressmaker' — all skills likely to come in handy in the colony. Eight women, rather surprisingly, had no designated occupation, and although they were probably housewives or servants by some clerical oversight were not so recorded. The four with other occupations included Johannah Reid or Laing, the 25 year-old Edinburgh brothel keeper (whose story is retold here later) and three public house servants.[8] Apart from regular and respectable employment how many women were likely to have been on the town as prostitutes? The evidence for Edinburgh and Glasgow suggests quite a high proportion for many women arrested in the cities were on the town. However, as far as can be gathered, none were ever transported from Scotland for the offence of prostitution alone.[9]

Where then were the criminal districts? This sample of women convicts confirms the evidence of earlier surveys that crime was overwhelmingly concentrated in Edinburgh and Glasgow (Table 9), where nearly 70 per cent of offenders were tried and convicted. Of the remainder most convictions were recorded in Perth and Aberdeen, while rural circuits in Stirling, Ayr, Dumfries, Inveraray and Jedburgh, together accounted for 11 instances. Crime amongst Scottish women was primarily a feature of the towns, though at the same time it must be said that there is nothing that positively distinguishes urban from rural offences as occurs with male crimes, for example, sheep and cattle stealing. South of the border ten Scots women were convicted in English courts, four in London and six in the North, for the usual range of petty offences like stealing clothes or picking pockets. Jane Milne, a 20-year old nurse from Aberdeenshire, was typical, being sentenced to seven years at Newgate and transported in the *Midas I* to New South Wales in 1824.[10]

Discounting a quarter of the women about whose criminal offences no information has been recorded, the great majority (see Table 10) were convicted for theft of property — money, clothes, food or drink. Typical of dozens of such offences are entries in the records like 'Stole Money', 'Stole Blankets' or 'Stole Wine'. Stealing clothes was a predominantly female crime, given the opportunities presented by domestic service; and much like thieving of food is a telling indicator of the poverty that was the general lot of these women. Even the bare bones of the record reveal some tragic cases like that of Nancy Moonie or Agnew, a 57-year old Catholic widow from County Derry ('All Work; Feeble') with nine children and one previous conviction who had stolen a mantle and was sentenced at Glasgow to seven years transportation in 1833. Five years earlier two of her sons, John and Henry, had also been transported, but whether or not she was ever reunited with them in the colony we have no way of telling. Just as pathetic was the case of Catherine McGilvray, a 30 year-old dairymaid from Skye, with no previous record, convicted at Edinburgh for stealing some milk and also transported for 7 years.[11]

103

The next most significant group of offences come under the heading of robbery either from the person or less typically also involving assault — a more obviously male crime. Often described in the record as 'Man Robbery', this first offence was usually theft of money or watches, probably by pick-pocketing. Assault and robbery was regarded as a serious crime and usually dealt with severely by judges, sentences of 14 years and even life being common. Typical was Agnes or Nancy McMenamy of Paisley, a 23-year old illiterate country servant, who had been repeatedly punished and sentenced to life at Glasgow in 1833 for man robbery; and earlier Elizabeth McDonald, about whom we have no personal details, given life at Edinburgh in 1828 for assault and stabbing.[12]

Housebreaking was another offence ill-regarded by the courts, even though it was an assault on property rather than the person. Fifteen offenders we know about in the cohort — mainly from the cities — were sent down for terms of up to 14 years, depending on previous convictions. One, Margaret Russell, a 26-year old muslin clipper from Calton, Glasgow, who stayed with her father, an inkle weaver, had a male accomplice, William Ogilvie, a shoemaker. One night after she and Ogilvie had taken a few drams they broke into the house of Ogilvie's master and stole a trunk containing money and other items. Ogilvie later declared himself 'very much intoxicated' — but to no avail. Both were ultimately transported to Botany Bay (Russell on *Midas I* arriving 12 December 1825), though unlike most, as we will find, did not entirely disappear from the record.[13]

Less significant numerically were a number of offences relating to forgery, receiving and most serious of all, murder. Uttering base coin or forged notes was quite a common male crime — often committed by those with relevant skills like blacksmiths or clerks — and it seems likely that the three women offenders just happened to get caught passing coins or notes rather than manufacturing them. There seem to have been regular suppliers of forgeries and criminals made their living by buying fake half-crowns from dealers and passing them off as the real thing — often at fairs and markets where detection was less immediate than perhaps in shops or pubs. Women offenders, some of whom had previous convictions, were dealt with just as rigorously as the men, one, Elizabeth Dickson, a Paisley dressmaker, getting a 14 year sentence at Glasgow for uttering base coin in 1832. Mary McDonald, a 32-year old spinster and servant of no fixed abode, is another case in point. She was convicted of 'offences relating to the coin', sentenced to seven years transportation at Glasgow on 6 January 1844, and shipped later that year to Hobart aboard the *Tasmania*. Receiving, a very common occurrence among the criminal classes, was perhaps even more difficult to detect than forgery. Among the cohort there are only two offences on record, both equally trivial, for receiving stolen clothes.[14]

Murder, by comparison, was a serious offence and many women convicted were likely to pay the extreme penalty. In other cases sentence was commuted to transportation, the judge might be influenced by mitigating circumstances (as often arises in cases of manslaughter), though transportation was invariably for life with the recommendation of a minimum period under close supervision in the colony before a ticket-of-leave would even be considered. We have only one instance on record here, that of Janet Stewart, a 29-year old tinker turned country servant from Perthshire, sentenced to life at Perth Court. Her story highlights life among the Perthshire tinker community — in this instance an encampment near Birnam, Dunkeld. According to the evidence of Duncan Stewart, Janet's husband, the family, including his brother, David, travelled the country and had stopped in a field to finish some spoons for sale. The party got drunk and a furious argument — mostly, it seems, in Gaelic — broke out among the company. Blows were struck and Stewart attacked her brother-in-law, stabbing him with a knife. A married women with three children, she had a five-year old on board the *Buffalo*, which transported her to New South Wales in 1833.[15]

The other crimes are a mixed but interesting bag including arson, incest and sacrilege. The first, arson or wilful fire-raising, was regarded by the courts as a serious crime against property and was severely dealt with. For example, Helen Stewart or Murphy (about whom more presently), a 34-year old married servant with four children, got life at Ayr Court for this offence in 1830.[16]

Table 8.
Occupation

Domestic	129
Country	17
Industrial/Factory	16
Other	4
None stated	8
No Data	26
	200

Table 9.
Distance of Native Place from Place of Conviction

	Instances	%
Environs	57	41
Up to 50 km	31	22
51-199 km	14	10
Over 200 km	37	27
	139	100

Table 10.
Offence

Theft	105
Housebreaking	15
Robbery	10
Assault/Robbery	7
Uttering Coin/Note	3
Receiving	1
Murder	1
Other	9
No Data	48
	200

Table 11.
Length of Sentence

7 years	126
10 years	13
14 years	44
Life	12
No Data	5
	200

Incest (and invariably exposing a child to perish) was probably not infrequent among both urban and rural society — but was certainly less frequently detected or reported to the authorities. Of course in Scotland it was typical of the sort of moral crime likely to reach the ears of the Kirk Session, which might deal with the matter directly itself and make no recourse to criminal proceedings. Sadly proceedings were brought to court in the instance recorded here, that of Ann Knox, a 22-year old unmarried housemaid from Renfrewshire, with one child. She was convicted with her half-brother, Andrew White, and sentenced to 14 years at Glasgow for the offence. Was White the father of her child and had their liaison been discovered as the result of her pregnancy? Even the evidence in the precognitions of this interesting and detailed case of incest in a mining community near Old Monkland, Lanarkshire, leaves the obvious questions unanswered. Collier neighbours and their wives all gave evidence of the cohabitation but Knox herself swore that 'the child was got in a field near Parkhead' (on the Glasgow road) — the father being one William Knox, a mason from port Dundas on the Forth & Clyde Canal. After White's wife died Ann had gone to live with him, ostensibly as house keeper, but prying eyes had caught them in bed together on more than one occasion. According to the marginal note against Ann Knox's entry in the *Earl of Liverpool's* indent, White was 'expected out' and might well have joined his step-sister and her baby in the colony. The single instance of sacrilege, by one Betty Ann Blair, we will examine presently as one of a series of case histories.[17]

While the records are often defective in personal data the sentence is invariably noted — so we have this information on all but five of the women. As indicated in an earlier survey the actual length of sentence (Table 11) was largely academic — given the fact that few convicts could hope to return from transportation. The length of sentence broadly reflected the seriousness of the offence and previous convictions and all the evidence indicates that sentences became more draconian with the passage of time. Yet the data show that nearly two-thirds of women received seven year sentences, while the longer sentences were reserved for the more persistent or violent among their number. Does this perhaps support the view that the Scottish judiciary resorted to transportation as a convenient (and cheap) means of disposal of the criminal classes — at the same time obliging a colony with acute labour and female shortages? To answer this question we need to look at specific experiences in the colony later in this paper. Certainly previous convictions influenced the sentences judges handed down — for although the data are deficient in this regard — almost half the recorded instances had one or more previous convictions, some for multiple offences. Agnes or Nancy McMenamy, who got life at Glasgow for man robbery in 1932, had been 'repeatedly punished'; while Margaret Coates, dispatched later on the *Tasmania* in 1844, had no fewer than five previous convictions. Perhaps this also suggests an attitude of leniency on the part of Scottish judges, reluctant to resort to transportation. While there is some measure of truth in this assertion relative to the English and Irish experiences, we need to offset this impression against the relative pettiness of the majority of offences involved.[18]

As the examples quoted show, personal histories, where they can be reconstructed, are highly illuminating of prevailing social conditions, culture and moral norms. Here are some further examples which tell us much about the lives of peasant and urban working class women in the period — especially regarding mobility, marriage, child bearing, and even personal appearance. Highland and Irish migration to the Lowlands, as we previously observed, is a significant feature in the cohort. Take for instance the case of Euphemia McPhail, a 24 year old, who had migrated from Mull about 1820 and worked as a farm servant to James Russell of Floak in Mearns, Renfrewshire. She had left her previous employer, another farmer, William Clark at nearby Craigton of Mearns, because Mrs. Clark apparently 'used her badly'. For revenge she returned and stole £2 12 in cash, some silver spoons and clothes. According to her own statement, whisky was her ruin. Clearly it had gone to her head for when arrested on the road to Glasgow she was carrying a large bundle of clothes and was wearing two bonnets![19]

Again, the arsonist, Helen Stewart or Murphy, aged 34, had been born in Ireland, married at 18 and came to Scotland with her husband in 1815. They had lived in Ayr for eight years and in Irvine about the same length of time. Ultimately she lived as widow in a house at Friarscroft owned by one, John Grieve, a weaver turned grocer-publican. After getting notice to quit Stewart left with her two children, but later, on the night of 31 March 1830, returned and set fire to Grieve's house, which was nearly burned to the ground.[20]

Employment, as we saw earlier, was overwhelmingly domestic — an extension of the womens' traditional role. The majority in industrial occupations worked at textiles and were thus clearly exposed to the economic uncertainties of the times. One woman, Betty Ann Blair, aged 40 and a native of Ayr, had clearly fallen on hard times. She had once worked at tambouring but at the time of her arrest in Glasgow was of no fixed abode and had no regular employment. She had already been confined to the Bridewell a number of times for theft and believed — by her own admission — that she was banished from Glasgow on that account. One evening, 'when the worse of liquor', she broke into the Original Burghers Chapel in Glasgow and stole two bibles — committing sacrilege before the law. According to the indent of the *Earl of Liverpool*, on which she was transported for seven years in 1831, Blair was 44 years of age and widowed with one child.[21]

A quarter of the women for whom data are recorded were married — and a further 15 per cent widowed. For example, aboard the *Buffalo* were 14 married women of average age 35 and 9 widows, aged on average 45 — some with children. Among the married women on this ship, Margaret Hay or McCormel, a laundry maid ('All Work') from Berwickshire, was typical. She was 29 years of age, had two children, and had been sentenced at Jedburgh to seven years for housebreaking. Discounting those for whom no data are recorded 40 of the women had children, 31 of their number being either married or widowed. The average family size among the married or widowed women was three children. Janet Stewart, the tinker-murderess, is a good example in point, for she had three children (one five years of age) with her aboard the transport ship. Nine women were single with one or more illegitimate children, one of the youngest was 20 year old Bell Souter, a needle-girl ('All Work') with two children, who had been sentenced at Perth for stealing some clothes. Seven women had children with them on board the transport ships — mainly infants in arms or under ten years of age.[22]

One other interesting feature of the Australian convict record is its attention to physical appearance and distinguishing marks — both highly significant to the authorities in an age before photography became widespread. For example, Euphemia McPhail, whom we met earlier, was a petite 5ft 2ins. tall, with black hair and blue eyes — according to the remarks by her entry in the indent of *Mary III*, which arrived at Sydney Cove on 18 October 1823. Again a later description of Jean Aitken, an 18 year old Edinburgh kitchen maid, is even more detailed.

> '5 feet tall and ruddy and freckled complexion, with dark brown hair, dark hazel eyes, two scars on centre of forehead, mark of burn under left jaw, scar on back of right wrist, scar on inside left wrist.'

Many women sported tattoos, no doubt momentos of old flames or husbands. These were a useful means of identification for the colonial authorities so the details were invariably recorded accurately. One, Sarah Diamond, a Glasgow girl sent on the *Buffalo* had a series of tattoos on her right arm including two diamonds, a heart and three stars, and the initials HDAC and DRAH — presumably former lovers.[23]

What befell these hapless women after they had been through the courts and sentenced? The sequence of events was roughly as indicated in the earlier survey: the collection of convict transportees in central gaols, notably in Edinburgh and Perth; shipment south to hulks on the Thames or penitentiaries in London; and thence dispatch to Australia on convict transports, a voyage of perhaps two to four months.[24] The time between sentence and dispatch could be considerably extended by delays in Scotland. In the early days this might be as much as three years (one woman, sentenced at Aberdeen in 1787, waited four!), but latterly incarceration for about a year before transport was the norm. The practice was to assemble 20 or 30 women for trans-shipment in a group — and because of the relatively small numbers involved before the 1830s — this often took some months. Prisoners from the north were invariably shipped via Aberdeen direct to hulks or gaols on or near the Thames or Solent. By the 1820s the majority of women transportees were not confined in the hulks but held in London gaols, prominent being the Millbank penitentiary (opened 1816). All the convict women shipped in the *Tasmania* during 1844 started their journey from Millbank. Finally, ill-health or pregnancy might be further causes for delay. Evidently the authorities exercised some humanity in returning sick or pregnant women to gaol even after they had been taken aboard ship.[25]

Women, as we saw, made up a relatively small portion of the convict population before the early 1800s and consequently no special provision was made for them during the voyage. On board the transport women were separated from the men, though liaisons were apparently commonplace, especially with the crew and soldiers accompanying the prisoners. While some women were no doubt as anxious as men to strike up relationships with the opposite sex (and many took partners during the voyage), others found themselves open to exploitation. Inevitably the middle-class officers and even the sailors and soldiers regarded the convict women as prostitutes whether they were or not — a view that also prevailed in the colonies for much of the period under review. The exploitation of women as virtual prostitutes no doubt continued undetected after the 1820s when women were at least being transported in separate ships; though a general tightening of discipline certainly reduced it.[26]

The voyage itself was potentially hazardous and frightening, though often plain-sailing and boring. Conditions on board seem, in general, to have been better than in the gaols and much better than in the hulks. So although accommodation in the ships' prisons was cramped and uncomfortable adequate bedding clothes, food and water were made available. Provided a woman was and remained healthy she would survive the voyage. Statistically the chances of survival were good — perhaps one in a hundred died on the voyage. Passing from Europe to Australia could take anything up to five months. The transport *Mary III*, for example, had a four month passage, sailing from London on 10 June 1823 and reaching Sydney Cove on 18 October that year. On board were 58 women, two Scots among their number being the luckless Euphemia McPhail and a Catherine Smith, aged 54, from Leith. According to the muster, taken on arrival, all the women appeared in good health, 'declared themselves well treated' and 'have been well spoken of by the surgeon and commander'. Again, *Midas I*, with 109 women aboard, left England on 24 July 1825, reaching Hobart Town four months later on 23 November. Disembarking 50 of her cargo there, she sailed north to New South Wales, arriving in Sydney Cove on 17 December — a passage of nearly five months in all. One woman had died, the remaining 58 (including two Scots) being healthy when mustered at Sydney.[27]

The bare bones of voyages like these can be fleshed out in one remarkable instance through the log-book of the *Tasmania*, which transported 186 convict women to Van Diemen's Land in 1844. William Black, the ship's master began his log on 1 August that year, reporting the ship ready at Deptford Dockyard. The next three weeks were spent taking water and stores and awaiting government orders. The convicts came aboard from Millbank on the 29th and 30th — 190 women and 26 children — accompanied by two matrons 'to superintend arrangements'. Mess women were immediately appointed from among the convicts, each being responsible for upwards of a dozen of her comrades; while others were to assist the cook and the nurse. One women was returned as unfit to make the voyage — and with clothing distributed the ship set sail on 8 September.[28]

The regime was well-disciplined, though severe when fighting and quarrelling disrupted good order. From the master's view point the best reports read 'Quiet and Good' or simply 'Quiet' — 25 of the 37 Scots women aboard were so described. It seems unlikely that every instance of indiscipline was recorded — there were a total of six in a 3½ month voyage. Mary Thompson, a 23 year old mill girl from Paisley, is case in point. She was put in the solitary box for striking a fellow convict and had a bad record of violence and abusive language throughout the voyage. She was released the next day on promise of 'governing her temper and not committing any more assaults'. Later another convict, Jean McKerdy, was 'sent to the poop to cool' for 'behaving in a dirty manner (p-----g) in another woman's bucket'.

A typical day in the ship's prison began at 8 am when beds were raised and cleaned and breakfast taken. This was followed by a routine of further cleaning, mending and washing of clothes, exercise on deck and leisure time, interspersed with lunch and tea. The prison was generally locked at 6 pm. Rations seem to have been adequate — with sherbert and lemon juice distributed regularly. The boredom is emphasised by the lack of incidents. Sailors apparently fraternised with the women but when detected such liaisons were reported to the master and the men punished. The log records the deaths of three women and one child. Saddest of all was the story of Margaret Coates, a 22 year old bleacher, who died on 3 October following premature labour and the birth of a still-born child. Another girl tried to commit suicide by strangling herself with tape from her dress — but was saved in time and sent to the ship's hospital to recover.

Quite how typical of the time this voyage was is hard to tell, but the passage of the *Tasmania* from London to Australia was clearly well-organised and the treatment of convicts relatively humane. Certainly when she entered the Derwent and anchored off Hobart Town on 20 December the master was able to deliver 186 women into the hands of the Deputy Comptroller General for Prisons in Van Diemen's Land — there being 'no complaints from the prisoners about their treatment'. Apart from a brief call at Dunchal the ship had made no other landfall until reaching the far side of the Indian Ocean — for a direct voyage from England was regarded as preferable for the health of the convicts — rather than putting in at Rio de Janeiro or the Cape of Good Hope. It had been thought best to push on provided there was a good supply of water aboard.[29]

What was the fate of women in Australia? The lynchpin of the penal system and a vital element in the economic fabric of the colonies until the 1840s at least was assignment — and for most convict women this meant domestic service. Colonists could apply to the government for assigned servants and be given their allocation as and when available. For example, some months prior to the arrival of the *Buffalo* in 1833 upwards of a dozen requests from different parts of New South Wales were received in Sydney. Hearing of the *Buffalo's* cargo of convict women the Superintendent of Police at Windsor wrote that 'sixteen can be disposed of immediately', including two middle-aged women who can milk, three dress-makers, five house servants, five laundresses and one nurse-cum-housemaid. Other requests indicated that similar numbers could be sent to Maitland, Newcastle, Port Macquarrie, Goulbourn and Wollongong. Word had evidently got round that the *Buffalo* carried only English and Scots women for the correspondence was full of complaints about the Irish. Donald Mackellan of Strathalan particularly requested that any assigned female 'may not be Irish' — as his wife had been 'much plagued by all the servants we have had from that country'.[30]

From the evidence that survives it seems probable that the majority of women sent to New South Wales and Van Diemen's Land were assigned either by on-the-spot selection or by requests of the kind that preceded the arrival of the *Buffalo*. In New South Wales the remainder — often the worst offenders, the physically or mentally sick, or the least attractive — were dispatched upriver from Sydney to the Female Factory Parramatta.[31] This establishment, opened in 1821, was a cross between a penitentiary and hospice. Several of the 200, including Janet Grenlees, a 23 year old housemaid from Paisley, ended up in the Female Factory, where she was recorded by the New South Wales census in 1828. A comment by her name in the indent of the *Midas I*, which took her to New South Wales in 1825, noted that her husband — under the name of Matthew Wilson, was soon expected to arrive in the colony. Were they thus able to start a new life together in Australia?[32] Another group — servants who did not give satisfaction or misbehaved — were invariably sent by local courts for secondary punishment at the Female Factory. They would not be assigned until they had served their sentences. Similar arrangements were made in Van Diemen's Land — with all the Female Factories doubling as maternity hospitals for women who fell pregnant — as many apparently did.

Almost invariably — given the random nature of assignment — some women ended up as virtual slaves toiling for a hard master and even being sexually exploited. While women were less likely to abscond than men (the ratio was roughly 1:8) some did and occasionally more than once. In 1835, for example, the New South Wales Government Gazette reported 53 Scottish convict runaways (including one Donald Donnachie) — no fewer than ten were women. Jane Gale, a 23 year old Edinburgh girl ('All Work'), who had arrived in the colony late the previous year, ran away from her master, George Graham, in early January; and again from a new master, a Mr. Windeyer, at the beginning of February. Catherine Maxwell, aged 25 and from Glasgow, already 'a notorious runaway', absconded twice during the year, latterly from a Captain Hunter of Sydney. Generally runaways were quickly apprehended, women being as unlikely as men to escape detection in a heavily policed society where a form was needed for everything, especially moving from place to place. A woman's chance of escaping detection was certainly poorer than a man's — since the latter might make it to the bush on foot or perhaps sail coastwise in a stolen boat, thereafter managing to survive and keep his anonymity. But for both sexes the lure of urban society — with its attractions of drink, sex and crime — was stronger than the risk of fighting for survival in the bush. Over the 'thirties as a whole no particular pattern of absconding can be detected — though for the women it was consistent at 10-15 per annum on a seasonal cycle favouring the spring and summer months.[33]

For some women marriage was the only means of escape from domestic service or the govenment Factory. If it did not bring relief from drudgery as an assigned servant it at least promised something of a new life with a family and some measure of freedom brought with a ticket-of-leave. Marriage was thought to make the colony more 'moral' — but the treatment of women and the operation of the 'marriage market' was often far from moral. In the early days women were lined up on arrival for selecion as wives or assigned as servants by soldiers and freemen — and this sort of selection procedure continued much later at the Female Factories. Convicts — male and female — were themselves encouraged to marry and could petition the governor to do so. If they had served their sentence or the greater part of it they might be granted a ticket-of-leave and hence be exempted from public labour and allowed to work for their own benefit within a prescribed district.[34] Mary Ann Conroy, who had been sentenced to seven years at Glasgow in April 1835 and arrived in Van Diemen's Land in October that year, is a good case in point. She was assigned to a Mr. Green in Bothwell but within two years was married to William Williams, a freeman — having petitioned the Lieutenant-Governor for this indulgence.[35]

Surprisingly, family relationships from home were sometimes re-kindled by transportation. Some of the women had relations among the convict colonists of New South Wales and Van Diemen's Land. Catherine McFarlane, sent on the *Earl of Liverpool*, already had a brother, Dan, in New South Wales — transported 12 years previously; Helen Russell's brother, Robert, had gone free to Van Diemen's Land in 1829 — four years before her own arrival at Sydney on the *Buffalo*; while we noted earlier that Nancy Mooney had two sons, John and Henry, both transported five years before she herself arrived in the colony. Again, the case of Ann Knox is not without interest in this regard, for she and her step-brother, Andrew White, had been jointly convicted. He too had been sentenced to transportation and was expected to arrive in the colony soon after her.[36]

Although we have been able to cite a few interesting examples, personal case-histories of experiences in the colonies are even harder to reconstruct than lives at home — often because the record is so scant that it raises more questions than it answers. Take the case of Margaret Russell, a 27 year old housemaid, sentenced to 14 years at Glasgow in September 1824. She arrived at Sydney Cove on the *Midas* in December 1825 after a five month voyage. According to the note in the ship's indent her husband, William Ogilvie, was already in the colony, having arrived earlier on the *Minstral*. Margaret Russell subsequently appeared in the New South Wales census of 1828, then aged 29 and described as a government servant and nurse in the employ of Henry Radford of Paterson's Plains. A William Ogilvie was living free and farming at a place called Merton in the Hunter Valley. Was it Margaret's husband and had they been re-united?[37] Jean Wise, aged only 15 when convicted at Edinburgh of stealing some money, is another about whom we know more than most — mainly because of her secondary punishments. She arrived on the *Buffalo* in 1833 and subsequently committed a number of offences in the colony. She twice received stolen goods — in 1835 and 1838 — each time being sentenced to 6 months gaol. She later spent some time in the Female Factory at Parrammatta and in the Sydney Hospital, being granted a conditional pardon in 1844, when she would have been 26 years old. She had probably managed to stay out of trouble and maybe even married in the interim.[38]

In Van Diemen's Land records of conduct are more detailed and highlight the twin problems of indiscipline and prostitution among convict women. A good case in point is that of Elizabeth Clark, sentenced at Edinburgh to 14 years for theft and transported in the *Sir Charles Forbes*, arriving in Van Diemen's Land in January 1827. By the time she had seen out ten years of her sentence she had been in trouble no fewer than 16 times for offences which included: being absent without leave; absconding; drunk and disorderly conduct; violent assault; keeping a disorderly house; found dancing in a public house; found in a public house bed with her master; having men on her mistress's premises; and leaving service under pretence of illness. Nevertheless she was ultimately granted a ticket-of-leave and may well have reformed her ways.[39]

While many of the fallen women among the 200 were wrongly regarded as prostitutes, others had been earning their living 'on the town' for long periods — mainly in Glasgow and Edinburgh — before committing the crimes that sent them to Australia. Johannah Laing or Reid, the Edinburgh brothel keeper, had an interesting career, as the brothel provided ideal cover for theft. She and her associates, Catherine McIntosh and sisters, Mary and Helen Barnet 'four of the worst characters of the kind in Edinburgh', operated a notorious brothel in Leith Street. Laing, 24 years old, had been born in Aberdeen and was married to a traveller with whom she was estranged. Here associates were apparently all country girls, moved to town. Their victim on the night of 23 November 1843 was James Fraser, a young engineer, whom Helen Barnet had picked up earlier outside the Theatre Royal. On discovering he had been robbed of a £2 note and 2 sovereigns, Fraser got the constables and all four women were arrested. Subsequently both Laing and Barnet were transported to Van Diemen's Land on the *Tasmania* — but whether or not they continued their life of prostitution is unknown.[40] Much of the women's story will never be told. Although their origins and crimes are generally well-documented, their journey to and arrival in the colonies meticulously entered up in ships' indents and in muster rolls, many disappear from the record soon after arrival in Australia. Some found it more difficult than others to eschew their former lifestyle and hence continued their criminal activities in Sydney or Hobart rather than Glasgow or Edinburgh. Some were almost certainly condemned to the same sort of drudgery as assigned or government servants they would have experienced at home in domestic or country service. Some were able to marry soon after arrival and quickly merged into the lower ranks of colonial society. Most of those who stayed out of trouble could expect a ticket-of-leave within a few years — four on average — and might later be awarded a conditional pardon. While we have no information on 19 out of the 50-odd women transported on the *Buffalo* in 1833, 25 we know of ultimately received conditional pardons and another six held tickets-of-leave.[41]

Were the Scottish convict women the worst of a bad lot as officials of the time maintained? The fact that many had previous convictions and the traditional reluctance of Scottish judges to resort to transportation combine to suggest the truth of this assertion. English and Irish women were often transported for relatively trivial offences — or at least had shorter criminal records! Van Diemen's Land certainly seems to have received the worst offenders — many of them Scots. Whatever the truth of the matter, the convict women were condemned to an uncertain fate on the other side of the world, at worst virtual slaves of a brutal penal system, at best enforced settlers in a male-dominated colony with an acute female-shortage. As Lloyd Robson's pioneering study of *The Convict Settlers of Australia* demonstrated so vividly, the convict's prospects at home were probably gloomy.[42] So transportation gave the opportunity for a fresh start in a new environment. The surviving evidence on the 200 suggests that a minority at least grasped that opportunity and made some sort of new life for themselves in the colonies. To add more flesh to the bare bones of the story sketched here could call for a major exercise in archive linkage between Britain and Australia. Such a project would undoubtedly help to explain a great deal about the social context of crime and the lives of working class women during the first half of the ninetenth century.

Notes:

[1] This article first appeared in *Jorals* Vol.8 No.1. 1988. I am most grateful to colleagues and associates in the Department of History, University of Sydney for helpful advice and to the Australian Studies Centre, University of London for funding a Visiting Fellowship to Australia in 1985. I acknowledge the assistance of congenial staff in the Public Record Office, London; Scottish Record Office, Edinburgh; National Library of Scotland, Edinburgh; State Archives of New South Wales, Sydney; State Library and the Mitchell Library, Sydney; State Archives of Tasmania; Hobart; and the La Trobe Library of the State Library of Victoria, Melbourne.

[2] I. Donnachie, 'Scottish Criminals and Transportation to Australia, 1786-1852', *Scottish Economic and Social History* vol.4, 1984, pp.21-38; I. Donnachie. 'The Convicts of 1830: Scottish Criminals Transported to New South Wales', *Scottish Historical Review*, vol. LXV, 1, 1986, pp.34-47.

[3] Based on data derived from Convict Indents and Musters in the Archives Office of NSW (AONSW) — cited fully in later references. For the two earliest transportees in the cohort see AONSW 4/4003A, Indents 1788-1800.

[4] AONSW X642A, Printed Indent of *Surrey* 1842; ibid. 4/4016, Indent of *Earl of Liverpool* 1831; ibid. 4/4018, Indent of *Buffalo*, 1833; Donnachie, 'Scottish Criminals', p.26.

[5] On convict origins and convict society generally see L. L. Robson, *The Convict Settlers of Australia*, Melbourne, 1965; A. G. L. Shaw, *Convicts and the Colonies*, London, 1966; and J. B. Hirst, *Convict Society and its Enemies*, Sydney, 1983. On women in particular see H. S. Payne, 'A Statistical Study of Female Convicts in Tasmania', *Tasmanian Historical Research Association Papers and Proceedings*, vol. 9, no.2, 1961, pp.56069; D. Beddoe, *Welsh Convict Women*, Barry, 1979; J. Williams, 'Irish Female Convicts and Tasmania', *Labour History* (Australia), 44, 1983, pp.1.17.

[6] Though there was no actual test of literacy and the data need to be treated with some caution (because some convicts certainly lied), they nevertheless remain valuable. On early literacy and literacy testing in the Scottish context see R. Houston, 'The Literacy Myth?' Illiteracy in Scotland 1630-1760, *Past and Present*, 1982, pp.81-102; and his *Scottish Literacy and the Scottish Identity*, Cambridge, 1985.

[7] For Mary Kelly see AONSW 4/4016, Indent of *Earl of Liverpool*, 1831.

[8] For Johannah Reid or Laing see Mitchell Library (ML) A1722, Indent of *Tasmania*, 1844.

[9] Robson, pp.76-82; Donnachie, 'Scottish Criminals', p.32-3.

[10] For Jane Milne see AONSW 4/4009A, Indent of *Midas*, 1825.

[11] For Nancy Moonie ibid. 4/4018, Indent of *Buffalo*; and Catherine McGilvray ibid. 4/4016, Indent of *Earl of Liverpool*.

[12] For Agnes McMenamy ibid. 4/4018, Indent of *Buffalo*; Elizabeth McDonald ibid. 4/4014, Indent of *Lord Melville*, 1829.

[13] Scottish Record Office (SRO), Records of the Lord Advocate's Dept. AD/14/176, Precognitions in the case of Margaret Russell and William Ogilvie, 1824; AONSW 4.4009A, Indent of *Midas*.

[14] AONSW 4/4018, Indent of *Buffalo*; ML A1722, Indent of *Tasmania*

[15] SRO, AD14/32/6, Precognitions in the case of Janet Stewart, 1832; AONSW 4/4018, Indent of *Buffalo*.

[16] For Helen Stewart or Murphy see AONSW 4/4016, Indent of *Earl of Liverpool*.

[17] SRO, AD14/222, Precognitions in the case of Andrew White and Ann Knox, 1830.

[18] Shaw, pp.36-7 and 164-5 and Donnachie 'Scottish Criminals' p.23 both indicate that the relatively lenient attitude of Scottish judges was partly influenced by a mixture of ideas about natural justice and economics of transportation.

[19] SRO, AD14/22/45, Precognitions in the case of Euphemia McPhail, 1822, AONSW 4/4009, Indent of *Mary III*, 1823.

[20] SRO, AD14/30/139, Precognitions in the case of Helen Murphy, 1830; AONSW 4/4016, Indent of *Earl of Liverpool*.

[21] SRO, AD14/30/210, Precognitions in the case of Betty Ann Blair, 1830.

[22] See in particular the Indent of the *Earl of Liverpool*, *Buffalo* and *Tasmania*. Children also accompanied earlier transportees.

[23] AONSW 4/4009 and 4/4018, Indents of *Mary III* and *Buffalo*.

[24] Donnachie, 'Scottish Criminals', pp.23-4; Beddoe, pp.85-91.

[25] PP 1810 XIV Account of Male and Female Persons Transported to New South Wales 1787-1809; W. B. Johnson, *The English Prison Hulks*, Chichester, 1970; S. McConville, *A History of English Prison Administration*,. vol.11, 1750-1877, London, 1981, p.136; ML, A1722, Log of *Tasmania*.

[26] Robson, pp.76-82. For another interesting view see M. Sturma, 'Eye of the Beholder: the Stereotype of Women Convicts, 1788-1852', *Labour History* (Australia), 34, 1978, pp.3-10.

[27] AONSW 4/4009, Muster of Female Convicts on Transport Ship *Mary III*; ibid. 4/4009A, Indent of *Midas*.

[28] ML A1722 Log Book of Hire Convict Ship *Tasmania*, 1844 for this and subsequent account.

[29] J. Ritchie (ed.) *The Evidence to the Bigge Report: New South Wales Under Governor Macquarrie, Vol.1, The Oral Evidence*, Melbourne, 1971, pp.122-4, evidence of James Hunter, in charge of Convict Transports 1818-20.

[30] AONSW 4/2180.3, Papers re: the Assignment of Female Convicts per *Buffalo*, 1833.

[31] See A. Salt, *These Outcast Women: The Parramatta Female Factory 1821-1848*, Sydney, 1984, for a useful account of this institution.

32   AONSW COD246, Census of NSW, 1828; ibid. 4.4009A, Indent of *Midas*; her Conditional Pardon, 39/1468, 1839.

33   *NSW Government Gazette*, 7 January, 4 February, 18 March, 10 June 1835. Estimate of overall numbers and annual averages from *NSW Government Gazette*, 1832-40. The fate of the runaways is discussed in C. Sweeney, *Transported in Place of Death: Convicts in Australia*, South Melbourne, 1981, pp.-142-151; and by Hirst, pp.125-7, 140-42.

34   Robson concludes that marriage rates among women were not as high as might be expected and Hirst, pp.79-80 generally agrees. This view was certainly expressed by many in evidence to the Select Committee on Transportation, PP 1837 XIX.

35   PP 1837-38 XLII Communications re: Convict Discipline in Van Diemen's Land, App. 15, Abstract of Petitions for Marriage, p.29.

36   AONSW 4/4016, Indent of *Earl of Liverpool* and 4/4018, Indent of *Buffalo*. Janet Anderson, sentenced at Edinburgh in 1822, is another interesting case, because she was allowed to leave Van Diemen's Land for Sydney with her husband, who arrived free at Hobart in 1828, AONSW 4/4008, Indent of *Lord Sidmouth*, 1823.

37   AONSW 4/4009A, Indent of *Midas*; ibid. COD246, Census of NSW, 1828.

38   AONSW 4/4018, Bound Indent of *Buffalo*; Conditional Pardon 44/1633.

39   PP 1837-38 XLII App. 15, Abstract of Petitions for Ticket-of-Leave, p.70.

40   SRO, AD14/44/222, Precognitions in the case of Joan Laing or Reid, 1844; ML A1722. Indent of *Tasmania*.

41   AONSW 4.4018, Conduct Reports of the *Buffalo*, 1833.

42   Robson, pp.128-9 and 145-6.

CHAPTER 7

A People's Plan: A Study of the 'Max Lock' Survey & Plan for Middlesbrough, 1943 and 1946

Jim Leonard

At a time when many apsects of planning are being questioned and often attacked, and when the whole relationship between government, locality, and people is being redefined, it is interesting to compare a situation well within living memory when a totally different atmosphere prevailed. I refer to the attitudes and hopes for local, regional and national planning which emerged during the Second World War, and found a kind of fruition in the immediate post war years. My example is that of Middlesbrough and its adoption of the Max Lock Plan, officially called the *Middlesbrough Survey and Plan.*

This topic will be examined in three phases. Firstly, the long-term context in which the Survey and Plan took place; secondly, attention will be given to Max Lock and his team: the composition, methods, strategies and final conclusions; and finally some long-term views of this episode will be considered. In this last regard I am fortunate in that I have access to some recent views on the matter by members of the original team.

Middlesbrough's town planning history (be it comprehensive or in-cremental) is one to inspire both awe and despair. From its inception in the second quarter of the nineteenth century, the town has presented a kind of Janus vision. One much publicised ingredient, both then and ever since, was the original town plan, drawn up by Richard Otley[1] and commissioned by the father of the town, Joseph Pease.[2] This grid-iron pattern influenced later extensions to the town and can still be seen today.[3] Conversely there is the tradition , equally remarked upon, of non-planning, and sometimes summed up in the phrase, the Infant Hercules. This description has often been used by nineteenth century politicians and historians to obscure rather than to enlighten the recipient's vision.[4] It was at a unique phase of its experience that Middlesbrough sought its most comprehensive and far-sighted town plan to date.

The years of the Second World War presented a mass of contrasts for the British people. Alongside the fears, toil and grief were the hopes and apparent possibility of creating anew the quality of national life in a spirit of unity and social equality. For Middlesbrough along with all the other towns that had over-specialised in the nineteenth-century staple industries, the post war boom had soon given way to inter-war depression.[5] Not only were there all the problems of a speedily constructed urban fabric but the wherewithal to rectify this was not apparently available. The economic largesse that had enabled the entrepreneurs of Victorian Middlesbrough to build not just one but two towns (the first based on coal, the second on iron), had given way to depression, poverty, squalor and under-privilege.[6] The war however created full employment, and enabled the town's leaders to think about far-reaching reconstruction after hostilities.

Serious destruction by bombing in the early years of the war forced some towns to propose large-scale plans for urban renewal. Middlesbrough was not heavily bombed but the quality of its development cried out for renewal.[7] Some modification had occurred in the inter-war years but not a lot. If we look at a working scenario of the impetus behind inter-war urban change, Middlesbrough does not compare well with many other industrial urban centres.[8] Taking housing as the most obvious example, one can detect mixed attitudes to tackling glaring problems, both in the public and private sectors. Looking at Council housing first, we can note some of the attitudes and achievements made possible by the range of housing acts from Addison to Greenwood.

A 1926 census of housing over-crowding showed that only 108 new houses were needed to overcome the worst level of congestion in the town. In retrospect such an amount seems ludicrous but at the time it was said that Council schemes had already created the near completion of 86 of this required number, and therefore 'there is at last a real prospect of quite intolerable overcrowding being banished from Middlesbrough'. It was stressed that 'the town may very well be among the very first in Great Britain to make such a boast'. It was shown that the houses built by the Council since the Armistice reached almost 2000, and thus 'the next housing service which awaits the Middlesbrough Corporation is a systematic clearance of the slums, as distinct from the banishment of the general over-crowding evil'. Nevertheless three years later a radical councillor, Mrs. Coates-Hansen, showed that over-crowding persisted.

She quoted a remark to the local press that had been made to her by a grocer from one of the northern wards. He had voiced the cheerful platitude that they, the grocers, were 'the butlers of the poor people' and that such shops were 'their pantries'. The councillor's remarks confirmed the gloomy findings of the Sanatorium Committee which confirmed that 75% of cases who returned home with the promise of health, died through bad diet and environment. She described one house in which twenty-four people lived in four rooms (in one case eight children sleeping in one bed) and paid a total of 36s a week in rent. She showed scores of letters which described the terrible conditions of housing in the worst parts of town.

The councillor invited a reporter to look out of the window at a tap in the middle of the street; this tap served all the eighty-five inhabitants of Durham Place. Although she had protested against this unsanitary practice in 1912 she added that 'women still fill their bread-bowls at it'. Returning to the grocer's remarks, Mrs. Coates-Hansen pointed out that the shopkeeper was cynically right. There were hundreds of homes in Middlesbrough where over-crowding precluded a pantry. She showed that food was often stored under beds, so that even if people could afford to buy food they had no real place to store it. Consequently they bought in ounces and pennyworths, and the grocer's shop really was their pantry. Her advocacy was for far more houses to be built, especially of the three bedroom variety.

Within three years of this particular analysis of the over-crowding problem, the Council could show that since 1921 the town had built nearly 3000 houses at a cost of £1,500,000. Falls in the house building prices were given as one cause of the speed-up in building. It was shown that houses in Acklam Garden City, built in 1921, cost over £1000 for the three bedroom parlour type, whereas the current three bedroomed house on the Whinney Banks Estate cost £350. Nevertheless some considered that enough had already been done. When the Housing Committee proposed to build 200 houses and twelve bungalows, Councillor Carter asked the Committee to call a halt as far as building operations on a large scale were concerned. He maintained that the town had 'done more in re-housing than any other municipality in the North of England, and that the Corporation would get out of its depth'.

Almost at the end of the inter-war period the town could claim some limited success in its five-year slum clearance programme. This contemplated the demolition of over 1100 houses and the displacement of over 5000 people. At the start of 1938 the town could boast that since the Greenwood Act, fifty clearance orders and one compulsory purchase order had been confirmed by the Health Ministry. This meant that 756 properties had been or were being demolished, and that 3371 persons had been rehoused from slum clearance areas. The current batch of orders covered areas on the north side of the town, between the railway and the river. Chronic adverse reports from the Medical Officer of Health high-lighted some of the characteristics of this sort of old housing. The fabric was decayed and in bad repair, and dampness was general. Air space was lacking, the streets were often narrow, and yard areas were deficient in size. Many of these yards were communal with a common water supply and sanitary accommodation. The lack of an internal water supply was usual, and, for the most part, baths, sinks, and suitable food stores were absent.

Nevertheless there were objections to such demolitions, mostly from property owners. Usually a three-fold strategy accompanied such resistance. Firstly there was an assertion that the property was fit for human habitation; or that the property was to be converted for business purposes; and finally that the property would be repaired. The Town Clerk usually pointed out that 'sympathy for the owners cannot cloud the issue and condemn tenants of working-class property to continue to live under intolerable conditions'. Yet notwithstanding such realism a final submission by the owners' representative included the statement that the end of slum clearance in the town had been reached, and that the owners thought that the Corporation officials, encouraged by previous successes, had gone further than they need have done.

****

Turning now to private housing, one can see parallel contradictions. In the mid-thirties a large scale suburban development was undertaken along Green Lane in Acklam. This scheme was reported as holding a 'unique place in the country' on account of its rapid execution. In spite of some of the aspects of this estate revealing the speculative builder at his most unimaginative, many points came in for praise. One reporter, for example, had played tennis only the year before where the suburb was then being developed. He mused that 'few people

would have visualised when they were serving love-all on the ground last year...
that within twelve months not only would houses have sprung up on those very
courts, but that people would be living in them, cultivating charming gardens
where the ball then bounced'. These somewhat select houses sold for £550,
boasting a tiled bathroom, ample cupboard accommodation in a spacious
kitchen, and a good sized washhouse; features such as these enabled the local
press to stress that a 'woman might have planned them, they are so
conveniently arranged'. The value of these houses was founded on a wide range
of refinements; from the 'stainless taps and bakelite switches and door fittings
to the Middlesbrough-made steel casements which make the windows a picture
of neatness'. Attractions which converted the 'passer-by' into the 'looker-on',
who in many cases became the 'stopper-on'.

Nevertheless only a few months earlier in reference to this and similar
developments, a correspondent castigated the growing suburbia as the 'new
ugliness'. With no green belt provision in Middlesbrough, the once pleasant
fields and beautiful roads that led out of the town had given way to ribbon
development. Even worse was a prevalent house-type; a 'villa of pretentious
tastelessness that is being repeated over and over again along all the main
roads'. This writer was amazed that 'with all the regional planning schemes and
all the powers possessed by the local authorities' the ordinary citizen remained
so powerless. Given the great opportunity that Middlesbrough had had in the
previous century to create a well planned town, the writer feared that the same
mistakes would be repeated in the 1930s because those in authority were blind
to the fact that 'aesthetic values are real values, and are as important to the
community as commercial ones or the values set up by individual greed'. This
particular contribution closed with the hope that the powers-that-be would
open their eyes to some of the really good building schemes both here and on
the Continent.[9] It was sentiments such as these, unfettered in the years
immediately following the Battle of Britain, that provided the impetus behind
schemes on the heroic scale of the Max Lock appointment.

In contrast was the rather mediocre performance in inter-war housing on
Middlesbrough's part. For example, nowhere was there the almost God-like
conception of any scheme such as Quarry Hill Flats;[10] not only were flats
treated with suspicion but were positively shunned.[11] Of the three substantial
suburban estates that the Council created in this period, much forethought was
lacking, although here the town was not unique.[12] Similarly private housing
provision augmented the Victorian and Edwardian suburbs as well as
stretching the essential make-up of the town well beyond the official municipal
boundaries. As with the corporation estates, the lack of true comprehensive
development made for new problems as well as apparently solving old ones.[13]

Not surprisingly few developments of note appeared in the town centre.
Some new departmental stores came but were restricted to the currently
accepted modes, unlike a number of grander creations in nearby centres.[14]
Similarly the main shopping street of the town detracted from, rather than
enhanced, the ability of the town centre to meet the growing needs of a deeper
consumer market: instead of providing a larger scale, compact development,
this main street, Linthorpe Road, took shoppers away from the centre. The road

developed piecemeal in a southerly direction and so stretched its facilities far too thinly.[15] At the same time attempts to modernise shop fronts tended to present a superficial if not a transient image.[16] Similarly while some towns sought to meet the newly developing traffic congestion of the inter-war years[17] by bold schemes of road widening,[18] Middlesbrough tended to allow development that often exacerbated this inner city problem. However at the sub-regional level, the 1930s saw a new road bridge over the Tees slightly up river from the notorious Transporter Bridge. This improvement in the western approaches to Middlesbrough[19] was matched by the town's first trunk road leading eastwards to the coastal settlement of Redcar.

Some new institutions did appear to meet new needs or at least to meet vastly changed former needs. In education Constantine Technical College was officially opened in 1930, and has remained the main academic institution in the Teesside sub-region ever since. Even here however, it is not hard to find aspects of the development which suggest that this innovation came too late and embodied too narrow a vision.[20] At a lighter level, a whole array of cinemas appeared throughout the town and both met and created an exploding popular demand.[21] When one considers the more established popular arts, both music and theatre fared badly in the town.[22]

It was thus as a town with many problems inherited from its recent as well as from its more distant past that Middlesbrough experienced the Second World War. Some solutions had been provided but the trend was often too little and too late. The same sort of rearguard approach epitomises the town's early reactions to the needs of war.[23] However, in 1943 a Reconstruction Committee was set up, and, following this, the town assumed an avant-garde position in post-war town planning.

****

The appointment of Max Lock as Planning Consultant, and the composition of his team, encompassed a number of historic quirks and ironies. The original suggestion for a Reconstruction Committee came from an independently minded member of the ruling Conservative Party, Eli Watley.[24] He further proposed that a Master Plan for post-war reconstruction be drawn up, somewhat in the manner of a number of fairly well publicised pre-war surveys by such practitioners as Adshead and Abercrombie.[25] The choice of the young and progressive Max Lock as Planning Consultant was better than the town fathers of Middlesbrough could have hoped for.[26] Other applicants for the post included Professor Abercrombie, and that scourge of tentacle-like suburbia, Clough William-Ellis.[27] Nevertheless the Reconstruction Committee agreed unanimously on Lock's appointment.

For an inclusive fee of 800 guineas Lock was to prepare a comprehensive report and survey for the replanning of the town. Particular reference was to be made to the reconstruction of the built-up areas of Middlesbrough, and proposals were to be included on the best use of undeveloped land. The comprehensive nature of the undertaking was stressed, as was the need to illustrate the survey, analysis and recommendations with plans and diagrams. The Council agreed to furnish all the data necessary and to cover the costs of office accommodation, maps, and staffing. The chairman of the committee, Sir William Crosthwaite, would give no estimate of how long the work would take nor what the costs would be apart from Lock's stated personal fee. It was recognised that Lock would have to deal with an area that was wider than the actual town boundaries, and, accordingly, his services would be placed at the disposal of the other Teesside authorities, in order to get a complete survey of the whole Teesside area, both north and south of the river. In the event the scope of the undertaking from its inauguration in March 1944 until the final presentation of the detailed reports in September 1945 never really extended beyond Middlesbrough.[28]

Lock's team with himself as Director and Town Planning Consultant fell into six uneven parts. Half consisted of four town planners and architects along with their twelve assistants. Then came a sociologist with five assistants, a geographer with four assistants, and finally a consultant analyst, a model maker with four assistants, a perspective artist, and a secretary with two assistants. Further help came from the Association for Planning and Regional Reconstruction, and from the Ministry of Information's Wartime Social Survey.[29] Some recent information by members of the team on background recruitment circumstances is given in the notes.[30] By the normally accepted standards of the time Lock's team members were young, came from a wide range of disciplines, and included a high proportion of women.[31]

Soon two further characteristics were evident. The team built up a close identity with each other and with the town on which they were working; from start to finish the commitment and enthusiasm that the team engendered did not flag. Lock himself recently recalled that 'Middlesbrough Corporation looked after us very well by letting us use a very nice house with ten or eleven bedrooms, so we could live as one team, with the same housekeeper who had been looking after me and some of my students in Hull.'[32] Another recalled that 'we all lived together at Moor Close in Linthorpe, and I think most of us were fired with what you might call the planning ethos which was just emerging out of wartime experiences'.[33] A third member noted that there was an enormous sense of commitment which manifested itself not only in the architects working at night at the end of a project', but also some of the young office staff putting in extra time without ever being asked or even being really part of the team.[34]

From the outset, the aim was to bring the study of urban needs to that degree of scientific method as would be applied to any other complex undertaking then relevant, such as the running of a large industry or the co-ordination of resources for the armed forces or the Home Front. The main thrust of the work came from three of the teams already mentioned: the architects and planners under Jessica Albery, the sociologists under Ruth Glass, and the geographers and economists under Arthur Smailes.[35] All the survey work was planned to be completed between March and December 1944, and from early 1945 the town planners and architects would remain in post for a time in order to complete the plan on the basis of the whole range of reports already submitted. These covered, for example, public health, education, youth and adult clubs, neighbourhood life, and retail shopping.[36] In addition to the actual survey work a vast amount of statistical information from many local government departments was collated by Lock and his colleagues.

It was considered very valuable to get information down in map form. Many sheets of statistics were finally reduced to maps. These were usually transparencies of standard size which could be superimposed on a particular locality in order to show an accumulation of particular characteristics. Such a breaking down of information in this way was considered essential in that the plan of the town could finally emerge on the basis of verified facts and proven needs. For the specific feed-back from the ordinary people four lots of questionnaires were used, in addition to a visit from a team member. There was firstly, a questionnaire for industrialists, another for shopkeepers, a third for club leaders, and finally a much more comprehensive one for households. For the latter, both the housewife and the chief wage-earner were consulted separately; this last survey was carried out by the Wartime Social Survey.[37] An example of the comparative information obtained can be seen from the following table:[38]

| Neighbour-hood (Population) | Rating for indices of: | | | |
	Neighbour-hood intergration	Geographical demarcation	Living conditions	Institutional equipment
St. Hild's (5399)	6	1	1	6
Whinney Banks (7079)	4	2	4	2
Mid Linthorpe (2408)	1	4	6	3

Source: Ruth Glass, *The Social Background of a Plan* (London, 1948) p.40.

The survey work was finished on time, and, from early 1945, the reports on the ten major aspects of the work were compiled together with planning proposals and a master-plan. In July 1945 a three week long exhibition was held in the town in order that the citizens could see the details of the survey and plan, and even at this late stage, make further suggestions.

Many sections of the local community were represented at this event. It was commonly felt that Lock had siezed on all the good points of the town and sought to eliminate all the bad ones. The Marquis of Zetland, who opened the exhibition, spoke of the need for more open space, better houses, greater facilities for cultural development and for recreation, and added that 'we want less grime, less dirt and no squalor'.[39] The Mayor declared that the day would go down in the history of Middlesbrough as a red letter day.[40] Mr. G. I. Pepler said that it must be obvious to all that only by team work based on survey and planning, could chaos and waste be avoided.[41]

Yet even at this euphoric stage there were notes of alarm. When the Council met to consider the mounting of this exhibition, some doubts as to cost were raised. The Council had already spent £7000 on the undertaking, and some members wanted to consider the implications of the Lock proposals more fully, at least before such proposals were seen by the public at large.[42] Nevertheless, Eli Watley once more came to the rescue and pleaded that the exhibition was essential as the public had a right to see, criticise and make recommendations.[43] Four months later some councillors raised similar objections in regard to the financing of the exhibition in London; this was on the grounds that 'the plan had been a means of condemnation on the town in that it suggested that Middlesbrough was tremendously behind the times'.[44] Once more the popular will prevailed and the exhibition was mounted in London with great success.

Lock's main recommendations were cast in three periods of time from the inception of the plan: five, fifteen and thirty years. Thus at the end of thirty years all the problems detected by Lock and his colleagues would have been dealt with, and moreover Lock considered that the actual building volume would hardly be greater than that of the previous thirty years. Regarding land use, it was proposed that the inner areas of the town be redeveloped at lower densities than then obtained; the shopping centre was to be regrouped; new estates were to be developed on the outskirts, and wedges of open space were to be brought through and between these estates right to the town centre. There was also to be a buffer of green space between the central housing areas and industry.

Regarding industry, the predominant iron and steel bases was to be augmented by new industries. Accordingly potential development areas in the sub-region were proposed for new locations. In transport, new road links were proposed in order to supplement the existing water and rail connections. The unsatisfactory mix of road traffic was to be reorganised into four categories: through traffic was to use new east/west arterial parkways, industrial traffic to use an improved road south of the railway line, main town traffic to use subsidiary radial roads, and finally local traffic to run on by-roads.

However the core of the problem facing the town was that of bad housing. This was to be cleared and redeveloped in three main phases whereby the very high densities then common were to be changed to forty-one to fifty persons per acre in the central areas, the same densities in the inner suburbs, and twenty-one to thirty in the outer suburbs. The layout of the houses was to be related to discernible neighbourhood patterns. Open spaces were to be created on a more equitable basis than formerly. New health services were to be provided, and the system of education re-organised and updated. Shops were to be rearranged into four kinds of groupings: the chief centres, the sub-centres, local centres, and strictly local centres. Finally the town centre was to be replanned around the late Victorian town hall with provision for cultural and entertainment centres, and zones for business, marketing and warehousing, as well as the provision of clubs, swimming-baths and car-parks.[45]

Ominously the Council did not immediately embrace this plan. New housing proposals were held up in the Autumn of 1945 because they did not conform to the Lock Plan. The newly formed Town Planning Committee pressed the Council to come to an early decision regarding the acceptance or otherwise of the Plan,[46] and by mid January 1946 the Council accepted the Plan in principle. Yet even then the former Mayor, a strong Lock supporter, said that he was not prepared to accept the proposals as the final plan on which Middlesbrough must develop. He was prepared to accept it as a splendid sketch plan on which they could build after much more consideration than had been possible to the present.[47] Not surprisingly the Plan was soon modified. Such modification followed the requirements of the 1947 Act which led to a new development plan for Middlesbrough in 1948.

****

Yet even now, after forty years, the Max Lock Plan will somehow not go away. It has become part of the local folk lore, and there is a lot of varied opinion about how much, if any, of the Lock Plan came into being, albeit under other guises. It is interesting in this respect to tease out the opinions of Lock himself and his immediate colleagues. Towards this end I will make use of two further visits to Middlesbrough by Lock.[48] The first was in 1968 when he was retained by a group of traders who were resisting the gradual denuding of shops in part of Linthorpe Road;[49] the second was a much more elaborate affair, when the aim of a three-day visit was to review the original Max Lock Plan. On this second occasion Lock was accompanied by other members of his original team.[50]

In 1968 Lock was asked his views on the development of the town in the twenty-odd years since he submitted his plan. He responded by expressing a profound disappointment. He went as far as to say that 'nothing has happened — and other places have been allowed to get in first'. Considering that the town had been given everything on a plate, he stressed that they had missed their chances. All the more since Middlesbrough had offered him the space to work in, but then found the very simplicity of his plan too complicated for their comprehension. He emphasised this point by saying that 'everyone tries to be too elaborate' instead of doing what suits themselves best; thus whereas Middlesbrough had taken a leading stance in post-war planning, it had subsequently allowed itself to be guided by what other people were doing.

Lock considered that his plan had stood the test of time. It had, in his opinion, been based on a really viable answer to the problem: it had been 'surgery which could be carried out without killing the patient', and in some ways echoing his feelings over twenty years previously, he noted that there had been nothing really drastic about the entire scheme.[51] As far as he could see, the only real omission was the lack of multi-storey car park provision, which could easily have been rectified. Turning to the outside appreciation of the survey and plan, he pointed out that his book was to be found in most of the chief planning departments, planning schools and universities in the world; sometimes in fact the work being referred to as their bible. He had moreover lectured at Harvard in 1957 entirely on his work in Middlesbrough; and similarly in Rio de Janeiro in 1960 where the Middlesbrough Plan was seen as the opposite side of the coin to that of Brazilia. Tactically he considered that it had been a pity that Middlesbrough had not kept in touch with the consultants to ensure continuity and capitalise on their researches.[52]

Twenty years later Lock and others from the original team were in Middlesbrough.[53] This visit must, in the circumstances, be the first and last major inquest into the Max Lock Plan. Fairly lengthy interviews brought three things to the surface in regard to the failure to adopt the 1946 Plan.

A major weakness on the part of the team was a lack of knowledge regarding future economic plans. The problem arose because of the war-time need for secrecy. Thus the strict control imposed on the steel and chemical industries also hid future schemes for expansion. Thus the planned development of ICI at Wilton was not disclosed to the team, and so 'this major underpinning of the whole area was a closed book to us'.[54] Moreover not only was this ICI expansion being considered during the time that the team was working in Middlesbrough, but massive expansion to the steel producing capacity of Dorman Long's were being planned.[55]

At a more general level the 1947 Act came in for some blame. This particular milestone in British town planning had led to a build up of elements of bureaucracy whose relative inexperience could mean delays. In the case of Middlesbrough there had been euphoria following the acceptance of the Plan, public enthusiasm, and financial promises. Lord Greenwood had said that they, the Government, would 'pump millions in' to see the plan carried out. Nevertheless nothing was done.

Following the 1947 Act, Middlesbrough Council appointed a planning staff. As a consequence the Plan didn't get off the ground because of joint resistance by these officers and their Council. The original team considered that these new appointees were conscious of the fact that they 'were the planners now'. To implement the Plan would have meant a lot of administration that the planners did not understand, having not done it before. On the other hand the Council did not want to pay an independent team to carry through the Plan when they were already paying the salaries of their own planning officers. Consequently most of the advantages that the town could have derived from the services of the team, free of all administration and procedure, were largely thrown away.[56] Lock himself summed up this by suggesting that it was 'a sad case of arrested development of the best made post-war plan "of mice and men" and women'.[57]

There are many ways of looking at this seemingly spectacular failure on the part of the Middlesbrough Council. One could trace a kind of historical continuity in the town's urban development whereby the possession of a plan was more important than any implementation, where in fact civil rhetoric mattered more than bricks and mortar. It could also be suggested that the wholesale reconstruction of a town centre was never really on, except in the case of badly bombed city centres. Middlesbrough opted instead to be in no way exceptional, and move with or slightly behind prevailing trends. Development has been incremental and sporadic, and some responsibility must lie with the radically changing local government status of the town over the last twenty years.

****

The town looks far more modern now than in the late war years but not in the way that Lock intended. Middlesbrough has really become like many other

places which feature such developments as new shopping centres, multi-storey car-parks, and substantial tracts of city centre pedestrianisation, in some ways a further extension of that shift to sameness that Asa Briggs detected in the late nineteenth century Victorian city.

Yet in spite of everything, the Max Lock document retains an importance in a number of ways. A kind of historical continuity was preserved in that the strong Quaker element of the local team resembled that of Joseph Pease and his colleagues who established the town in the first place. However, apart from the vastly different social context in which the two groups operated, the Lock team brought a special kind of socially aware, feminine scrutiny to this rather insensitive and very masculine town. For many of these team members, their eighteen or so months of work and residence in Middlesbrough changed their lives irrevocably. They had seen bad housing before, but not in such stark proximity.[58] Finally, the document remains as an illustration of those enthusiastic values that came out of the Second World War; values that we can compare and contrast with those of our own times, and remind ourselves that sadly, many parts of that post-war vision never became reality.

Notes:

[1] Richard Otley was agent for the owners of the Middlesbrough Estate, the founder firm of Middlesbrough. For details of his plan see William Lillie, *The History of Middlesbrough* (Middlesbrough, 1968).

[2] For a standard account of the life and works of Pease see *Lillie*; for a more critical assessment of Pease and a full biography see J. W. Leonard, 'Urban development and population growth in Middlesbrough 1831-71' (unpublished D. Phil. thesis, University of York, 1975).

[3] Many nineteenth century booster historians have praised the symmetry of the original town's grid-iron layout, while ignoring the many imperfections of early infilling. Grid-iron simplicity and convenience predominated later nineteenth century growth, and gave the town centre, in the eyes of some observers, an American appearance, while others saw only monotony.

[4] The 'Infant Hercules' remark was part of an after dinner speech made by Gladstone, as Chancellor of the Exchequer, in Middlesbrough in 1862. The remark really referred to the spread of industry in the town since 1850 but was soon adapted as being praise for the urban growth also.

[5] Even in this period prior to the First World War, Middlesbrough's backwardness had not gone unnoticed in academic journals. See, for example, F. Tillyard, 'English Town Development in the Nineteenth Century', *The Economic Journal*, 23 (1913). Here Middlesbrough's public health provisions are compared unfavourably with those of Birmingham, and even more unfavourably with those of Leicester.

[6] For the shock horror of an outsider's first impression of the town in the mid-twenties see D. Goldring, *Gone Abroad* (London, 1926); and for a no less horrifying impression from the late thirties see G. Orwell, *Keep the Aspidistra Flying* (Penguin reprint, 1962), pp.98, 102, 107.

[7] There is occasional discussion in the town as to how heavily or lightly Middlesbrough was bombed; opinion varies widely. For an authoritative account

see A. Robinson and A. Scott, *Middlesbrough at War: 1939-1945, the Home Front* (Middlesbrough, 1986), for a detailed account of how the town prepared for and experienced early bombing see G. W. Bailey, 'Preparing for the Blitz' (unpublished M. A. dissertation, Teesside Polytechnic, 1988).

[8] Note the sweeping changes in Leeds during this period. See F. J. Fowler, 'Urban Renewal, 1918-1966', in *Leeds and its Region* edited by M. W. Beresford and G. R. J. Jones (Leeds, 1967), and a later amplified account M. Meadowcroft, 'The years of Political Transition, 1914-39' in *The History of Modern Leeds* edited by D. Fraser (Manchester, 1980). In this latter account Meadowcroft describes the Leeds changes as a period of innovation, a phrase that not even the most loyal citizen could apply to Middlesbrough.

[9] *North Eastern Daily Gazette* (hereafter *NEDG*), 30th July 1926, 21st February, 1929, and 5th December, 1932, *Northern Echo* (hereafter *NE*) 22nd November, 1932 and 26th January, 1938.

[10] For the scale and conception of this scheme see A. Ravetz, *Model Estate* (London 1974).

[11] At the beginning of the thirties the Plans Committee objected to a scheme by a private developer to convert business premises into residential flats for the poor, especially as the conversion was in the old, northern part of town. The deputy town clerk pointed out that neither the Housing, Plans nor Sanitary Committees could prevent this legally correct scheme, as, in spite of objections, the builder would no doubt go on with the work, *NEDG* 19th March 1931. Similarly in the middle of the decade the Housing Committee were reminded of a low rise experiment in Dacre Street, also in the old town where flats were built primarily for riverside workers but only one such worker was actually in residence. It was only when the income standard of the applicants had been raised, and the catchment area extended as far as Billingham, that the development had been filled. *NE* 26th February, 1935. In some respects, this false start resembles the similar hopes in Leeds in regard to market workers occupying Quarry Hill Flats.

[12] For some of the mobility problems of the residents of two large inter-war Council estates see R. Glass, *The Social Background of a Plan* (London, 1948), and for the even more serious problem of relative malnutrition caused by having to pay higher rents see G. C. M. McGonigle and J. Kirby, *Poverty and Public Health* (London, 1936).

[13] See comments by *Glass* on high degrees of privacy but low provision of services in the private housing developments in the southern parts of the town.

[14] Note for example the opening of Lewis's store in Leeds in 1932 following earlier developments in Liverpool, Birmingham and Sheffield. A. Briggs *Friends of the People* (London, 1956).

[15] See comments by *Glass* on the linear pull of Linthorpe Road which detracted from the more desirable nucleation of Middlesbrough's centre.

[16] A writer who spent part of her early professional life in the town, described the main streets as giving a sense of impermanence, and looking as if most of the shops had been erected hastily, like a 'set for a film'. N. Jacob 'Middlesbrough: Child of England's greatness but no bonnie bairn', *Yorkshire Life Illustrated*, II (1957), 4, pp.13-14.

[17] For general information see C. L. Mowatt, *Britain Between the Wars* (London, 1955); and J. Tetlow & A. Goss, *Homes, Towns & Traffic* (London, 1965).

18 See for example the development of the Headrow, Leeds in *Meadowcroft*.

19 Almost inevitably the new bridge itself became congested with the continued build up of traffic.

20 For analysis of this development see J. W. Leonard, *Constantine College* (Middlesbrough, 1981).

21 See R.E. Flavell, 'The development of the cinema with special reference to its establishment in Middlesbrough' (unpublished B. A. dissertation, Teesside Polytechnic, 1984).

22 In spite of the beer and football image of the town in the inter-war period, Middlesbrough was the first municipality to create a 'little theatre' in the post-war period. For details see *Lillie*.

23 See *Bailey*.

24 For a brief account of some of the main personalities, including Watley, in this dramatic phase of the town's fortunes, see D. Walsh, 'Planning for Peace: the Middlesbrough Experience' (unpublished B. A. dissertation, Teesside Polytechnic, 1988). This author's own experience as a district councillor gave him useful insights for this piece of work.

25 For much of the work of these pioneers in the Teesside area in the inter-war period see D. Gunby, 'The south Teesside joint town planning committee: the early years, 1920-1930' (working paper, November 1981), and 'Statutory town planning in the 1920's: the experience of Thornaby 1922-26' (working paper, December 1981). This author is currently Implementation Group Leader, Economic Development Division, Cleveland County Council.

26 For short accounts of Lock's appointment see *Walsh*, and V. Cunningham, 'Middlesbrough's housing plans and achievements, 1945-1951' (unpublished B. A. dissertation, Teesside Polytechnic, 1984). Sadly Max Lock died on 2nd April 1988; for details of his career before and after his Middlesbrough appointment see various obituaries in the serious and professional press.

27 See particularly his work in *England and the Octopus* (London, 1928), and *Britain and the Beast*, (London, 1937).

28 In regard to the failure to extend the scope of the undertaking, Lock commented on this when interviewed in Middlesbrough over forty years later. He agreed that the planning team pushed for a remit to cover the whole of Cleveland, but the nearest that they came to this was at the end of the Middlesbrough work. They were then snapped up by the Hartlepools. Thus the team crossed the river. Afterwards they went south to Portsmouth to do a sub-regional scheme, and finally to Bedford, ending their shared experience as a kind of 'travelling circus'. This interview was held at Dorman Museum, Middlesbrough, on 3rd April 1987, hereafter cited as DM.

29 For personal details see M. Lock, *The Middlesbrough Survey and Plan* (Middlesbrough, 1947) p.7.

30 The first major influence on Lock was not an architect but a sociologist, Patrick Geddes, who favoured the social survey as the starting point rather than the secretiveness of many architects of that time, and the mechanical nature of many of the grand designs of the engineer. He had already supervised a civic diagnosis of Hull and translated the information in map form. However the planning stage was not carried out. Instead Lock preferred the challenge of Middlesbrough; a town

more suitable for his scope than the larger and more complex city of Hull.

Griselda Rowntree's background was that of a young social scientist rather than a planner. This was her first job after graduating in modern greats at Oxford. She knew of Lock through family connections, and, after meeting him socially, was invited to join the team.

Barbara Foster Sutton was working for the Wartime Social Survey, currently on a household survey of Middlesbrough. Contact with Lock was made, and within a short time, she was invited to work alongside Griselda Rowntree and others as an assistant to Ruth Glass, who herself came from the Association for Planning and Regional Reconstruction.

Jessica Albery qualified as a planner just before coming to the town. She'd studied in the evenings at Regent Street Polytechnic, where, as part of her course, she had to do a plan of the town. She chose her father's constituency, Gravesend, and, following this experience of despoilation by the cement industry, she felt qualified to participate in the Middlesbrough endeavour.

All this information from DM.

31 The youthfulness came both from Lock's preferences and the circumstances of the wartime call-up. The range of disciplines reflected Lock's interpretation of the outlook of Geddes. The large proportion of females came from the war situation of women doing 'men's jobs'. Jessica Albery suggested that without the shortage of qualified men, women such as herself would never have had these career opportunities. She went on to join the newly formed Ministry of Town and Country Planning.

32 DM. In 1944 a *Picture Post* article included a photograph with the caption 'The team lives together too', explaining that while the survey continued, the specialists live in Middlesbrough, identifying themselves with the town as a living organism. 'How to play your town'. *Picture Post*, 28th October, 1944.

33 Griselda Rowntree went on to emphasise that people were living for something beyond their own immediate interests, and felt that resources could be planned for peace as well as war. She added that the ethos gripped many of them, and made participation in the survey and plan such an exciting venture at that time. DM

34 Jessica Albery was here referring to the fact that they 'recruited two very young things from the High School to come in and do the typing and secretarial work, and they came into the office very early too. DM

35 Currently on loan from London University where he lectured in geography.

36 It is interesting to note how aspects of the work related to other parts, and, in fact, sometimes changed their form. Griselda Rowntree looked at education (not so much the quality which was suffering from wartime constraints), but at relative opportunities. Not too surprising she found that children from the poor northern parts of the town had almost no chance of secondary education, whilst children from the Council estates had more chance, and children from the southern private suburbs had most. Much of her work in this aspect of the survey was concerned with the incidence of head lice. She noted that 'this was very common in those days — people had fewer baths in the home and less opportunity to wash... and the incidence of head infestation was a measure of the adequacy or otherwise of housing circumstances'. DM

37 Due to the good Offices of the Ministry of Information, this Wartime Social Survey group consisted of twenty-five female investigators. They sampled 1400 families, one in twenty-three households, and recorded facts and opinions from

both housewives and wage-earners on housing, shopping, transport, recreation, and town improvements. For the specific report on shopping see Barbara Foster Sutton, 'Retail trade' in *Lock*; for the household survey see D. Chapman, *A Social Survey of Middlesbrough* (London, 1945); and for a full analysis of this data by the chief sociologist see *Glass*.

38 This is a shortened version of the original. St. Hilda's was the original coal port, and one of the most run-down parts of the town. However, the close-packed nature of the housing lay behind the high dregree of neighbourliness, and its close proximity to the town centre made for ample institutional equipment. Whinney Banks was a Council estate immediately to the west of affluent Linthorpe. It retained some of the neighbourliness of the working-class areas of the town, enjoyed the benefits of low density housing, but was located far south of significant institutional resources. Linthorpe was the main middle-class area within the borough boundary. Here privacy was at a premium, living conditions were good, and a regular public transport system, apart from private vehicles, was available for journeys to the centre, where the main institutional facilities could be sampled.

39 NEDG, 16th July, 1945.

40 The Mayor, Councillor R. R. Kitching, was himself a qualified architect, and gave Lock his fullest support throughout the survey and plan.

41 Pepler was Chief Technical Officer to the Ministry of Town and Country Planning.

42 Final cost actually came to £7269, and was made up as follows: staffing £5850, accommodation £988, modernising the O.S. map £351, and taking the atmospheric survey £80.

43 *NE*, 9th May, 1945.

44 *Evening Gazette* (hereafter *EG*), 11th September, 1945.

45 The fullest details are of course given in *Lock*.

46 *EG*, 26th November, 1945.

47 *EG*, 18th January, 1946.

48 This is not to imply that Lock did not make other visits to the area in a professional or social capacity. See for example an account of his appearance at Teesside Guild of Arts at Ormesby Hall in 1958 when reference was made to his plan and the overseas demand for his book. *EG*, 15th November, 1958.

49 Lock successfully helped this group of traders retain their premises on a section of the eastern side of Linthorpe Road. There had originally been a plan to extend the polytechnic site westwards as far as Linthorpe Road. Ironically Lock's success in this regard ran counter to his 1946 plan, which advocated a concentrated shopping area in the town centre as opposed to the drawn-out southwards pull of the shops in this particular location.

50 For brief details of this occasion see D. Gunby, 'Max Lock returns to Middlesbrough', *Planning History Bulletin*, 9 (1987).

51 In spite of Lock being a modernist, as were many others of his generation, he nowhere advocated the sort of high-rise glass and concrete which became common from the 1950s to the 1970s. His proposed buildings tended to be low rise, in small groupings, with a judicious amount of external decoration.

52 Interview with Malcolm Race, *EG* 20th September, 1968, under the heading 'What ever happened to the Max Lock plan?'

53 Under the heading, 'Max Lock returns', a short item on behalf of the Middlesbrough Economic Development and Property Department summarised the situation. It is noted that the post-war outer estates of the town had been built on locations indicated by the Lock team but sadly remarked that much of the town centre rebuilding had never happened. Nevertheless it considered that the plan retained a vitality and freshness, and represented the hope for the new Britain that emerged from the People's War. *Middlesbrough News*, February, 1987.

54 DM

55 Dorman Long & Co. had plans for a new universal beam mill between Grangetown and Warrenby on the south bank of the Tees, at a cost of £9,000,000. The capacity would be 350,000 tons of steel sections per annum. *EG*, 26th November, 1945. ICI also had plans; a five year project for an entirely new complex at Wilton, again on the south bank, at a cost of £10,000,000. This plant would be for manufacture of heavy organic chemicals. *EG*, 10th December, 1945.

56 DM

57 Letter sent to me by Max Lock.

58 Griselda Rowntree, for example, saw houses that seemed to be actually crumbling and decaying before her very eyes; Max Lock noted that the housing was 'exceptionally dense with 200 to the acre'; and Jessica Albery, in Middlesbrough at the time of the 1945 Election, went round the better parts of the town saying, 'I've been converted — so should you'. DM

CHAPTER 8

Regional Variation in Maternal & Child Welfare Between the Wars: Merthyr Tydfil, Oxfordshire & Tottenham

Elizabeth Peretz

This essay is an example of how necessary regional studies are for a fuller understanding of social welfare history in Britain. The case studies include a rural, metropolitan, and urban/industrial authority's services which are described as they had evolved by 1937. The factors which had influenced their shape are then examined. The picture that then emerges is one where local variation in service provision prevailed, and where the Ministry of Health favoured a mixture of well-supervised voluntary and local authority maternity and child welfare throughout England and Wales. These services were expected to be inexpensive to the provider, some of the real costs being passed on to the user as fees, some being borne by ratepayers, and some through national grants, and consequently can be regarded as conforming to a pluralistic model. The schemes of each district took on their shape as councils and voluntary committees responded on the one hand to local social, economic, and geographical factors, and on the other to central ministerial recommendations.

Defining and redefining problems is part of a historical researcher's stock-in-trade. Some definitions seem particularly resistant to change. One such definition is that attached to origins of the welfare state in Britain; arguments for a peaceful revolution, in which voluntary activity gradually made way for the state machinery, obstinately persist. The autonomous workings of pre-war local government is given little attention; local authorities are seen as simple agents of the state. Voluntary bodies are complimented on their innovations, and then assigned to the wings.[1]

Maternal and child welfare services play a key role in this analysis; they have been described as some of the most advanced or complex of the inter-war state welfare services.[2]

Some researchers have challenged the view that there were effective public health and welfare services in the inter-war period. Charles Webster, in his first volume of the official history of the British National Health Service, throws doubt both on the completeness of the welfare state which came into being in 1948, and on the growth of a national state welfare service in the years after World War I.[3] He also argued that welfare systems could only be as good as the localities administering them could afford, that little help came from Westminster despite government rhetoric, and that depressed areas therefore could not provide necessary health and welfare measures for their inhabitants.[4] Lewis and Macnicol have argued that the state family welfare system of the inter-war period was inadequate for the existing needs of those with low incomes; they suggest that state welfare machinery, at a government level, was inhibited by employers' opposition to a minimum wage, professional opposition from the medical lobby, and a persistent distrust of intervention in the family amongst those in power which was coupled with a belief in self-help.[5]

These authors have gone a long way to shake the myth of a steady progress to the welfare state, and the effectiveness of inter-war public welfare services. However, it has been left to other recent researchers from the field of geography to look at whether the inter-war services could really be termed 'state' services with the homogeneity and central planning this suggests. These writers have looked at central-local government relations in the inter-war period, and have pointed to the vital role played by local authorities and local rates in 'state' health and welfare services.[6] Described from this geographical perspective, the inter-war relations between central and local government seem like those between a supervising and aiding authority, and a group of loosely federated towns and counties. Local government made its own decisions about a wide range of services including welfare and housing; in these matters national legislation was permissive, and the Ministry of Health at Westminster was only a grant giving and advisory body. Using this perspective, which distances local authority initiatives from national ones, I would argue that a number of local histories of inter-war welfare need to be undertaken to examine central-local relations, local circumstance, connections between the voluntary and statutory sectors on the ground, local need and local service. What needs examining is not, as was thought, the early days of a state service and its inexorable growth, so much as the transition from diverse local authority services, and their relations with the voluntary sector and central government, to a more cohesive central system with its voluntary connections.

What follows, then, is a description of maternal and child welfare, seen at the time and subsequently as one of the best developed 'state' services, in three contrasting local authorities in inter-war Britain. Relations with the Ministry of Health, connections between the statutory, voluntary, and private sectors, local circumstance and need, are all examined. Although the conclusions rest on only three geographical areas and their relations with Westminster, they go one more step towards illuminating the reality of 'state' welfare between the wars, and the origins of the welfare state.

National government was actively involved in debating and enacting policy connected with the health and welfare of mothers and infants from at least the turn of the century.[7] The most important acts of parliament are usually taken to be the Midwives' Acts of 1902 and 1936, the Notification of Births' Acts of 1907 and 1915, and the Maternal and Child Welfare Act of 1918. In chronological order, these established a standard of practice and training for midwifery with a national register of Midwives, a mechanism for officially notifying all births within 36 hours of their occurrence (the permissive Act of 1907 was made statutory in 1915), a mechanism for any group to obtain grants for work with mothers and children, a committee in every local authority to take responsibility for maternity and child welfare with at least two female members (1918), and a national midwifery service mounted and supervised by local authorities (1936). There were other significant enactments; the formation of a Ministry of Health with a Department of Maternity and Child Welfare in 1919, the provision whereby general practitioners called in by midwives in an emergency were to be paid in the first instance by the local authority (1918), the Nursing Home Registration Act of 1927, and the 1929 Local Government Act which brought all the Board of Guardian's responsibilities under the local authorities, and changed the procedure for obtaining government grants.

This legislation was supervisory and administrative on the one hand, and on the other enabling, or permissive. There was no statutory obligation on local authorities to provide health visitors, clinics, maternity hospital care, birth control, or any other services and personnel associated with the health and welfare of mothers and children; local authorities and voluntary societies which wanted these services and could pay for at least half of their cost from rates and fees could apply to the Ministry for a 50% grant before 1929, and after 1929 persuade the local council to release a similar proportion of the block grant received from the Ministry.

The maternal and child welfare department at the Ministry of Health dealt with grant applications from local authorities and voluntary organisations, produced memoranda for distribution to these agencies, and sent supervisors to assess and advise in localities. The department dealt with over 200 local authorities in England and Wales and probably as many voluntary associations. This gave the Ministry a certain limited power in overall policy, although even this was further limited by Treasury dictates. But they were mainly confined to dealing with requests, and trying to respond to them in years of economic stringency. Their ability to generate new services where local authorities or voluntary groups were unwilling was very limited. Where this was felt necessary, memoranda were sent out — this happened over the provision for toddlers in the late 1920s, and birth control in the early 1930s.[8] Those authorities who did nothing were, on occasion, visited by a Ministry official for report and discussion; if a local authority made no effort to respond to Ministry recommendation they faced the threat of difficulties over the following year's Ministry grant. But teeth were seldom bared; after all, services absent meant money saved. Following the Local Government Act of 1929, the Ministry set up Public Health Surveys as a more formal method of monitoring and recommendation to local authorities. These recommendations did begin to have some effect, particularly as larger grants and more capital projects began to be centrally aided as money became more freely available in the later 1930s. But even then, schemes presented to the Ministry could be made to seem more comprehensive than they were.[9]

While local rates and local charitable effort determined the scale of public health and welfare services, those people who were the policy makers throughout the nation were those who fixed the rates, controlled the local councils who determined how these rates should be spent, and provided, collected and administered the charitable donations for health and welfare bodies like voluntary hospitals, nursing associations, or the infant welfare associations. These were usually the financially powerful of an area, the landowners, or works owners and their wives, who were in turn influenced by local traditions, cultural patterns, and working class organisations, as well as the more practical considerations of geography and level of prosperity. Gillian Rose has examined these patterns of power in relation to local government in Poplar, and Jane Mark Lawson in two towns in the north-west.[10]

Below is a brief outline of the services available to mothers and infants living in the three local authorities to be compared in 1937, the year the Midwives' Act came into full operation. The comparison reveals discrepancies in provision which are then discussed in context. The concluding section draws out some underlying common themes.

Maternal & Child Welfare Services in Merthyr Tydfil, Oxfordshire & Tottenham in 1937

Tottenham

Of all the three areas discussed here, Tottenham provided the fullest and most accessible service for its mothers and infants in 1937.[11] A mother in financial need, whether on unemployment benefit of simply in a low income household could obtain the following help from the borough's public health department. On suspecting pregnancy, she could walk to her nearest ante-natal clinic. With a choice of three in the borough open three afternoons and one morning a week, all staffed by an obstetric specialist and health visitors, and all within two miles of the furthest citizen, mothers had choice as well as availability. The visit was free to all comers. At most, a mother might be asked a penny for a cup of tea, or encouraged to join a thrift club. Of all expectant mothers in Tottenham, 41.1% attended ante-natal clinics in 1937.[12] If all seemed straightforward to the obstetrician who examined her, she could book a midwife at the town hall, during office hours; the town hall was no more than a mile from any part of the borough. In April 1937, the council agreed that midwifery charges would be 42/- a case for first children, 31/6 for second and later children, more than the 30/- maternity benefit payable to those mothers covered under National Health Insurance through their own or their husband's work. A generous 'scale of eligibility' was offered for mothers on low incomes. Those women whose cases were not thought to be straightforward, either because of poor home facilities or because of obstetric problems, were advised to go into hospital. Some Tottenham mothers elected to go into hospital themselves. Charges were around 42/- for a ten day stay, so there was little financial incentive to stay at home, particularly since those in the low income bracket were eligible for free hospital treatment and free home helps to look after their families in their absence. It was reported to committee in January that an average of around 40% of Tottenham mothers were delivered in the North Middlesex Hospital or the Mothers Hospital in Clapton in the three years 1934-6. If an emergency developed during confinement, whether at home with a domiciliary midwife, or in hospital, an obstetrician was called in, or a general practitioner, whose fees were paid in the first instance by the Council. The Council expected little to be recovered; in February 1937 it was estimated that only £20 of the £120 allowed for under this heading in the budget would be recovered from patients. (Doctors and consultants fees for these cases might be anything from £1 1s upwards depending on the case).[13]

Post natal clinics, held at the ante-natal clinics 'to make it easy for them' (the patient), and less alarming, were held, and a gynaecological clinic was attended by well over 100 women with a wide variety of problems, the most common being 'menstrual irregularities'. Convalescent treatment for mothers was available in the Borough and in Hampshire; here, as with the other services, there was a generous scale of eligibility. This was a full service for 1937, but even so Dr. Kirkhope, the Medical Officer of Health, wrote in his Annual Report of 1937 'Complete as these services appear to be, there are still ways in which they can be further improved.'

Infants fared as well as their mothers. A full home visiting service by health visitors ensured supervision of the majority of infants from the last midwife visit to school entry at five. Infant welfare centres, well equipped and situated in their own council premises were open almost every morning and afternoon of the week in all corners of the borough. During 1937, a purpose built Council Health Clinic was opened for school, maternal, and child preventative health. This building was a matter for civic pride, with its modern architecture, splendid equipment, trees and fountains. All clinics were staffed with paediatric staff, health visitors and volunteers who gave advice on infant care, clothes and feeding. Mothers' committees played a prominent part in these clinics. The health visitor could authorise a low income mother to have free treatment for herself or her infant at the dentist, the minor ailment clinic, the ear nose and throat clinic, the orthopaedic clinic, the artificial sunlight clinic, the opthalmology clinic, or the local X-ray department. Free butter, virol (a patent strengthening food for babies), milk (at a generous $1\frac{1}{2}$ pints a day) cod liver oil and malt were all available to such mothers. Working mothers could use the Council's daily crèche in the south of the borough, where the fees were the lowest and the proportion of trained staff the highest compared with those of neighbouring Councils'. The list of good facilities continues; Vale Road Nursery School, another cause for civic pride, built on model lines, had just been opened in the north of the Borough, for a small number of 2-5 year olds. Infants needing hospital or convalescent treatment could obtain this free on a generous scale of eligibility. (This was paid for partly by the local Invalid Children's Aid Association and partly by the Council). The take up of these services was enhanced by a widely publicised annual Council public health week, when all the institutions mentioned marked the occasion with open days, posters, films, baby shows, and school competitions.

Merthyr Tydfil

Merthyr Tydfil's 1937 service was in marked contrast to that in Tottenham. Here a mother had no easy way of finding her council midwife; she might have to travel four or five miles by bus to the ante-natal clinic, only to find that this makeshift affair in a local chapel or club would not be open for another ten days. If the mother was checked — in this case by the public health assistant medical officer of health for M&CW — and thought to be in need of hospital treatment, she might be referred to the maternity wing of the local public assistance infirmary, where she would be kept under the intermittent inspection of Professor Strachan from Cardiff, an obstetrician who was paid to make the 20 mile journey for Merthyr's obstetric abnormalities. Merthyr's domiciliary midwifery service was in place in 1937, with all the midwives employed directly by the Council. Although this was a paying service, in practice many families received free midwifery; after much Council debate, it was agreed that families of three persons earning 30/- or less a week after deduction of rent should get midwifery free, and so should families of five persons earning 50/- or less.[14] Hospital costs were normally 42/-, compared with the home midwifery charge of 25/-. After emergencies, however, mothers might be faced with steep charges for doctors or specialists which they had to pay back to the council; one woman paid off over £20 in instalments of 1/- per week.

A rather thinly spread service of health visitors covered the precipitous terrain of the neighbourhood to provide home visits to mothers; often an infant would only be visited once before entering school. However, mothers could get cod liver oil and milk free at the infant welfare clinics until a child's first birthday, on production of an unemployment benefit card. Informants have remembered this distribution as the main — if not the only — function of the clinics.

This service was not easy to get to, and neither were the clinics for artificial sunlight treatment, orthopaedic treatment, or minor ailments held in the centre of the Borough. Bus fares were occasionally paid, as were the train fares for polio sufferers going for treatment to Cardiff. There was one nursery school, for 20 children, for which mothers had to pay 1/- a week; this was poorly placed for much of the borough, several miles distant, and was almost totally maintained by voluntary donations.[15]

Oxfordshire

In Oxfordshire, the poor mother had an even less attractive deal in 1937 than her counterpart in Merthyr Tydfil.[16] No ante-natal clinics existed. A mother could ask a private general practitioner to examine her twice during her pregnancy free, but for those mothers with no regular habit of paying for consulting a doctor this would have been hard to arrange. The 'council' midwife was in reality employed by the local district nursing association who worked under loose contract for the local authority. These midwives were mainly district nurse-midwives, with only an 18 months to 2 year training, rather than SRN. A mother paid 25/- for a confinement provided she contributed 2d a week insurance money for the local nursing association. If not, she paid 30/-. Only 1 in 10 deliveries took place in hospital. For mothers who preferred this route, and for those who were referred, hospital could make a large hole in the family budget. Mothers had to attend ante-natal sessions in Oxford, which might easily involve both bus fares and child care, and special clothes and nightclothes were expected for the fortnight's hospital stay. The Council paid few bills, and reclaimed what it could. The only real help given was in the payment of doctors to attend in emergencies at home; less than a third of this money was ever recovered, despite several attempts to improve collection.[18]

After the baby was born, a health visitor — a busy woman with five separate responsibilities and a patch of 70 square miles to cover, often without a car — paid at least one visit. A mother was then invited to a makeshift baby clinic open once a fortnight for a few hours, where she could obtain expert advice from a visiting general practitioner or the health visitor. She also risked scrutiny by the village elite, from the church or manor, who came to the clinics to do their voluntary work, make tea or sell cost price dried milk or virol. Free milk could be given, though it seldom was. Hospital or minor ailment treatment could also be paid for by the council, as could home helps, but only a handful of families were helped in these ways each year.

Why were there such differences in services as those described above? Was it something about the localities themselves and their citizens, or to do with central/local relations between local public health departments and Ministry of Health? Do they reflect local response to rates of infant and maternal mortality? Who instigated the growth that took place in each locality's maternal and child welfare service? Below, these questions are examined in turn, in each locality, before concluding with some speculations about the wider picture of maternal and child welfare between the war.

****

Table 1.
Birthrate 1921, 1931 & 1937

	Tottenham	Oxford	Oxfordshire	Merthyr Tydfil	England & Wales
1921	22.8	16.47	19.8	27.5	22.4
1931	14.1	15.04	15.8	15.9	15.8

Table 2.
Infant Mortality Rate 1921, 1931 & 1937
(deaths under 1 year, per 1,000 live births)

	Tottenham		Oxfordshire		Merthyr Tydfil		England & Wales	
	No.	rate per 1,000	No.	rate per 1,000	No.	rate per 1,000	No.	rate per 1,000
1921	231	67.9	146	55.9	205	90	70,250	83
1931	124	52.9	59	30.7	120	105	41,939	66
1937	126	63.9	87	42.4	71	79	35,175	58

Table 3.
Scales of Eligibility for 1pt. Free Milk
From Local Council for Family of Five

	Tottenham (a)	Oxfordshire (b)	Merthyr Tydfil (c)
1921	37/6	32/6	35/-
1931	39/-	32/6	35/-
1937	39/-	32/6	45/-

a. For 1.5 pts. through pregnancy up to 5 years old.
b. For 1pt.
c. For 1pt. in last three months of pregnancy and up to 1 yr. old.

Derived from:

Minutes of Maternal & Child Welfare Committee, Tottenham Borough Council/Metropolitan Borough Council 1919-39

Minutes of the Health Committee, Oxfordshire County Council 1919-39.

Minutes of the Maternal and Child Welfare Committee printed in the Annual Council Minutes Books, County Borough of Merthyr Tydfil, 1919-39.

Figure 1. Population in England & Wales 1921, 1931 & 1937

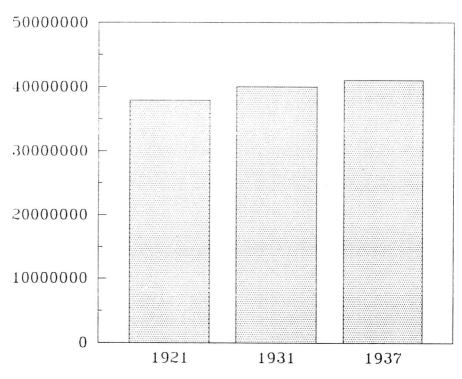

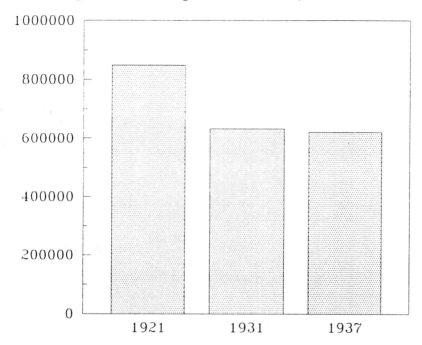

Figure 2. Births: England & Wales 1921, 1931 & 1937

Figure 3. Population Change in Tottenham, Oxfordshire & Merthyr Tydfil in 1921, 1931 & 1937

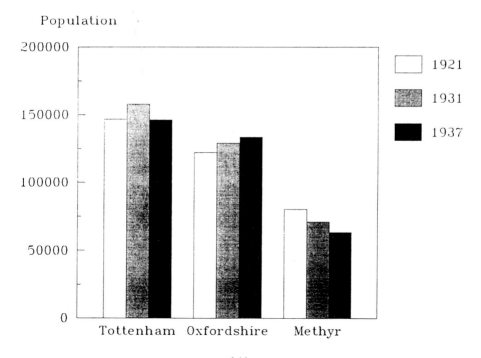

**Figure 4. Births: Tottenham, Oxfordshire & Merthyr Tydfil
1921, 1931 & 1937**

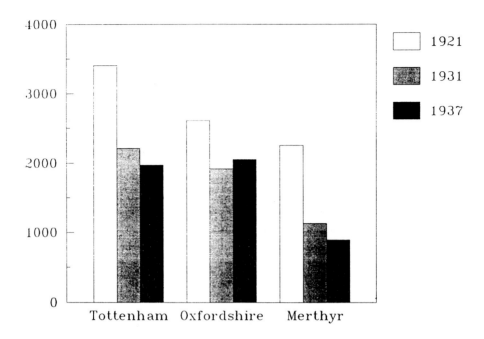

Source: Derived from Annual Reports of Medical Officers of Health for
Tottenham, Oxfordshire and Merthyr Tydfil, 1921, 1931 and 1937.

There was a reservoir of health expertise in the London area which benefited
public health departments like Tottenham; they employed part time specialist
obstetricians, gynaecologists, and paediatricians who worked in the London
teaching hospitals; they had access to specialist institutions — including
maternity hospitals, which they could and did buy into; they could attract
professionals who were well trained, and took advantage of further training
schemes in London. Tottenham's voluntary hospital kept a low profile in the
maternal & child welfare field, in contrast to several East End hospitals.[19] The
local newspapers heralded health weeks, new housing, institutions, and public
parks with great pride. Children were the symbol of Tottenham's future; the
council promoted special children's services, and the press devoted space to
reporting and photographing this.

The blue print of services outlined in the Maternal & Child Welfare Act of
1918 by the Local Government Board, and grant aided by the Ministry of
Health from its inception in 1919, closely resembled the service mounted by
Tottenham Public Health department under Dr. Kirkhope, a fiery Scottish
Barrister, chairman of his local NALGO branch, and continued from 1937 by
his successor Dr. Hamilton Hogben (Lancelot Hogben's brother). These were
both men of vision, empire builders, full of the rhetoric of preventative health
service and dedicated to its provision. They worked closely, and amicably, with

their councillors, and with the planners at the Ministry of Health, but had more than one collision with the financial part of the Ministry which wished to curb their spending and reduce their scales of eligibility. Voluntary associations which did operate in Tottenham did so to enhance the Council's service.

This was very different from Merthyr Tydfil and Oxfordshire's experience. Merthyr unemployment problems.[20] The age structure of the population changed as many young people left in search of employment. Births fell. (see Table 1). Although Merthyr had become a county Borough in 1912 it was geographically more like a string of villages perched on the precipitous sides of two high mountain valleys. Ordinary environmental health services were difficult and expensive to provide.[21] A special reservoir was constructed by Merthyr Tydfil at a time of expansion, which put the Council badly in debt from the 1920s. By the time the iron works at Cyfartha had closed, and the population diminished, much of the water from this reservoir, Taf Fechan, was superfluous, but it still had to be paid for. Drainage, subsidence, streets, street lighting — all these services were expensive. The area comprised in the borough was 16 square miles, spread out in long fingers up the valleys. Glamorgan, the surrounding County Council, took on none of the public duties of Merthyr; as a County Borough, Merthyr had responsibility for all its services. This was in contrast to the more prosperous Tottenham, first an urban and then a metropolitan borough, which had many duties taken off its hands by the County of Middlesex. After 1929 Merthyr also took on responsibility for the poor law administration within its boundaries; until then this function had been shared by several towns and villages in the areas. Provision of out relief for the high number of chronic unemployed was very expensive; between 1931-36 the average sum paid out was £581,004 13s 4d p.a. The people of Merthyr faced a difficult task in providing public services at all; they faced this problem because of economics and geography, not because of trying to provide a full service. Widespread unemployment faced them with yet more difficulties. Rates provided a small revenue because of empty houses and non payment; through bankruptcy and unemployment to the point where the rates in the £ had to be set at 29/6. The political complexion of the Borough Council put them in opposition to many of the local magnates, which only served to worsen their position. The Councillors, a majority of whom were labour from the early 1920s onwards, faced hostility from the local ratepayers to the extent that a public assessor was employed by the government in 1935 with a view to disbanding the Borough altogether. There had been three deputations of angry ratepayers to Whitehall since the end of World War I. It is instructive that at the end of a year, the assessor, Sir John Rowland, seconded to the Borough to help them out, had nothing but admiration for the Council. Miners and steel workers were the dominant groups in Merthyr; the Labour Party was dominated by miners and their wives; their culture was a male one at work and in public affairs, and in this aspect of their belief they were conservatives, and so were their wives, who were proud of their housekeeping and large families. This predominantly working class district had its landowning and works owning minority, who continued to exercise power through the distict; their views dominated the newspaper, the trades, and the professions. They had wider influence, too, in Cardiff and London. The voluntary movement, led by the iron and coal owners and their wives, was persistent in Merthyr Tydfil. Voluntary work represented a channel for civic pride and citizenship in contrast to the Labour demands for jobs, fair wages, and proper unemployment pay. The maternal and child welfare movement occupied a very particular position in Merthyr as a result of these circumstances. The most outspoken political champions of the system were the liberal professional women who used the needs of women and children as a political platform to oppose the Labour call for proper unemployment pay and the end of the means test.[25] One such towering female figure was Mrs. M. A. Edmunds who came into politics in the Edwardian period as a school board member dedicated to teaching housekeeping in schools; she was opposed by the working class councillors who felt their wives and daughters were good enough housekeepers already. Such people as Mrs. Edmunds saw Council Maternal and Child Welfare provision as an extension to voluntary provision in the area; another way to claim government grants or obtain rate support for targeted self help exercises. However, they were not in control of the council; their influence rested in encouraging money and resources from national voluntary bodies, like the Save the Children's Fund, Pearson's Fresh Air Fund, the National Birthday Trust fund to help provide holidays, nursery schooling, boots, Christmas treats, and patent strengthening foods to Merthyr. The Council Maternity and Child Welfare service itself was used by the Labour majority largely as a way to get central government grants to supplement food for the unemployed with young families; milk was consistently the largest item on the M&CW budget, and the recipients were agreed every week by a committee of one or two councillors, Liberals included.[23] The other parts of maternal and child welfare such as those offered to mothers in Tottenham were not ignored, but they were difficult to provide economically in such inhospitable terrain. The concerns Medical Officers of Health brought to the Council meetings were environmental, often to do with housing which was very poor in the borough. One energetic assistant medical officer for M&CW concerned herself with the polio outbreak and orthopaedics, and also with the effect of goitre on local mothers. Dealing with infectious outbreaks, the effects of malnutrition, and the effects on health of long term unemployment and poverty on a shoestring left little room for the niceties of corrective and preventative infant and maternal services.

Oxfordshire, a large, prosperous county in the heartland of England, covered a large area — 736 square miles — of scattered villages, small towns, with considerable floodland and few major roads or railways. Agriculture was on the decline, and between 1912-1936 the proportion of the working population in agriculture fell from a third to a quarter. The car works in Cowley, Oxford, which grew dramatically in the inter-war period, recruited from the countryside. The result was that the county's population continued to rise, unlike that in many rural areas. Poverty, in this situation, was very uneven; agriculture was particularly poorly paid in Oxfordshire, while Morris's car works paid well provided the market was good, but frequently put employees on short time or suspended employment. Oxfordshire had a substantial

landowning class; in 1937, 50 of the 66 villages surrounding Oxford were one quarter owned, and 20 of the 50 entirely owned, by one landlord.[24] It was this landowning class that dominated the county council throughout the inter-war period. Three quarters of the 60 members were landowners, the rest mainly professional men from the small towns. It remained Conservative throughout. There were only at most four women on the Council.[25] The voluntary associations of the county were predictably growing in strength in the inter-war years, particularly the Oxfordshire Nursing Association, the Oxfordshire Federation of Women's Institutes, and the Oxfordshire Rural Community Council. The committees of these associations were dominated by the landowning class; Lady Jersey, the Viscountess Harcourt, Mrs. Morrell of Headington Hall, Miss Ashurst of Waterstock, Lady Parker, Lady Mason. Connections between the voluntary associations and the council were strong; Mr. Ashurst was for many years chairman of the County Council and at the same time of the Oxfordshire Rural Community Council. Keeping the rates down was seen as a priority here as in other Conservative areas. They were remarkably successful in this; where on average British local authorities owed 7d a head for public service loans in 1937, Oxfordshire only owed 4d per head. The Public Health department of the Council was small; it comprised a Medical Officer of Health who was also School Medical Officer, a supervisor of Midwives and Health Visitors, 7 Health visitors (rising to 14 by 1939), and one midwife in Henley. Midwifery was done under contract by the Oxfordshire Nursing Federation, which was in comparison a much more powerful public body, employing 63 District Nurse Midwives, most of whom had been trained under their charge at the Plaistow Maternity Charity and Nursing Home.

The Medical Officers of Health did not concern themselves over maternal and child welfare, except briefly during the First World War when some 7 county midwives were employed. The first MOH was seen as slothful by the visiting Ministry official in 1931 and the second was more interested in Tuberculosis and Venereal Disease than M&CW work.[26] They neither of them championed causes on the council's public health committee; Mrs. Morrell was a much stronger agent of change here in maternal and child welfare than the officials.[27]

****

Are there any general points to be made about how these services, which played such different parts in their locality's lives, were constructed? Could policy emanating from the Ministry be seen as formative?

Between 1917 and 1921 there was a burst of enthusiasm nationally for maternal & child welfare. This reflected the overlap of the 'save the babies' fervour of the last years of the war, and 'the homes fit for heroes' fervour of the first years of peace. The voluntary movement which produced the National Babies' Weeks also pressed for government support for working class families, and even their housing.[28] This Liberal supported period of expansion came to an abrupt end with retrenchment. However, its effects were nationwide. In Tottenham the Medical Officer of Health won the assent of his new Maternal & Child Welfare Committee to combine the existing voluntary and local authority provision into a completely overhauled council service in 1919-20. He won what grants he could from the Ministry of Health for the Crèche, Cot Centre, Infant Welfare Centres, and staff, and approached the Carnegie Trust when the central government refused to give any more. The end of these years in Tottenham was marked by Dr. Kirkhope's angry letters and deputations to Whitehall when the Ministry cut the grant for free milk for mothers and infants.[29] In Merthyr there was little attempt to build a maternity and child welfare service in these early years; housing was seen as the most pressing need, and council efforts went into council housing plans, which were thwarted by the Ministry. However, the cutting of the milk grant produced a letter of protest from the Council here as well.[30]

In Oxfordshire, very little milk had been distributed under the Milk Order of 1919, and no protest followed the grant reduction. However, there was protest when the Ministry threatened to withdraw the grant for the seven county midwives, employed to plug the gaps in the voluntary association's network, in 1916 and in 1922; the protest was resisted by the Conservative Councillors. The Public Health maternity and child welfare service here, as we have seen, remained almost skeletal.

When the Local Government Act was passed in 1929, all local authority services, which until then had received backdated yearly 50% grants, were allotted new block grants on a 3 year plan. One of the objects of this act was to provide more uniformity of public service from the local authorities. But it had flaws from the start. Despite a complicated computing scheme which was meant to improve grants to poorer authorities, the 3 year's projections were mainly based on the local authority's past budgets.[31] In Oxfordshire and Merthyr this left little room for manoeuvre.

Public Health surveys were conducted by the Ministry of Health to encourage change; officials could always produce the threat that funds would be discontinued. Oxfordshire and Merthyr both had more than one such survey; Tottenham apparently escaped without one, possibly because of its status as urban or metropolitan rather than County Borough.

Merthyr was engulfed in problems of unemployment and massive public assistance bills and produced very little change in the M&CW service in these middle inter-war years. The Ministry of Health carried out two separate surveys of maternal and child welfare provision criticising the service, and as a result some changes were made to provide a hospital service for maternity cases and a little more health visiting. However, as the M&CW Officer said herself in a council meeting, infants in her care needed boots, not cod liver oil — but the government would not provide grants for boots, so she had to make do with cod liver oil. In Oxfordshire the 1929 Act produced no change at all — except a slight drop in population to visit with the extension of Oxford City boundaries.

Oxfordshire, with a more meagre public service than either of the other areas looked at here, were only asked for minor adjustments after their Public Health Surveys, despite damning comments on the laziness of the Medical Officer of Health. They were asked for — an obstetrician to call in emergencies, and the increase in health visitors already being demanded by the county's public health committee itself. The named obstetrician made no domiciliary visits in the first two years of his appointment.[33] From 1937 onwards there was a general increase across the country in capital investment in maternal and child welfare, and an extension of services.

Plans for purpose built maternal and child welfare centres were put forward for two sites in Merthyr, and two in Tottenham. In each case the plans were generated with Council enthusiasm to consolidate school and infant health departments. Both authorities met opposition from the Ministry of Health, over sites, extravagance and plans. Tottenham had two centres built, one in 1937 and the other in 1939.[34] Tottenham also put forward plans successfully for a purpose built nursery school, opened in 1937. Oxfordshire had no such plans for capital investment, and received no chiding on this from the Ministry. the 1936 Midwives Act bound local authorities to provide an adequate midwifery service for their population; this in aggregate was the basis of the acclaimed national Maternity Service. Tottenham employed as many midwives as they were allowed by Central Government; they asked voluntary associations to submit plans, according to Ministry directions, but only accepted contracting for a minority of the service in this way. Merthyr employed all its own council midwives; there was no nursing association with enough funds to help support a midwifery service. Oxfordshire, on the contrary, contracted out for all midwifery needs to the Oxfordshire Nursing Federation, except for one anomalous County midwife employed since 1917. Voluntary hospitals and private practitioners had contracts with the Council to provide the rest of the referral services. this scheme, which relied so heavily on the voluntary sector, received the Ministry's approval rather more readily than that in Tottenham; the 'state' service represented in Oxfordshire was little more than a voluntary system under local authority supervision.

****

What conclusion can be drawn? First, that in these three areas, 'maternal and child welfare' followed a different pattern, occupied a different place in the political agenda of public life, and formed such different services with such different champions that it is hard to carry out more than a superficial comparison. It is likely that more regional studies of services will produce some useful generalisations; Conservative Counties may have mainly adopted the voluntary model, Labour enclaves with a male dominated work force and working class culture may have shied away from extensive preventative public health which apparently undermined their families, and have encouraged instead workers' health insurance schemes for all ill-health, and schemes for housing and education; Jane Mark Lawson's contention that working class communities with a substantial female work force produced a full maternal and child welfare service, with crèches and hospital provision, may well be shown to be correct, although Tottenham is only a slightly muddled example of this. Central government did little to even out such fundamental differences between services.

The experiences of maternal & child welfare in these three local authority areas reflects the dominant themes of the localities, and the relations of these local councils with the Ministry of Health. They do not reflect simple

147

explanations for uneveness of service. A simple connection between the needs of the mothers and the children themselves, as measured by mortality rates or by relative poverty, is not evident. The Ministry seem to have been a reluctant spender throughout, in a service in which they encouraged the voluntary and the makeshift more than the public funded professional and institution.

This study goes a little way to expose the myth of the steady growth of inter-war state welfare, although the real shape of the maternal and child welfare 'service' and the national public health system as a whole awaits regional study. Myth or not, it was on this uneven service that the overall national health system of the welfare state was based, and in the political climate of the early 1990s it is to be feared it will be that uneven service to which we return.

Notes:

[1]   G. Newman, *Building a Nation's Health* (HMSO, 1939); C. L. Mowat, *Britain Between the Wars 1918-1940* (Methuen & Co. 1955). For a discussion of this point see C. Webster, 'Health, Welfare and Unemployment During the Depression', *Past and Present*, No.109, 1985, pp.204-.30.

[2]   C. Webster, *The Health Services Since the War* (HMSO 1988), p.9.

[3]   ibid.

[4]   Webster 'Health, Welfare and Unemployment during the Depression'.

[5]   J. Lewis, *The Politics of Motherhood* (Croom Helm, 1980), J. Macnicol, *The Struggle for Family Allowances* (London, 1980).

[6]   G. Rose, 'Locality, Politics, and Culture: Poplar in the 1920s', Environment & Planning: Society & Space, 1988, Vol.6. pp.151-68. R. Lee, 'Uneven Zenith: towards a geography of the high period of municipal medicine in England and Wales' *Journal of Historical Geography*, 14, 3 (1988), pp.260-80; J. Mark-Lawson, M. Savage, A. Warde, 'Gender and Local Politics', in *Localities, Class, and Gender*, ed. Lancaster Regionalism Group, (Pion Press, 1985). pp.195-215.

[7]   see J. Lewis op.cit.

[8]   See J. Lewis op.cit.

[9]   L. Peretz 'Towards a National Maternity Service: the inter-war experience of Oxfordshire and Tottenham' in *The Politics of Maternity Care*, ed. J. Garcia et.al. (OUP. 1989).

[10] J. Mark-Lawson, G. Rose, Op.cit.

[11] Minute Books of the Maternal & Child Welfare Committee, Tottenham Metropolitan Borough, 1937; Annual Report of the Medical Officer of Health for Tottenham, 1937.

[12] Annual Report of the Medical Officer of Health for Tottenham, 1937.

[13] Minutes of the Maternity and Child Welfare Committee Tottenham 17.2.37; 20.1.37; 21.4.37.

[14] Minutes of the Public Health Committee, Merthyr Tydfil, 29.6.37.

[15] Annual Report of the Medical Officer of Health for Merthyr Tydfil, 1937.

[16] Annual Report of the Medical Officer of Health for Oxfordshire, 1937.

[17] ibid.

[18] L.Peretz, op.cit.

[19] L. Marks paper read to the Wellcome Unit for the History of Medicine, Oxford, January 1989.

[20] Public Health Survey for Merthyr Tydfil, 1936 PRO, MH 96/384 129028.

[21] See C. Webster 'Health, Welfare and Unemployment...' for a full discussion of this.

[22] This section relies heavily on Reports in the Merthyr Express, 1919-39.

[23] Minutes of the Public Health Committee, Merthyr Tydfil County Borough, 1919-39.

[24] Barnett House Committee Social Service in the Oxford District, Vol. 1 (OUP 1938).

[25] *Yearbooks*, Oxon. County Council, 1919-39.

[26] Oxfordshire Nursing Federation Minute Books, 1919-39.

[27] Public Health Survey of Oxfordshire, Ministry of Health, 1931. PRO MH 66/191 129028.

[28] J. Lewis, op.cit.

[29] Annual Reports of Medical Officer of Health for Tottenham, 1919-21; Minutes of Maternal & Child Welfare Committee for Tottenham UDC. 1919-21.

[30] Minutes of the Public Health Committee, Merthyr Tydfil 30.8.21.

[31] Minutes of the Public Health Committee, Oxfordshire County Council 10.1.23.

[32] Annual Reports of the Chief Medical Officer of Health to the Ministry of Health, 1937-9; Annual reports of the Medical Officers of Health for Tottenham and for Merthyr Tyfdil, 1936-9.

[33] L. Peretz, op.cit.

[34] Minutes of the Maternity & Child Welfare Committee, Tottenham Metropolitan Borough Council, 1937.

CHAPTER 9

Adult Education and the Development of Regional and Local History: East Yorkshire and North Lincolnshire, c.1929-1985

Margaret Noble and Jan Crowther

The current appeal of regional and local history is demonstrated by the wealth of books and journals, town trails and heritage centres, and a growth in the number of formal qualifications in the subject as evidenced by its appearance in the school curriculum and degree and diploma courses. The establishment of local history, family history and civic societies, the increased use of record offices and local history libraries, all attest to this developing interest. The growth in the subject is due to many factors: amongst them the desire of people to find out about their environment in a period of rapid change, the growth of leisure time in which to pursue such interests, and the greater availability of local documentary material through the establishment of record offices. The collection and indexing of documents has facilitated the identification of topics and areas which provide fruitful material for researching regions and localities. In addition in recent years the advent of the photocopier has revolutionised such study, enabling students to examine copies of original sources.[1]

These developments have involved both professional and amateur historians, and indeed those with no previous interest in the subject. Academics have seen the value of researching regional and local society in order to facilitate comparative analyses and to understand more fully the relationship between local and national experiences. Furthermore, the study of local areas is now seen as important in establishing a national framework of change and development, and there has been a tendency, therefore, for the professional historian to produce work which might be described as regional and local history.

Adult education has played a major role in stimulating the study of regional and local history, and in providing opportunities for the development of teaching, research, and necessary skills in the subject. This chapter traces the twentieth century development of regional and local history, and examines chronological and spatial patterns of provision, within adult education in the area of East Yorkshire and North Lincolnshire. No attempt has been made to look at the University Extension Movement, which had been active in the region since the 1870s. The chapter attempts to evaluate the developing importance of regional and local history, and to assess its relationship to adult education. The period of study is from the early decades of this century until the mid-1980s, and the main focus is on the Workers' Educational Association and the University of Hull, which jointly provided adult education in the region from the late 1920s. This study concentrates primarily on non-certificated part-time courses; more recent courses leading to formal qualifications have not been analysed in any depth.

Methodology and scope

The main source of data on adult education provision is found in the annual reports of the Yorkshire North District of the W.E.A. and the University of Hull, together with ancillary material such as statistical tables of classes, correspondence, and committee reports.[2] Discussions were held with tutors, past and present, in order to amplify this material. Due to the lengthy time span of this study it was decided to extract data on classes at five-yearly intervals, beginning in 1929/30 and ending in 1984/85, giving a total of twelve sample years. Data were gathered of the four main types of courses: namely tutorial, that is courses of three years duration; sessional, courses normally running for at least twenty meetings; terminal, courses of ten to twelve meetings; and short, courses of nine or less meetings. These types of courses were administered in three ways: first by the two organisations working together under the auspices of the Joint Committee; secondly by the University Extension Committee; and thirdly by the W.E.A.

The area served by both institutions was extensive, stretching from the northern part of Lindsey in the south to the Cleveland area of the North Riding in the north (Figure 1). The eastern part of the W.E.A. Yorkshire North District is of far larger extent than the University Extension Committee area, but for the purposes of this study data have been principally collected and analysed only for that area served by both bodies.

One difficulty faced in extracting information relating to local history courses is that there is a necessary reliance upon the descriptive title contained in the annual report, and it is possible therefore that some classes may have been incorrectly included or omitted. For example, for a course described as 'Social History' or 'Archaeology' it is impossible to ascertain, unless one had detailed knowlege of that class, whether local material formed an important part of the syllabus. In the general absence of such information a decision was made to include only those courses where the title, or background information, indicated that a substantial portion was devoted to regional and/or local history.

The early development of adult education in the region

In the early years of the twentieth century adult education in Yorkshire was principally provided by the W.E.A. and the Universities of Sheffield, Leeds and Oxford. At this time Yorkshire was part of the north-western district of the W.E.A., and it was not until 1914 that it was created a district in its own right. It was administered as a single unit until 1929 when it was divided into two districts, North and South, although for administrative purposes councils for eastern, western, and southern sections, had been established seven years previously.[3]

In the very early years nearly all the W.E.A. provision was concentrated in industrial West Yorkshire, and the extensive area of East Yorkshire with its

Figure 1.
Adult Education Boundaries in Eastern Yorkshire and North Lincolnshire

large rural population was unserved. The problem of providing adult education in this area was recognised and the 1917 W.E.A. report stated that 'it is unlikely to be solved unless it is given special treatment'. Some initial developments included the formation of W.E.A. branches at Hull and York in 1917; student groups also existed at Grimsby and Selby. However, it was not until a special scheme was introduced to develop classes that any comprehensive system of provision emerged. The W.E.A. began work in the North and East Ridings in 1920 by appointing a full-time organising tutor, Ernest Gitsham, whilst the University of Leeds appointed George Gibson as staff tutor. The two tutors apparently divided the responsibility for tutorial and sessional work. Mr. Gibson undertook the tutorial work, devoting three evenings a week to that task, and spent the rest of his time giving courses of six lectures in villages. Sessional work was taught by Mr. Gitsham, and he also undertook terminal and short courses. Initial response to the programme was very good and by the end of 1920 classes were running in seventeen centres. In fact demand outstripped supply. By 1928/9 there were nineteen tutorial classes and thirty-eight sessional and terminal classes.[4]

This extension scheme was funded by voluntary grants provided by the following — a group of sympathisers known as the Yorkshire Group, the Cassel trustees, and the East Riding County Council, whilst some assistance was also given by the Board of Education and Leeds University Joint Committee. Early funding was, however, problematical and the future was rather uncertain, and by 1925 financial support had fallen. The East Riding L.E.A. threatened to withdraw their funding of £75 p.a. unless Mr. Gitsham, who had been accused of making "indiscreet remarks" and of teaching "socialism", was dismissed. The L.E.A. apparently wished to confine the W.E.A. to less damaging subjects "such as literature". The W.E.A. fought off this attack.[5]

The founding of Hull University College in the late 1920s was of great significance in the development of adult education provision in the region. The University College had a deliberate strategy of trying to attract students from its regional catchment area and the importance of extra-mural work in the early years in achieving this aim was recognised by the fact that the first professor to take up an appointment in the University was Professor T. H. Searls in Adult Education. The Department quickly established itself and by 1939 had a staff of seven, which by 1949 had increased to fifteen.[6]

When founded the W.E.A. had the two-fold aim of stimulating and co-ordinating 'all working-class efforts of a specifically educational character', and of developing a partnership between the working-class movement and the universities.[7] This worked well with the University of Leeds, which was initially responsible for serving East Yorkshire, and the W.E.A. in its 1928 report stated that 'we feel there is much to gain by having a joint committee [with the new University College] in close contact with the developing area around the Humber and the East Riding'. However the University College of Hull saw this relationship in a different light. Its main objective was not to co-operate but 'to show the flag and extend its influence ... into the East Riding and part of the North and West Ridings and Lincolnshire'.[8]

Table 1.

Local History Classes in East Yorkshire and North Lindsey
1929-1985

| Date | Hull University[1] | | | W.E.A.[2] | | |
	No. of Loc. History Classes	Total[3] all claims	%	No. of Loc. History classes	Total all claims	%
1929/30	2	31	4.9		N.A	
1934/35	7	110	6.3		N.A	
1939/40	8	106	7.6	4	74	5.4
1944/45	1	97	1.0	3	56	5.4
1949/50	6	176	3.4	8	107	7.5
1954/55	16	154	10.4	21	88	23.9
1959/60	9	144	6.3	37	179	20.6
1964/65	22	189	11.6	30	195	15.4
1969/70	48	254	18.9	41	295	13.9
1974/75	37	256	14.5	49	347	14.1
1979/80	36	216	16.7	60	447	13.4
1984/85	39	181	21.5	90	447[4]	20.1

[1]   Including Joint Committee.
[2]   Figures used for the W.E.A. in this table are those for the whole of the Yorkshire North District.
[3]   Totals are for certificate, tutorial, sessional, terminal, and short courses only, and exclude day release, summer school, and residential courses.
[4]   Including 127 special provision courses, 13 or 10.2%, of which were in local history.

Table 2.

**Types of Local History Courses in East Yorkshire and North Lindsey
1929-1985**

Year	Tutorial No. %	Sessional No. %	Terminal No. %	Short No. %	Total all Classes
1929/30	0	0	2	0	2
1934/35	2 (28.6)	0	5 (71.4)	0	7
1939/40	1 (8.3)	3 (25.0)	8 (66.6)	0	12
1944/45	0	1 (50.0)	1 (50.0)	0	2
1949/50	1 (8.3)	3 (25.0)	6 (50.0)	2 (16.6)	12
1954/55	3 (10.7)	14 (50.0)	5 (17.8)	6 (21.4)	28
1959/60	2 (5.7)	10 (28.6)	12 (34.3)	11 (31.4)	35
1964/65	6 (15.4)	13 (33.3)	11 (28.2)	9 (23.1)	39
1969/70	12 (17.1)	15 (21.4)	18 (25.7)	25 (35.7)	70
1974/75	5 (9.4)	19 (35.8)	12 (22.6)	17 (32.1)	53
1979/80	7 (11.3)	28 (45.2)	12 (19.3)	15 (24.2)	62
1984/85	6 (8.0)	24 (32.0)	27 (36.0)	18 (24.0)	75
	45	130	119	103	397

The area served by both institutions contained only a few major centres of population. The philosophy from the outset was to try to run classes in small villages, and therefore the Joint Committee, and bodies such as Womens' Institutes, the Rural Community Council, and parish councils, were important vehicles in their strategy. Despite the tension between the two institutions, by 1931 'valuable headway' had reportedly been made and 'co-operation between the College (Hull) and the Association ...[was] of a very cordial nature'.[9] In 1935 a co-ordinating body was established to cover all organisations working in the East Riding, and proposals for one-year and terminal courses were submitted to this committee for consideration. However relations between the University College and the W.E.A. were not always harmonious in the early years. Two aspects of the new University College's policy were particularly objectionable to George Thompson, the W.E.A. District Secretary: the provision of one-term courses, which he regarded as the W.E.A.'s province; and the choice of 'deliberately popularised subjects nearest to recreational interests [presumably drama and theatre]'.[10] In 1940 the W.E.A.'s annual report stated 'there is some dissatisfaction with the adult education scheme of the University College, which is not in the best interests of the W.E.A.'

Whilst joint work continued to develop, both the University College and the W.E.A. considerably expanded their own work in the period after 1940. By 1939 a W.E.A. tutor, Mr. Eames, had been appointed to conduct one-year and terminal classes in Lindsey. From the end of the Second World War full-time tutor-organisers were appointed for the Yorkshire North district of the W.E.A., and by 1950 eleven tutors were responsible for adult education in this region. Employment as organising tutors helped to launch the educational careers of many who served in these posts. Some later took up appointments in extra-mural departments.

The development of local history provision

Local history did not figure in early W.E.A. adult education classes. Government, economics, the industrial revolution, and literature, were the subjects most in demand in the first two decades of the twentieth century. These subjects were seen to fit into the philosophy of the W.E.A. and were also deemed to be 'suitable' for university extension work.[11] Most history classes were in either industrial history, or economic history. At annual summer schools of the W.E.A. the emphasis was also on these subjects, together with social philosophy, and general history. Early history classes held in eastern Yorkshire included a class at Scarborough in industrial history and economics, and one at Great Driffield in social history. Apparently regional and local history was not at this time a subject studied in its own right, but it is probable that it played a role in many of the more general history classes. Mr. Gibson wrote in his reminiscences of his work in East Yorkshire, of the problems of acquiring books for terminal and short courses, and the necessity therefore of concentrating 'largely upon local history or current affairs.'[12]

Throughout the 1920s most history courses continued to be of a largely general nature, but in the middle of that decade several classes specifically

Figure 2a
Location of Tutorial Courses 1929-85

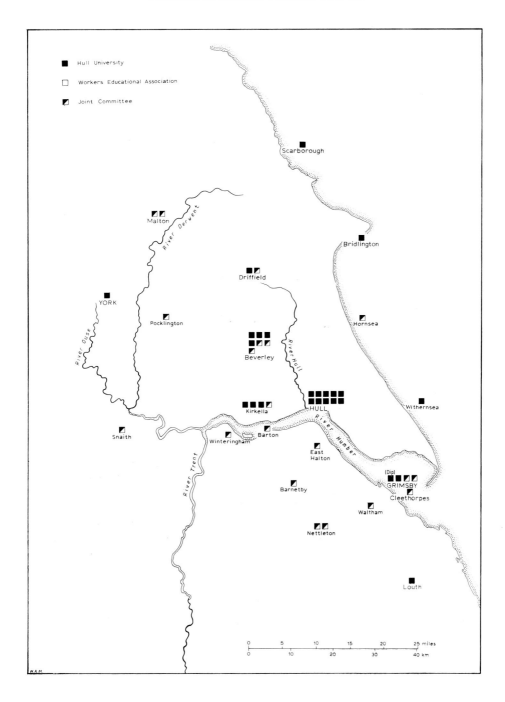

Figure 2b.
Location of Sessional Courses 1929-85

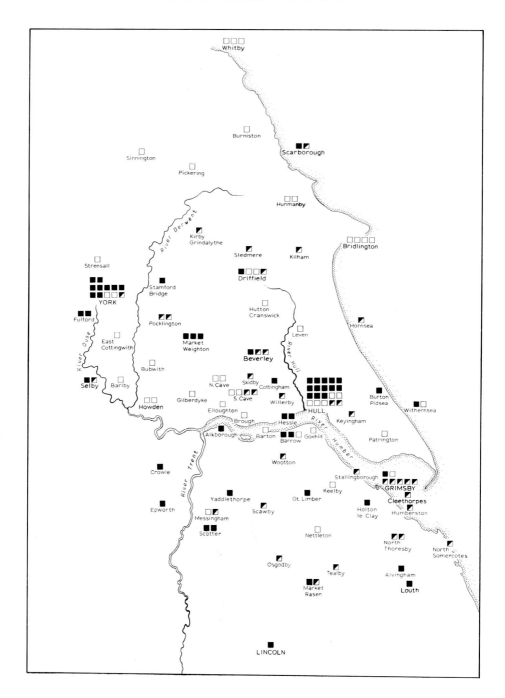

Figure 2c.
Location of Terminal Courses 1929-85

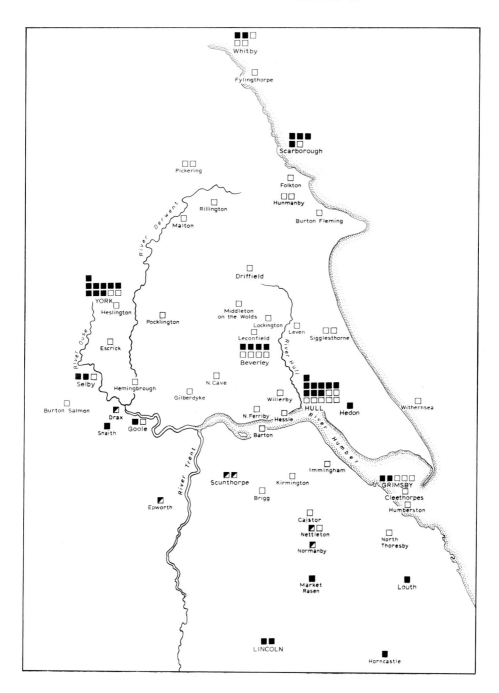

Figure 2d.
Location of Short Courses 1929-85

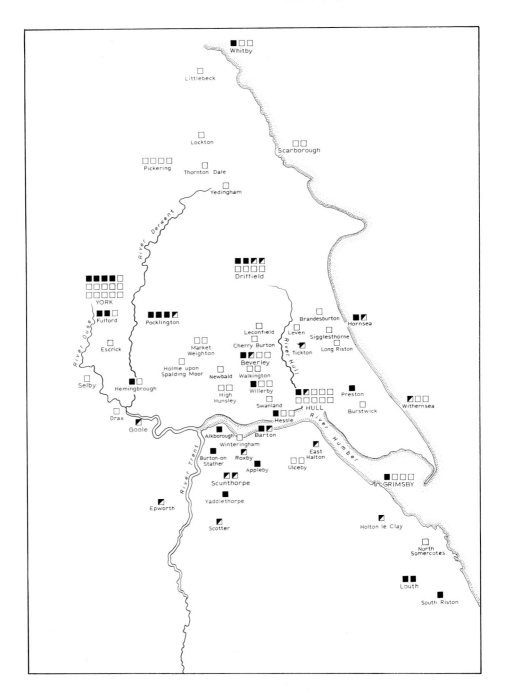

Table 3.
Subject Content of Local and Regional History Classes

SUBJECT	1929-1950						1954-1970						1974-1985					
	Tu	Se	Te	Sh	Tot	%	Tu	Se	Te	Sh	Tot	%	Tu	Se	Te	Sh	Tot	%
Local History/ Local Studies	4	7	5	1	27	77.1	11	28	24	23	86	50.0	4	17	14	16	51	26.8
Sources	-	-	-	-	-	-	2	1	1	3	7	4.1	1	4	3	3	11	5.8
Archaeology	-	-	2	-	2	5.7	5	3	6	9	23	13.4	1	4	7	1	13	6.8
Regional	-	-	4	-	4	11.4	3	6	3	3	15	8.7	5	18	8	6	37	19.5
Countryside/ Landscape	-	-	1	-	1	4.5	-	6	4	2	12	7.0	-	4	5	1	10	5.3
Individual Town	-	-	-	-	-	-	1	4	1	4	10	5.8	4	10	11	11	36	18.9
Individual Village	-	-	-	-	-	-	-	-	4	-	4	2.3	1	7	1	3	12	6.3
Architecture	-	-	-	-	-	-	1	3	2	3	9	5.2	-	1	-	6	7	3.7
Other	-	-	-	1	1	2.8	-	1	1	4	6	3.5	2	6	2	3	13	6.8
TOTAL	4	7	22	2	35		23	52	46	51	172		18	71	51	50	190	

Tu = Tutorial
Se = Sessional
Te = Terminal
Sh = Short
Tot = Total
% = Percentage of all classes for each period devoted to particular subject content

devoted to the study of regional and local history began to appear. Under the tutorship of R. W. Crosland classes in 'Old Yorkshire' were held at Appleton le Moors, Kirby Misperton, and Wetwang, in 1925/26, and at Lastingham, Bridlington, and Wold Newton, in the following year. All these early classes were terminal courses of twelve meetings, and they attracted between twenty and thirty-five students each. At the time of the founding of the Hull University College there were thought to have been only fourteen local history extension courses in the country; these were mostly short courses of four to six lectures taught by part-timers, who were often local antiquaries.[13] Under the Hull University Extension Committee the first local history classes in East Yorkshire were terminal courses conducted by F. W. Brooks in 1929/30 at Tickton and Hornsea and the first tutorial class in local history began at Beverley in 1937, under the tutorship of H. S. Rogers.

Local history was relatively slow to expand in the inter-war period for two main reasons: the popularity of subjects of more contemporary concern, and the lack of suitable tutors. The influence of the war years made the study of international affairs, economic problems, and reconstruction, very popular. In 1930/31 there were only three classes in the Yorkshire North district devoted to the study of international relations, and just one in the University, but by 1936 there were nineteen and eighteen respectively, rising to fifty-one and twenty-five in 1938, and eighty-seven for the W.E.A. in the following year. However in the post-war period demand for such courses dramatically declined and by the start of the 1970s there was an 'almost complete lack of interest in international affairs ... easily the most discernible trend in adult education in the last two decades'.[14] The shortage of tutors qualified to teach local studies was recognised from the outset, and indeed the University of Hull Local History Committee, formed in 1930, was sufficiently concerned about this problem to make the training of new tutors one of its principal concerns.[15]

From slow beginnings the provision of local history classes steadily expanded. As Table 1 shows there were only a handful of such classes in the region in the period before 1950, accounting for on average nine per cent of W.E.A., and just six per cent of university provision. As in earlier years it is difficult to estimate what proportion of the apparently general history courses listed in annual reports was devoted to local and regional study. The H.M.I.'s 1954 report on adult education courses in history and the social sciences in the North and West Ridings made the following interesting observation, 'The strongest classes were among those taking courses in social and economic history ... It is however, characteristic of Yorkshire students that they appear to prefer works of scholarship or even text-books to the attractions of 'petite histoire'.[16] This latter comment presumably refers to local history, and we might speculate whether students in rural East Yorkshire and North Lincolnshire found such study more attractive.

From the 1950s absolute and relative increase in local history classes occurred in conjunction with the general increase in part-time adult education courses. It is interesting to note that local history classes were of far greater relative importance in the W.E.A. than in the university sector. In the 1950s more than one fifth of all W.E.A. classes were devoted to local history compared to no more than one tenth of university classes (Table 1). Whilst in the W.E.A. sector there was some decline from these levels in the following two decades, local history continued to account for at least one in seven of all classes. Classes run by the Extension and Joint Committees expanded considerably during the 1960s and in 1969/70 forty-eight local history classes were provided, accounting for nineteen per cent of courses. The following years, however, saw some decline from these levels, although by the present decade more than thirty local history courses were still provided in most years by the two bodies in East Yorkshire and North Lincolnshire. The mid-1980s witnessed a marked increase in the relative importance of local history classes. The reasons for the fluctuating importance of local history are complex, but it is evident that the availability of part-time tutors, and the interests of tutor-organisers and University staff played a significant part.

Types of classes

The number of local history courses steadily increased over the study period (Table 1). For the Yorkshire North District of the W.E.A., this rise was continuously sustained. However, University provision reached a peak in the year 1969/70, and then declined in the early 1970s, before enjoying renewed support from the start of the present decade. Within the study region similar patterns are apparent, although the peak of provision was reached in 1984/85 (Table 2). As the latter table shows, the relative importance of the different class types as vehicles for the teaching of local history fluctuated over time. In the early years of the study period, tutorial and short courses in local history were largely non-existent and terminal courses were arguably of greater importance than sessional. From the 1960s, however, the balance began to change and a greater proportion of all courses were sessional, whilst short courses also increased in importance. These general trends, however, obscure the fact that generally it was the University, and the Joint Committee, which took responsibility for tutorial and sessional courses, whilst the W.E.A., certainly in absolute terms, was responsible for more terminal and short courses.

Joint Committee classes were represented on each type of course, but until 1970 local history accounted for little more than ten per cent of such classes in any year: in fact in 1944/45 and 1959/60 there were no Joint Committee classes in local history. The Adult Education Department's Annual Report of 1960/61 commented that there was an almost 'total absence of classes in local history, from the Joint Committee list, and it is obvious that the work of the Department in local history is largely a result of its long and effective co-operation with local history societies. W.E.A. branches have informed the Department however, that they are keenly interested in local history, and it is possible that some W.E.A. classes in this field may be developed in the near future'. However this comment is not substantiated by the W.E.A. 1959/60 Annual Report which lists a total of 27 sessional, terminal and short courses in local history for East Yorkshire and North Lincolnshire.

The subject content of local history courses is clearly of interest. Table 3 shows a breakdown of classes by subject types for three periods viz, 1929-50, 1954-70 and 1974-85. At a general level it is interesting to note that classes

163

described as local history declined from over 70% of all provision in the pre-war period to just over 25% by the 1980s. At the same time the number of more specific courses began to increase. Archaeology, for example, was particularly important in the 50s and 60s, as were studies of the landscape and countryside. Clearly over time, as local history developed, the subject content of classes became more specialised and demanding. The W.E.A. Annual Report for 1964/65 commented that such classes 'make serious demands on the students, as witness the numbers of local histories being published, and are not provided for those who simply like to dabble in antiquarianism'. For the decade 1974-85 the most notable trend was in the growth of the number of classes devoted to studying individual towns and villages, and the increase of regional courses, both of which accounted for between one-fifth and one-quarter of all provision. The detailed breakdown into specific class types substantiates these general trends, but at the same time highlights some minor differences, and the considerable fluctuation in the popularity of the various fields of local history over the study period.

Not all local history provision was made through the types of courses discussed above: from the early days summer schools and residential courses formed a major part of adult education programmes, and in more recent years weekend courses and day schools have become major vehicles for teaching and research in local history.

From the mid-1960s new types of local history courses began to emerge: notably those leading to formal qualifications in the subject. In 1965 a three-year diploma course in local historical studies was instituted by the University, and continued until the late 1970s. At this time the University initiated a major policy for developing part-time degrees through its Department of Adult Education under the leadership of Professor Bernard Jennings. Given the strong tradition of academic local history within adult education it was a natural development for the diploma to be restructured into a two-tier certificate/degree course in regional and local history. The first intake of students was in 1980, and was run from two centres — Grimsby and Hull. This was the first undergraduate local history degree course in the country.[17]

Spatial patterns of provision

Over the course of the last fifty years local history classes have been provided in most towns and larger villages of the region. Patterns of provision however are far from uniform in both spread and number and types of courses (Figures 2-5). Tutorial provision has been overwhelmingly concentrated in the major urban centres of Hull, Grimsby, and Beverley, and whilst most market towns have also had at least one tutorial course during this period this is true of only a few villages, all located in Lincolnshire. The reasons for this pattern must in part be explained by University policy, which has seen towns as more viable locations for tutorial work, and in part by the active role in developing tutorial classes in smaller centres played by individual tutors, notably Rex Russell, and more recently Rod Ambler.

Sessional courses show similar patterns, with the majority of courses again being concentrated in the major urban centres and in market towns. It is interesting to note that University provision was predominantly concentrated around Hull and York on the north bank but on the south bank was more widely dispersed, perhaps reflecting the greater availability of tutors to take courses in this area. Joint Committee and W.E.A. work was more widely spaced and was particularly evident in the northern part of the region.

Terminal courses seem to have clustered in distinct parts of the region notably around York, Beverley, Hull and Pickering. Large areas of the region appear to have been largely unserved by terminal courses, particularly the area to the south of Grimsby and the broad expanse of the Wolds across to Bridlington. The reasons for this pattern are not altogether clear, but may in part reflect the work of local tutor-organisers of the W.E.A. and their network of local contacts.

As we have already seen short courses were taught largely by the W.E.A. in a range of communities stretching from Whitby in the north, to Burton Salmon in the west and Nettleton in the south. Whilst University provision of short courses declined into the 1980s earlier provision again concentrated on the main towns of the region with villages remaining generally unserved.

The predominant spatial pattern that emerges from these maps is a dichotomy of provision between the University and the W.E.A., the former concentrating most provision in towns and the latter, whilst also clustering to some degree in the towns, showing a far greater spread to rural centres of population. It seems clear that these patterns reflect both deliberate policy decisions on the part of the two bodies, and the interests and contacts of invididual tutors. There has been a clear division of labour in the region whereby the University has focused on towns and longer courses, due to its large staff base and the need for simple organisation, whereas the entrepreneurial W.E.A. tutor-organisers have largely promoted short courses in rural areas, seeing as part of their role the need to establish new centres.[18] However, the tendency for University work to concentrate in towns gave cause for concern. The 1981 Annual Report made the comment that there was an "increasing tendency for courses to be concentrated in large urban areas, and especially in the University. This increases the feeling of isolation of rural communities".

Tutors

Tutors undoubtedly had a major influence on the development of local history provision and on the nature of the subject and it seems pertinent therefore to consider the role played by tutors. The availability of tutors, and the interests of W.E.A. tutor-organisers, naturally affected the development of local history provision. The pioneer work in the teaching of local history in the 1920s and 1930s was undertaken by a small number of individuals. R. W. Crosland was the first tutor to take local history courses in the region. He was a Quaker based at Hutton le Hole, and worked for the W.E.A. The first person appointed in the University with specific responsibility for local history was H. F. Bing. Officially an assistant lecturer in the History Department from 1931 to 1934, he was appointed to carry out adult education, and devoted himself during this time to developing local history work, mainly in Lincolnshire. He was said to have been the first full-time tutor in local history in the country. In 1934 he was replaced by Maurice Barley, who again played an important role in developing the external work of the department, by both taking classes and organising classes for other tutors. The University clearly had a greater number of tutors upon which it could draw than did the W.E.A. Both full-time members of the Adult Education Department, staff from other departments, and individuals from outside the University worked on the extra-mural programme. A member of the History Department, F. W. Brooks, played a central role in the teaching of local history from 1929 until the 1970s. He was one of the longest serving tutors. Professor Mayfield, writing about the history of the Adult Education Department at Hull University said of the 1930s, 'the study of local history in the area would probably have developed [more quickly] and enthusiastically under the inspiring influence of the present Reader in Medieval History [F. W. Brooks] had the supply of available tutors for the subject allowed'.[19]

The early expansion was considerably curtailed with the onset of World War Two, when the number of staff tutors in the Adult Education Department was reduced from seven to one, with the result that local history work came to a standstill. However, development work continued after the war, and the establishment of a comprehensive network of tutor-organisers for the W.E.A. was significant in developing local history teaching for two reasons. First many of the tutor-organisers already had, or soon developed, interests in local history and were keen therefore to run courses in the subject; second their role led to the growth of a more formalised network of part-time tutors.

As demand for regional and local history grew many tutors responded, and began to develop an interest in the subject, even though they had no formal background in the area of history. Frank Nicholson was appointed in 1947 as tutor-organiser for the East Riding, and held this position for twenty years. He was a literature specialist, but quickly developed both his teaching and research in local history.[20] John Rushton, currently tutor-organiser for North Yorkshire, has a background in economics, but principally teaches courses concerning individual villages and towns.

Tutors were instrumental in influencing class location and type. Rex Russell was appointed as W.E.A. tutor-organiser in North Lincolnshire in 1951, moving into the University Adult Education Department in 1964. He developed and ran courses in many small villages, which otherwise might have remained unserved. Many of his tutorial classes resulted in group publications, which made a significant contribution to the development of research in the subject.[21] He continued this policy after he moved to the University. David Neave, successor to Frank Nicholson, was W.E.A. tutor-organiser in the East Riding for thirteen years, until he moved into the Department of Adult Education in 1981. His keen interest and training in the area of local history, led to his teaching in a wide variety of locations. His decision as to where to hold classes was often based upon the availability of sources for particular communities, personal interest in the history and development of specific towns and villages, and local contacts. This emphasises the importance of the tutors' influence upon spatial patterns and types of course provision.

From the early years of the twentieth century 'the whole tradition of university adult education and the policy of the W.E.A. was against the provision of courses leading to examinations, or the opportunity for students to obtain qualifications.'[22] However in the post-Second World War period universities began to shift their position, with the result that some adult education tutors began to play an important role in developing courses leading to formal qualifications in regional and local history. In this connection the contribution of Kenneth MacMahon, staff tutor in local history in the department from 1949 to 1968, and senior lecturer in the History Department from 1968 until his untimely death in 1972, was very notable. With his colleague, Edward Gillett, Adult Education staff tutor in history (with responsibility for north Lincolnshire), he was instrumental in developing and teaching the University's formal qualifications in regional and local history through the diploma course from the mid-60s. From the start of the present decade this work has considerably developed, with the establishment of the part-time degree. By the mid-1980s the Department had arguably the best-staffed local history section in the country, with three full-time lecturers in regional and local history, a lecturer in industrial archaeology, and a Professor of Adult Education with a strong research interest in the subject.

The individual interests and approaches of tutors working for the W.E.A. and the University undoubtedly had a major influence upon the development and nature of local history within the region. Some tutors saw their role and that of their class as developing research through transcription of documents and the writing of histories of localities. Such undertakings were particularly characteristic of tutorial work. David Neave, for example, produced a history of South Cave in 1974, Elisabeth Hall a transcription of the inventory of Michael Warton of Beverley in 1986, and Rod Ambler a study of workers and community in Scunthorpe in the 1870s in 1980, each the result of class-based research.[23] The work of some tutors, although not leading directly to class publications, was nevertheless significant, for it led to the production of many local history studies. Kenneth MacMahon, for example, produced several works relating to Beverley, and Edward Gillett a substantial history of Grimsby.[24] For many tutors, their major aim was, and remains, to develop the students' knowledge and understanding of local history through placing the study of localities within a wider framework, and through introducing sources and methods.

Summary

It is evident that adult education has had an important impact on the growth of and development of local history. Over the course of the study period the nature of the subject, in both teaching and research, has clearly changed. In general terms there has been a shift from a political perspective, and predominant emphasis on national events, to studying social and economic trends, and analysing their impact on individual communities and regions. The study of the local effects of national trends has clearly received greater attention in the post-Second World War period, as such important sources as census enumerators' returns, and the hearth tax, have become widely available locally.

In the early years there was an emphasis upon printed sources, such as pipe rolls, local histories, and the records of local antiquarian and archaeological societies. Research based upon original material such as parish documents and estate papers, was difficult, unless sources were available locally or arrangements could be made with their custodians. As sources became more readily available and xeroxing machines made reproduction easier,[25] new techniques of analysis emerged, and it became possible to establish a more comprehensive view of social and economic change within regions and communities.

A question which might be posed is to what extent has adult education developed the academic credibility of local history? Recent years have seen much debate on the subject's status: some would argue that if it has gained credibility it is because much current local history is not just about filling in gaps in our local knowledge, but is concerned with posing, answering and testing questions and hypotheses of more than local significance. Furthermore the development of research and the recent rapid growth in publications perhaps attest to its increasing intellectual rigour.

A second question relates to the extent to which the developing interest in local history can be attributed to the growth of adult education. Whilst much local history development has been led by 'academics', who have seen the benefits of researching topics of local and regional interest, it is undoubtedly true that without the interest and demand created by adult education classes our knowledge and understanding of regions and localities would have remained significantly underdeveloped. However it is evident that not all demand can be attributable to adult education, for a two-way process has been, and is still, at work. The formation of local history libraries and record offices, the establishment of local history societies, and publications have all stimulated interest in the study of local areas, and have in themselves created demand for further local history classes.

This paper has perhaps left many unanswered questions, but may also have raised others of more than local significance. The increased interest in local history and the response of adult education programmes to that demand has been questioned in some quarters. It has sometimes been argued that there has been too much local history in adult education programmes, leading to an imbalance.[26] This is an issue that needs to be addressed, both by those who organise and provide adult education, and by those who meet the demand for regional and local history.

Notes:

1   See for example J. D. Marshall, 'Teaching local history', *Journal of Regional and Local Studies*, 4 (1984), pp. 61-63, B. Stapleton, 'English local history: an educational exercise', *Journal of Regional and Local Studies*, 4 (1984) pp. 64-68, and B. Jennings, 'The teaching of local history', in A. Parker and G. G. Raybold, *University studies for adults* (1972) pp. 158-175. In the region under review several local history societies have been established, including the Lindsey Local History Society, and the East Yorkshire Local History Society.

2   The annual reports and records of the Yorkshire North District of the W.E.A. are kept at the West Riding Record Office, Sheepscar, Leeds. The archival material used for Hull University is in the Department of Adult and Continuing Education, and in the Brynmor Jones Library, University of Hull.

3   J. F. C. Harrison, *Learning and living, 1790-1960: a study of the English adult education movement* (London, 1961), p.269, W. E. Styler, *Yorkshire and Yorkshire North: the history of the Yorkshire North District of the Workers' Educational Association, 1914-1964* (Leeds, 1964), p.1 & p.14, B. Jennings, *New lamps for old? University adult education in retrospect and prospect* (University of Hull, 1976), p.1.

4   See George W. Gibson, 'Adult education in East Yorkshire in the 1920s: some reminiscences' *in* W. E. Styler, *ed., Adult education in East Yorkshire, 1875-1960* (Hull, 1965), pp.17-25, and annual reports of the W.E.A.

5   Styler (1964) op. cit. p.17.

6   University of Hull Annual Report 1949/50.

7   Quoted in B. Jennings, *Knowledge is power: a short history of the Workers' Educational Association* (University of Hull, 1979) p.1. See also Caroline Ellwood, *Adult learning today: a new role for the universities?* (London, 1976), p.50.

8   Harrison op. cit. p.293.

9   Styler (1964) op. cit. p.23.

10   Jennings (1976) op. cit. pp.15-16.

11   Harrison op. cit. p.291 *and* Ellwood op. cit. pp.49-51.

12   Gibson op. cit. p.24.

13   F. W. Brooks, 'Local history, 1930-1948', *Local Historian*, 10 (1972-3), pp.385-9.

14   Hull University Department of Adult Education Annual Report for 1970/71.

15   Minutes of the Research Sub-Committee of Hull University Local History Committee 1930/31, VC 3, Hull University Archives, Brynmor Jones Library.

16   Ministry of Education. Report by Her Majesty's Inspector, *Courses in history and the social sciences in the North and East Ridings of Yorkshire by the University of Leeds and the Yorkshire North District of the W.E.A., 1952-1954* (1954), p.28.

17   B. Jennings, 'The open-door university: a strategy for continuing education leading to degrees', *Studies in Adult Education*, 15 (1983) pp.47-59. See also J. D. Marshall 'A survey of courses in regional and local history in tertiary education', *Journal of Regional and Local Studies*, 6 (1986) pp.59-73, and 'More tertiary courses in regional history', 7 (1987) pp.65-71, for a wider discussion and subsequent developments.

[18]   David Neave, pers. comm.

[19]   G. E. T. Mayfield, 'The University of Hull Department of Adult Education, 1928-1960', in Styler (1965) op. cit. p.30.

[20]   Michael Hyde, 'Frank Nicholson, 1901-1986', *East Yorkshire Local History Society Bulletin*, no.37, Summer 1988, p.12.

[21]   Rex Russell's publications are too numerous to list, but they include four volumes on Barton on Humber in the 1850s, published by the Barton on Humber Branch of the W.E.A.

[22]   Ellwood op. cit. p.158.

[23]   David Neave, *South Cave: a market community in the 18th and 19th centuries* (South Cave, 1974), new edition Howden: Mr. Pye Books, 1984; Elisabeth Hall, *ed. Michael Warton of North Bar House, Beverley: an inventory of his possessions*, Hull: Centre for Regional and Local History, University of Hull, 1986; R. Ambler, *Workers and community: the people of Scunthorpe in the 1870s*, (Scunthorpe, 1980).

[24]   Kenneth MacMahon, *Old towns and cities: Beverley*, (Dalesman Books, 1973), plus many other studies; Edward Gillett, *A history of Grimsby* (Oxford, 1970). When he died Kenneth MacMahon was working on a history of Hull, which was taken over by Edward Gillett, and published in 1980, second edition 1989.

[25]   Though, as Rex Russell points out, the money available for xeroxing, buying census returns, air photos, etc. was very limited. Sometimes past classes' work might help to sponsor future work if local W.E.A. branches had money available from selling publications or from organising weekend schools.

[26]   This issue was raised in the 60s and 70s due to the very high demand for local history, see for example West Riding Record Office, W.E.A. 185, East Riding Adult Education Advisory Committee, 2.11.66, and W.E.A. Annual Report, 1974-5.

LIST OF PUBLICATIONS — ERIC M. SIGSWORTH

1952   Bradford 1830-1870, in C. R. Fay (ed), *Round About Industrial Britain 1830-70.*

1949   The History of Local Trade at Morley, *Journal of the Textile Industry* (ref. untraced).

1951   Fosters of Queensbury and Geyer of Lodz, *Yorkshire Bulletin of Economic & Social Research* Vol.3. No.2. pp.67-82.

1952   The West Riding Wool Textile Industry and the Great Exhibition, *Yorkshire Bulletin of Economic & Social Research* Vol.4. No.1. pp.21-31.

1957   *Black Dyke Mills, A History: with introductory chapters on the History of Worsted Industry.* (Liverpool University Press)

       with R. K. Wilkinson, A Survey of Slum Dwellers in Leeds, *Yorkshire Bulletin of Economic & Social Research.* Vol.15. No.1. pp.25-51.

       with R. K. Wilkinson, Slum Dwellers in Leeds, *New Society* (ref. untraced).

1965   Science & the Brewing Industry, 1850-1900, *Economic History Review* Vol.16. No.3. pp.536-550.

1965   The Distribution of Wool Textiles, in G. F. Rainnie (ed.), *The Wool Textile Industry: An Economic Analysis* (Oxford)

       with R. K. Wilkinson, Re-building or Renovation, *Urban Studies* Vol.4. No.2. pp.109-121

1967   Leeds in the Industrial Revolutioin, in M. W. Beresford & G. R. J. Jones, *Leeds and its Region.* (British Association, Leeds.)

1968   with J. Blackman, The Woollen and Worsted Industries, 1875-1914 in D. H. Aldcroft, *The Development of British Industry and Foreign Competition, 1875-1914* (London).

1970   Editor, Studies in Yorkshire and Humberside, *Yorkshire Bulletin of Economic & Social Research*, Vol.22.

       with R. K. Wilkinson, The Measurement of Deficiencies in the Housing Stock, *Yorkshire Bulletin of Economic & Social Research.* Vol.22. No.2. pp.143-163.

       Gateways to Death? Medicine, Hospitals and Mortality, 1700-1850, in P. Mathias (ed.), *Science and Society*

       The British Retreat from Pre-Eminence, *The American Benedictine Review.* pp.203-217.

1971   with R. K. Wilkinson, The Finance of Improvement, *Yorkshire Bulletin of Economic and Social Research* Vol.23. No.2. pp.113-128

       with R. K. Wilkinson, Some Effects of Re-Housing, *Journal of Social and Economic Administration.*

1976   with T. E. Wyke, Victorian Prostitution, in M. Vicinus (ed.), *Suffer and be Still* (Indiana University Press).

1978   with F. E. Finnegan, *Poverty and Policy: A History of Batley* (York).

1980   The Wool Textile Industry, in R. A. Church (ed.), *Studies in Victorian Entrepreneurship* (Allen & Unwin).

1981   with P. Swan, Para-Medical Provision in the West Riding 1841-1881, in *Bulletin of the Society for the Social History of Medicine*. No.29. pp.37-39

1982   with P. Swan, An Eighteenth Century Surgeon & Apothecary: William Elmhirst, 1721-1773, in *Medical History* Vol.26. No.2. pp.191-198

1984   Sir Montague Burton, in *Dictionary of Business Biography*, Vol.1.

William Elmhirst 1721-1773, Surgeon Apothecary and Medical Frontiersman, *Pharmaceutical Historian*. pp.6-7.

1986   Editor, with Valerie Brady, *The Ledger of William Elmhirst, Surgeon and Apothecary 1769-1773* (Centre for Regional Studies, H.C.H.E.).

1988   Editor, *In Search of Victorian Values* (Manchester University Press).

1990   *Montague Burton: The Taylor of Taste.* (Manchester University Press).

INDEX